At Home in the Hills

J. Turner Fleming
Photograph: Derek Lunn, Hawick

AT HOME IN THE HILLS

Sense of Place in the Scottish Borders

John N. Gray

Berghahn Books
New York • Oxford

Published in 2000 by
Berghahn Books
www.BerghahnBooks.com

© 2000, 2011 by John N. Gray
First paperback edition published in 2011

Photo credits:
Frontispiece photograph by Derek Lunn, Hawick. Used with permission.
Permission to use map 2 and 3, "Border Marches and Surnames," by James
Reed, *The Border Ballads*, pp. 46-47, courtesy *The Athlone Press Limited.*
Map 4, "Buccleuch Estate Lands, Seventeenth and Eighteenth Centuries"
is based upon Figure 8 and the historical narrative from Robson
(1977:52ff).

Library of Congress Cataloging-in-Publication Data

Gray, John, 1945-
  At home in the hills : sense of place in the Scottish borders / John Gray.
    p. cm.
  Includes bibliographical references (p.) and index.
  ISBN 978-1-57181-739-6 (hbk) – ISBN 978-0-85745-179-8 (pbk)
    1. Borders Region (Scotland)—Social life and customs. 2. Landlord and
  tenant—Scotland—Borders Region—History—20th century. 3. Rural
  families—Scotland—Borders Region—History—20th century. 4.
  Agriculture—Scotland—Borders Region—History—20th century. 5. Farm
  life—Scotland—Borders Region—History—20th century. 6. Family—Scotland—Borders
  Region—History—20th century. 7. Borders Region (Scotland)—Rural conditions. I. Title.
  DA880.B72 G73 2000
  941.3'7085—dc21   99-045151

British Library Cataloguing in Publication Data

A catalogue record for this book is available from the British Library.

Printed in the United States on acid-free paper.

ISBN 978-1-57181-739-6 (hardback)
ISBN 978-0-85745-179-8 (paperback)

For Turner

For Jacki

.

CONTENTS

ILLUSTRATIONS

PREFACE

In 1981 I began fieldwork in Scotland as a comparative counterpoint to my ongoing research in Nepal. I believed that by doing so I could rely on more than the relatively unreflexive knowledge of one's own cultural world that forms the usual and often implicit comparative framework for ethnographies of life-worlds of other people in other places. Except for a few references to my understandings of social life in a multicaste village in the southern reaches of the Kathmandu Valley, I have only partially realized this more rigorous comparative imperative in the following account of hill sheep farmers' sense of place in the Scottish Borders. Perhaps some of the suggestions I make in the Afterword about the embodied experience of self and place that I found in both the Nepali village and Borders hill sheep farming locality might provide a theme for a more penetrating comparative project on sense of place.

My field trips to Scotland were supported by periods of study leave from the University of Adelaide and research grants from the Faculty of Arts in a practical display of their dedication to the furthering of research and intellectual discovery. Through our Seminar Program and informal discussion, colleagues in the Department of Anthropology, University of Adelaide, have patiently witnessed and generously participated over many years in my growing understanding of the social world of hill sheep farming. I want to especially thank Deane Fergie and Rod Lucas for their valuable comments upon sections of the manuscript, Marian Thompson for her work on the index, Chris Crothers for her skills in drawing the maps, and Colleen Solly for her efforts in lightening my administrative responsibilities—and my spirit. Parts of the book were presented at the Congress of the European Society of Rural Sociology in Prague and the meetings of the European Association of Social Anthropologists in Barcelona and Frankfurt. I am grateful to Göran Djurfeldt, Henk de Haan, Miguel Vale de Almeida, Vered Talai, and Hastings Donnan as well as the Scientific Committees of the ESRS and EASA for their kind invitations to join in their workshops. Much of the writing of the book took place when I was a Visiting Associate at the International Social Sciences Institute (ISSI) of the University of Edinburgh in 1997. I remember the end-of-year formal dinner of ISSI when a fellow Associate spoke eloquently for the other Associates in thanking all the staff of the Institute for the warmth of their welcome and spirit of collegiality that we appreciated even more than the material facilities that they made available to support our research efforts. I am also very grateful to Andrew and Catherine Duncan who invited me to stay with them during the time I was associated with ISSI. We had met many years earlier when I purchased a car from them—not the usual basis for a long lasting friendship. And a very special thanks to Deema Kaneff for her sincere encouragement and wicked chocolate.

❦

The fieldwork upon which this book is based was conducted in Teviothead, a hill sheep farming locality in the Borders region of Scotland sixty miles southwest of Edinburgh on the A7 trunk road. My wife and I lived in one of two attached former workers' cottages on Falnash Farm for nine months in 1981. Rob Hislop, a retired manager and shepherd of Lymiecleuch Farm, was our neighbor and friend. He was always willing to help me understand the finer points of hill sheep behavior and stockmanship. In 1986, we returned to Teviothead for another nine-month period of fieldwork, this time taking up residence in what used to be the shepherd's quarters at the back of Falnash farmhouse where Sandy and April Fleming had recently taken up residence. I carried out another four-month period of fieldwork in 1991 alone. Sandy and April showed much kindness by inviting me to stay with them in the farmhouse; I became a part of their family and was enriched by our deepening relationship. They continued to extend the invitation for the shorter research visits I have made since then.

During these periods of fieldwork, I spent time on all of the farms in the locality. I walked the hills at least once with most of the shepherds and many times with some before the advent of the four-wheeled motorbike they now use for hill herding. I also engaged in other farming activities where I could be of some assistance—catching sheep for the clipping, helping with dipping ewes, jagging sheep, and cutting lambs, with the movement and shedding of sheep in the folds, and with general maintenance tasks around the farms. I went to numerous store and fat lamb auctions in Hawick, Anan, St. Boswells, and Longtown; to tup sales in Lockerbie and Lanark; and to local agricultural shows in Teviothead, Roberton, and Langholm. In addition, I was made to feel free to join farmers and shepherds in their leisure activities including companionable evenings at the local hotels, carpet bowls, and curling. The level of welcome and willingness to assist in my research was boundless. I take this opportunity to express to every person in Teviothead my heartfelt appreciation for their kindness and friendship. So universal was the warm reception we received throughout the years that I hope that the people of Teviothead will take this as a personal expression of our thanks to each and every one of them.

Among the people of Teviothead, there was as much lively interest in what I would write about their life-world as there was in their neighborly concern for each others' everyday affairs. Despite my assurances of confidentiality and my description of the strategies I would adopt to maintain it, they often told me that they were looking forward to the sport of deciphering the inadvertent clues to the identities of the farms and people I included in my writings. This was the fate of earlier published articles that I showed to people in Teviothead. It is an issue that lately has been the topic of a discussion thread on the Web site of the Society for the Anthropology of Europe (H-SAE 1998). Reading it has made easier my decision not to use pseudonyms for farms and people except where I believe I would be detrimentally breaching people's privacy and confidentiality. I apologize for any errors of judgement in this respect.

There is one person in Teviothead I want to mention individually. Everyone there knows the special friendship that I had with Turner Fleming. His picture forms the frontispiece to this book, which I dedicate to him. He and his wife Betty were two of the first people we met in Teviothead, and they offered a generosity of spirit to us and our research throughout all our stays in Teviothead. A lot of my understanding of sheep stockmanship and farming as well as of the community of Teviothead was gained from Turner during the numerous times we walked in the hills, prepared the tups for sales, clipped and dipped the ewes, enjoyed a farm-bred mutton dinner, or sat in front of a fire with a single malt whiskey on a cold winter's night. I could not have had a better friend and teacher. One of the last times I was with him he was judging sheep at the Royal Agricultural Show in Edinburgh—an honor recognizing his consummate stockmanship. Sometimes I regret that I never directly told him how grateful I am for our relationship ... but then, it probably wasn't necessary anyway because I believe he sensed how I felt.

I also dedicate this book to my wife, Jacki. Its intimacy and accessibility are testaments to the insights she inspired.

Map 1 United Kingdom and the Anglo-Scottish Borders

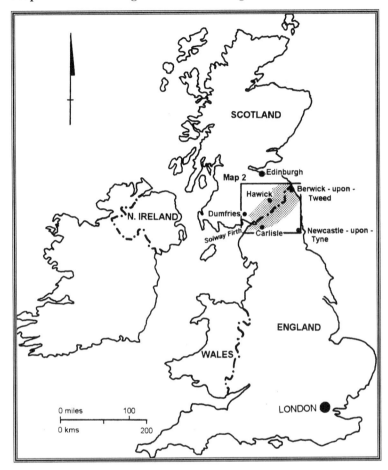

INTRODUCTION

Place-Making and Family Farms
in the Scottish Borders

'Tis blissfu' 'mang the hills to be,
Wi' lightsome steps to wander,
The sounds to hear and scenes to see
Of nature's wildest grandeur.
(From Song, Henry Scott Riddell [1871])[1]

I see the silver gleaming
of a peaty trout-flecked burn.
I see the heather steaming
on a grouse awakened morn.
And, in my half-sleep dreaming
I feel glad that I was born
where hills are hills and mountains,
where springs are gushing fountains,
where nature thrives, and burns and rivers flow.
(From *Pastoral*, Tim Douglas [c. 1980])[2]

This book is an anthropological account of people living
and working on hill sheep farms in the rural parish of
Teviothead near the town of Hawick in the Borders region of
Scotland. It follows their endeavors at "making a life" (Parish
1996) in the context of increasing interventions by the
British state and the European Community into agricultural
production as well as into family and rural community relations in the Borders. I focus on three interrelated dimensions
of making a life within this regional, national, and supra-

Notes for this section begin on page 20.

national context: the hill sheep farming activities of raising lambs for sale on the European market to produce a business profit; the family and labor relations whose aim is to keep the farm in the family; and most particularly the "place-making" practices (Basso 1996:5) that create the intimate association hill sheep farming families experience between themselves and their farms in the Scottish Borders.

Map 2 Anglo-Scottish Borders

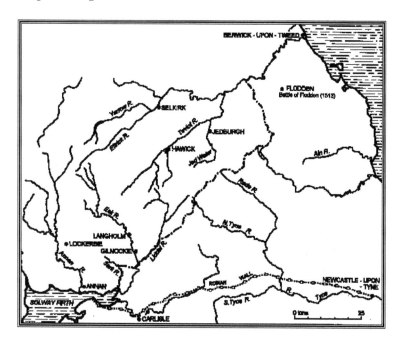

The Anglo-Scottish Borders is an area stretching across Great Britain from the North Sea to the Solway Firth and from the Lammermuir Hills in Scotland to the southern county lines of Cumberland, Westmorland and Northumberland. Teviothead is located in the central part of the region where the terrain is characterized by the rugged Cheviots Hills and Southern Uplands—beautiful or foreboding, depending upon whether or not you are a Borderer—that have served as a topographic synecdoche for its people and their way of life.[3] It is Border sheep farmers'

affinity with these hills that is the principal subject matter of my ethnography and differentiates it from others, such as Neville's (1994), that are based on social and ceremonial life in Border towns. During the course of several extended periods of fieldwork carried out over the past seventeen years, I came to understand the special, sensual, and intimate attachment of sheep farming people to the hills they spend so much time in—a feeling of being in their proper place that I try to capture with the phrase "being-at-home in the hills." I also came to realize that their sense of place was significantly different from that found among townspeople of the Borders. I spent a lot of time traveling with farmers and shepherds to agricultural shows and sheep sales around the Borders. During these trips, when we could more leisurely reflect upon life on hill sheep farms, they would often ask me how I liked living in Teviothead, knowing that I had lived in cities all my life; they were surprised when I said that I enjoyed living in both types of locations. Invariably, their response was that they could not live in a town or city because it lacked the pastoral scenery and the open space of the country that they found conducive to their feeling at home in the hills. "Just look out my [cottage] window," said one shepherd, "Here in the country you don't see another house the same as your own or near your own [implicitly alluding to the housing estates in Hawick]." This opposition between town/city and country, widespread throughout the United Kingdom (see Williams 1975), is given a particular spin in the Borders. It affects the way Borderers relate town and country in conceiving of the Borders as a distinct cultural and historical place and the way analysts portray the Borders as a place in the United Kingdom.

The study of the Borders region has been structured by this town-country opposition despite the economic interdependence of town and country.[4] Since the early work of Littlejohn (1963) on the sociology of a rural hill sheep farming valley neighboring Teviotdale, the major ethnographic work on Borders social life and identity—other than my own (Gray 1984, 1988, 1996a, 1996b)—has focused on the towns and in particular upon the well-known annual civic ceremonies known as "Common Ridings" (Neville 1979, 1989, 1994; Smith 1993, 1995, 1996). The opening sentence of Neville's excellent study of Selkirk and its Common Riding starkly presents a "town" perspective on the countryside as a natural, uncivilized, disordering, and foreboding landscape: "In the vast moorland known as the Borders of Scotland, the ancient towns, or *burghs*, are sentinels of civic order amid an otherwise sparsely populated expanse of heath and meadow dominated by hills and Cheviot sheep. These stately towns form commercial islands ..." (Neville 1994:3). Common Ridings or other analogous festivals, which are celebrated in most Border towns,[5] portray a town-country opposition in the form of a struggle over land (Neville 1994:4–6). The major event of Common Ridings is a ritual of place-making that marks out the boundaries of the town. It consists of a re-enactment of the annual patrolling on horseback around the towns' common lands to protect them from encroachment by rural-based landowners.

There is another layer of meaning to these festivals. In Selkirk, the Common Riding is also a ritual of remembrance of the town's boys killed in wars. This memorial is made through the festival's specific association with the Battle of Flodden (1513) in which Borderers bravely fought, died and lost their king, James IV, to the English armies in one of the innumerable battles of the three-hundred-year War of Independence between Scotland and England (Neville 1994:17ff). Hawick's Common Riding also recalls the Battle of Flodden. The town's common lands were granted to it by Sir James Douglas of Drumlanrig "in recognition of the faithful services of the men of Hawick at the Battle of Flodden, and in commisseration [*sic*] for the great loss they sustained" (Oliver 1887:108). In the festival, the banner carried by the young Hawick-born Cornet leading the ride-outs alludes to the story of the brave lads of the town who surprised and captured the flag of an English raiding party exploiting the post-Flodden English dominance of the region. The references to the Battle of Flodden in these festivals celebrate another important opposition in Borders town culture—the political opposition between Scotland and England epitomized by the long history of conflicts over Scotland's sovereignty that occurred in the Borders during the War of Independence. For both Neville and Smith this opposition is crucial to constructing a separate regional identity for the Borders.

Through combining both these oppositions in Common Riding, the theme of the defense of common lands by the towns against encroachment of rural landlords resonates with the defense of Scotland by the towns against the armed incursions of English so that both England and the rural countryside of the Borders are juxtaposed to towns. The effect of Neville's and Smith's analyses is to generalize to the whole Borders region a self-image derived only from the perspective of its towns and their histories. Excluded from their analyses of Borders people and their place-making practices are the inhabitants of the countryside and the distinct history of their experience as Scottish Borderers confronting England. This exclusion is particularly ironic in that Smith is careful in her work to be sensitive to the way in which the Borders region "is doubly marginalized: first by the invisibility of Scotland within England's Britain, and then lost within a Scotland marked out by its central belt, and signified by its Highlands and Islands" (1996:24). In this respect, the rural population, such as the hill sheep farming people of Teviothead, are triply marginalized and invisible within Neville's and Smith's town-based representations of the Borders.

Neither in Littlejohn's research nor in my own in Borders hill sheep farming localities did we find a high level of participation by farming people in these town-based Common Riding festivals. If from the perspective of its towns, the Battle of Flodden symbolizes Borders identity in opposition to England, I argue in Chapter 1 that raiding, or *reiving*, which was endemic in the Borders during the fourteenth to sixteenth centuries, plays the same role for people in the countryside. Reivers were rural-based landowning lairds—the very people whose encroachment on common lands the Common Ridings were meant to prevent—and the bands recruited from among their kin and dependants for the purpose of raiding, thieving, and blackmail. Both the soldiers of Flodden and reivers are "romantic" images of bravery and valor glorifying Borderers' resistance to domination by England during the War of Independence. These historical themes find contemporary objects for resistance in the region's continual appropriation by the British state and the supranational institutions of the European Community (see Nadel-Klein 1991). Thus, as I suggest in Chapter 3, for hill sheep farmers in particular it is the European Community's agricultural policies that have defined the Borders countryside as economically marginal in yet a further—quadruple—way because the region is classed as a "Less Favoured Area" for agricultural production (see Gray 1996b).

It is perhaps not surprising, then, that early on in my fieldwork in Teviothead shortly after the European Community Sheep Meat Regime had been introduced and its effects on "marginal" sheep farms were being felt, a farmer gave me a copy of Fraser's book, *The Steel Bonnets: The Story of the Anglo-Scottish Border Reivers,* saying that if I wanted to understand people of the Borders, I needed to know about reiving.[6] While reivers plundered on both sides of the Borders (Fraser 1971:9), in the historical imagination of contemporary people in Teviothead it was the foremost act of resistance that was distinctive of the Borders at a time when Scotland was struggling for its independence from England; for them reiving remains the symbol of that resistance to encroachments from external agencies and powers as well as the distinctiveness of the Borders region. This is the significance of those places in the hills that, as I describe in Chapter 6, shepherds associate with reiving. These places evoke a shared world of meaning derived from an image of the reivers, whose success in making a life in the Borders—using their intimate knowledge of the region to raid and evade capture by stealth—derived from being-at-home in the hills, just as it does for hill sheep farming people.

In describing the practices through which hill sheep farming people place-make a life and an identity in the hills of the Scottish borders, this ethnography also addresses two central issues in contemporary anthropology. First is the growing recognition among anthropologists (Appadurai 1988; Basso 1996; Dominy 1995; Feld and Basso 1996; Hirsch and O'Hanlan 1995; Jackson 1995; Rodman 1992; Weiner 1991) and cultural geographers (Agnew and Duncan 1989; Berdoulay 1989; Duncan 1990; Entrikin 1991; Pickles 1985; Relph 1976, 1981, 1985; Tuan 1977) of the importance of the spatial in social life and the processes through which people create places and imbue them with significance. Second is an intense awareness of the effects of global processes upon people's sense of place in social life and upon anthropologists' taken-for-granted assumptions about the location of culture (Appadurai 1991; Clifford 1997; Gupta and Ferguson 1992, 1996, 1997a; Olwig and Hastrup 1997). After a brief interlude in which I discuss my understanding of the concepts of space and place, I describe how these issues form the themes for situating my ethnographic account of hill sheep farming people making a place and a life in Teviothead.

Interlude: Space and Place

Space is not an abstract phenomenon—empty, neutral, homogeneous, and a priori—onto which humans map their action in the form of meaningful places.[7] Adopting a phenomenological perspective that describes human consciousness in its lived immediacy and "honors the actual experience" (Jackson 1996:2, 16), Casey argues the converse—that place is the primary human experience and is prior to space. Human being-in-the-world is fundamentally a being-in-place. We are always somewhere, in some location that is actively and constitutively perceived through the body's senses and movements so that the places we inhabit inherently have particular contours and meanings for us. In this respect, place and placedness are elementary "lived-experience" *(Erlebnis)* (Casey 1996:18). Our "modern" understanding of space, formulated explicitly in the seventeenth and eighteenth centuries as an abstract phenomenon (Casey 1997), is a distillation from this primary lived-experience of "being-in-place" (Casey 1996:16ff). In this respect, space is an a posteriori "secondary" experience deriving from a reflexive act upon "the already elapsed [lived] experience [of place] that is an object of analytical or abstract knowledge" (1996:18). Ironically, then, the seemingly abstract and objective notion of space decentered from human agency is itself a human product.

Casey draws quite a stark contrast between the a prior, specific, embodied, and meaningful experience of place and the a posteriori, abstract, dehumanized, and formal Western Enlightenment concept of space. His analysis is pitched at the level of universal human experience: the placedness that humans experience as a condition of being-in-the-world is contrasted with the abstract concept of space. However, the

relation between place and space takes on a different configuration and character when space in its eighteenth-century
abstract form is no longer universalized but particularized in
a historical and cultural context that is also an inherent condition of human being-in-the-world. While reversing the terminology, this was de Certeau's (1984:91ff) message.[8] For
him, *space* (in my terminology) refers to the distanced,
abstract, dehumanized, and totalizing spatial productions of
the cartographer or city planner—the agents of government.
In defining and organizing *spaces*, their maps, plans and built
forms are instruments for the exercise of power. De Certeau's
notion of *place* (in my terminology) refers to the sensual construction of meaningful locations by people consuming such
spaces through their everyday practices of moving about and
using them for their own purposes. In this respect, the same
geographical location has a different nature from the perspective of people in different social locations—what is *space*
for the cartographer or city planner becomes meaningful
place for the people using it. An important dimension of de
Certeau's practice perspective is that both producers of *spaces*
and consumers of *places* are historically and socially located.
His analysis reveals a weakness of a phenomenological
approach: its avoidance of the differentials of power in the
constitution of locations and our spatial experience of them
(see also Tilley 1994:11; Gupta and Ferguson 1997b:40).

I adopt an approach to the place-making of hill sheep
farming people in the Scottish Borders that is inspired by
Casey's phenomenological critique of the a priori conception of homogeneous space and by de Certeau's practical
incorporation of sociohistorical particularity and differential
relations of power in the production and consumption of
space. Thus "place" refers to the meaningful locations and
"frame of mind" (Thomas 1993:28) created by human "dwelling," the term Heidegger used to describe "the manner in
which we humans *are* on the earth" (Heidegger 1975:147,
italics original); and "space" refers to the humanly constructed settings of such place-making. Since the construction of space is historically and socially located, "there is no
[single abstract] space, only [historically and socially
specific] spaces" that are simultaneously the media for and
the product of human action (Tilley 1994:10; see also Soja

1989:70; Relph 1976, 1985). A central dimension of the historical and social contexts in which spaces are media and outcomes of action is that they are organized by differential relations of power between on the one hand external and/or global sites and on the other hand local sites of human action and experience—as Gupta and Ferguson write: "spaces have *always* been hierarchically interconnected, instead of naturally disconnected" (1997b:35). People at these two different kinds of sociopolitical sites can have different experiences and understandings of a location as a place or a space. This is another sense in which space and place are reciprocally related as different perspectives on the same location.

From the perspective of an individual or group living in their local context, the location they inhabit appears as a constraining medium for their action because it is the production of agents external to their locality. This is how I treat the Borders region in the first three chapters. In each I describe how governments in Edinburgh and London, landlords of large estates, and the European Community respectively shaped the Borders into historically distinct spaces through determining its boundaries, internal divisions, and distribution of people according to specific agendas of domination (Foucault 1977:141ff). *Space* is thus "a rationalized, expansionist, and at the same time centralized, clamorous and spectacular production" (de Certeau 1984:xii) of global forces, a historically specific medium within which people carry out their lives, make their local places, and reciprocally make themselves. This local place-making is the subject of the remaining chapters in which I analyze how hill sheep farming people perceive their farms and invest them with significance through their farming activities (Feld and Basso 1996:8). In this sense, then, I am reserving the notion of space for the location or setting that people experience as largely externally produced and that acts as a medium or constraining setting for their everyday actions. The notion of place is reserved for the personally, socially, and/or historically meaningful locations that people experience as the outcome of their own actions. Places then are the outcomes of local people's consumption (to use de Certeau's metaphor) of these spaces with respect to their own everyday practical ends that may be "foreign to the [externally-produced space] they had no choice but to accept" (de Certeau 1984:xiii).

A Predicament of Emplacement

> There's a place for us,
> Somewhere a place for us.
> Peace and quiet and open air
> Wait for us
> Somewhere.
> (Bernstein and Sondheim 1957)

I open with an epigraph of the song "Somewhere" from *West Side Story*. As part of their modern retelling of Shakespeare's sixteenth-century tale of *Romeo and Juliet,* Bernstein's music and Sondheim's lyrics capture a predicament of emplacement besetting the contemporary world. *West Side Story* is told in a different register than *Romeo and Juliet,* and this difference is marked by its title. Shakespeare's title names the *principal characters* who are the focus of complex human relations that he explores in the play. For Shakespeare, the problem for Romeo and Juliet inheres in the social relations they implicate by their relationship. The locale for the playing out of these relations is more a backdrop and less important than the fact that the characters are from different kin groups. Bernstein's title names *a place* suggesting that to explore the same complex human relations in the twentieth century requires more than a neutral setting where they occur because the problems for Tony and Maria are somehow inextricable from the place where they live. The West Side of New York City is where immigrants from Puerto Rico and Italy settled to make a new life, and an important part of making that new life is to create a sense of place by establishing an exclusive attachment to a territory—a place where they feel "at home in the world" (Jackson 1995). The song, sung by Tony and Maria, alludes to their relationship doomed in that place (and that time) because their love cannot be disentangled from the conflict between the Jets and the Sharks over control of space in the city. Their relationship is infused with the predicament of emplacement that afflicts the inhabitants of the West Side. Within this story, the song also expresses a more general longing for a sense of place that is dislocated by life in a society populated by uprooted people from many elsewheres. The post–World War II movement of people from their homelands to the "New World" led to a more urgent yearning for emplacement, a somewhere that gives meaning to life and is given meaning by life.

Nearly three decades later, anthropologists began to doubly sense this predicament of emplacement.[9] In a first sense, there is a recognition of an existential predicament in that the people whose lives are the focus of ethnography are increasingly subject to global processes that disturb, loosen, or sever the intimate and constitutive relation between being and place that is fundamental to person-in-the-world (Seamon 1984:45). Appadurai (1991) describes what he calls the process of "deterritorialization" in which specific territorial boundaries and identities are transcended by transnational corporations, large-scale labor migration, global movements of capital, and mass communication technology (cinema, television, videotape recorders). This "loosening of the bonds between people, wealth and territory fundamentally alters the basis of cultural reproduction" (1991:193). The result of these "brute facts about the world of the twentieth century" is that "groups are no longer tightly territorialized, spatially bounded, historically unselfconscious, or culturally homogeneous" (1991:191).[10] Gupta and Ferguson similarly argue that the realities of the modern world in the form of "the rapidly expanding and quickening mobility of people combines with the refusal of cultural products and practices to 'stay put' to give a profound sense of a loss of territorial roots, of an erosion of the cultural distinctiveness of place ..." (1997:37). Auge coins the term "supermodernity" for the late twentieth century characterized by an

> excess of space ... correlative with the shrinking of the earth... [where] rapid means of transport have brought any capital within a few hours' travel of any other. And in the privacy of our homes, finally, images of all sorts, relayed by satellites and caught by the aerials that bristle on the roofs of our remotest hamlets, can give us an instant, sometimes simultaneous vision of an event taking place on the other side of the planet. (1995:31)

This supermodern excess of space produces "non-places" to which people have difficulty in establishing stable attachments and where they have difficulty in sustaining ongoing relations with others. Jackson (1995) begins his book about his own and Australian Aborigines' experience of being-at-home-in-the-world with the following description of causes and experience of homelessness:

> Ours is a century of uprootedness. All over the world, fewer and fewer people live out their lives in the place where they were born. Perhaps at no other time in history has the question of belonging seemed so urgent. Since the end of the Second World War, millions of men and women have migrated from the impoverished countries of the south to cities of the industrialized north because they see no future for themselves at home. They sell their labor and hope to return to villages where they will become heroes ... The quarter we drop into the panhandler's Styrofoam cup on a freezing January afternoon betokens our own mood of estrangement even when we are well-housed and well-heeled. (1995:1–2)

Basso points to some of the same global processes that have "dislocated" the American Indians with whom he has spent so many years:

> In this unsettled age, when large portions of the earth's surface are being ravaged by industrialism ... when on several continents indigenous peoples are being forcibly uprooted by wanton encroachments upon their homelands ... when American Indian tribes are mounting major legal efforts to secure permanent protections for sacred sites now controlled by federal agencies. (1996:105)

Finally, Feld and Basso portray the contemporary predicament of emplacement in their characterization of the "now acute world conditions of exile, displacement, diaspora, and inflamed borders, to say nothing of the increasingly tumultuous struggles by indigenous peoples and cultural minorities for ancestral homelands, land rights and retention of sacred places" (1996:4).

In a second sense, anthropologists themselves are experiencing a reflexive predicament of emplacement with regard to their most cherished concept—culture. They are recognizing that the same global processes that dislocate people also undermine what Hastrup and Olwig called "the place-focused notion of culture," "the anthropological place fixation" (1997:

5, 6) or what Gupta and Ferguson refer to as the "assumed iso-morphism of space, place and culture" (1997b:34). By this they are referring to the pervasive assumption of ethnography that cultures are separate entities not only with unique customs but also with a pre-given, distinct, and bounded geographical loca-tion.[11] And two of the same authors who describe the disloca-tion of people also describe this concomitant dislocation of the concept of culture. Thus the processes that for Appadurai (1991) caused a loosening of the bonds between people and place also caused a deterritorialization of the *concept* of cul-ture. Because of mass communication, people now live in and identify with ethnoscapes—places where cultural differences are not so much spatially juxtaposed as interactively and imag-inatively constituted. Likewise, Gupta and Ferguson link the border crossings, multiculturalism, hybrid postcolonial cul-tures and interconnected global system that characterize the contemporary world to the "erosion of the supposedly natural connections between people and places" (1997:39).

Yet Hastrup and Olwig (1997:11) and Gupta and Fergu-son (1997:39) also recognize an irony: just as anthropologists are responding to their reflexive predicament of emplace-ment by questioning the place-focused concept of culture, "deterritorialized" peoples are responding to their existential predicament of emplacement by re-emphasizing the isomor-phism of place and culture as part of a self-conscious process of creating a sense of place and identity in the world. Nadel-Klein's analysis of the persistence of localism—"the continu-ing reference to place in assertions of a political or cultural will to distinctiveness" (1991:501)—in Scotland provides a concrete illustration of how the marginalizing and dislo-cating effects of a global political economy on local com-munities paradoxically produces "representations of group identity as defined primarily by a sense of commitment to a particular place and to a set of cultural practices"(1991:502). In this respect, place-making remains a fundamental process for humans; creating a place for the self and for one's group is central to personal and social existence. Losing one's place because of these global processes may be one of those post-modern ironies that engenders a heightened awareness (Basso 1996:107) not only of the place lost but also of the centrality of being-in-place to self and identity.[12] It is in this context that the yearning for a place so poignantly expressed in Bernstein's song is felt and the active quest for a re-emplacement commences—even if it must occur under conditions of deterritorialization, homelessness, uprootedness, diaspora, mobility, and the non-places of supermodernity. And one of the subtexts of many recent ethnographies is that anthropologists too are caught in the irony for we are also coming to treat place and space as problematic in our analyses rather than as the unquestioned and neutral locational background of our descriptions of social lives (see Basso 1996; B. Bender 1993; Casey 1996; Cohen 1982, 1985; Jackson 1995; Jedrej and Nuttall 1996; Rapport 1993; Tilley 1994; Weiner 1991).

Despite this growing awareness of dislocation and mobility disrupting the attachment of people, culture, and place, Herzfeld (1991) implies that there are other less spatially radical but no less deeply felt challenges to people's sense of place (see also Gupta and Ferguson 1997:39). Much like the Rethemniots of Crete, contemporary Border hill sheep people are not geographically dislocated migrants, uprooted refugees, or exiles confronted with the prospect of having to create and establish an attachment to a new place. The issue for their sense of place has been and continues to be "about battling the form and future of the physical environment, about shoring up familiar cultural spaces against the encroaching strangeness" (Herzfeld 1991:24) that has been a recurrent feature of their history and their location in the international borders between Scotland and England. I take up this theme in the first three chapters in which I construct a history of Anglo-Scottish border space in the form of an archaeology (Foucault 1970, 1972). In each I identify a historical rupture brought about by an encroaching strangeness in the form of a space-defining event for the Borders that produced a distinct episteme of relations between beings and place. I also use each of these opening chapters to introduce some aspects of contemporary hill sheep farming.

Chapter 1 is about the fourteenth to sixteenth centuries when the War of Independence between Scotland and England, devised in the distant capitals of Edinburgh and London but largely fought in the Borders, turned the region into a lawless international frontier of reivers. Organized by feudal relations to a local laird, reiver families became identified with the river valleys that were their strongholds as well as where they lived, and I suggest that this is an early indication of a sense of place in which person and place become refractions of each other. Another legacy of this period is that the Borders region remains a single and coherent space that spans the political boundary between England and Scotland. In the seventeenth to nineteenth centuries, it was the 1603 Union of the Crowns under James I and the transformation by his proclamation of the Borders into the "Middle Shires" that enabled the refashioning of the Borders from a lawless frontier into a disciplined space of capitalist agriculture on large landed estates in the center of the new kingdom. In Chapter 2, I trace the spatial effects of this shift from feudal to capitalist relations brought about by the administrative reform on the emerging estate of the Duke of Buccleuch centered in Teviotdale. I suggest that these reforms produced a metamorphosis of the earlier person-place association between extended reiving "families" and feudal territories to an association between tenant farming families and specific farms. Here I introduce a central motif of the book concerning how this person/s-place relation, this sense of place on a farm, is a fundamental dimension of the way hill sheep people understand their family farms. In the latter decades of the twentieth century it was Britain's membership in the European Community and its regulation by the Common Agricultural Policy that again redefined the Borders, this time as a peripheral rural space made up of politically and socially valuable but economically marginal family farms. In Chapter 3, I explicate the spatial consequences for the Borders region of the Common Agricultural Policy, how it was designed to maintain family farming because this type of production sustains not just rural society but society as a whole and how it codified a morally charged image of rurality. I describe the two different farming polices that Teviothead sheep farmers adopted to maintain the financial viability of their farms.

Place-Making and Family Farms in the Scottish Borderlands

Few areas of the world have experienced such a series of encroaching strangenesses over such a long period of time.

This is perhaps one of the consequences of the region's location on international borders where a fluidity of spatial and cultural identity is the result of "political negotiation and contest" (Donnan and Wilson 1994:7) between nation-states over the limits of their sovereignty. It is a negotiation that is still going on, now with renewed vigor after the New Labour government of Tony Blair began the process of devolution in 1997. The location of Teviothead in a borderlands space remains a significant dimension of the setting for the actions of hill sheep farmers, both constraining and enabling the way they make a life and a place in the Borders.

The main proponents of the borderlands concept—Adejuyigbe (1989), Alverez (1995), Martinez (1994), Donnan and Wilson (1994)—identify structural characteristics of spaces located at international boundaries that everywhere act as constraints or determinants upon the actions of people living in them.[13] They highlight two contrary attributes that derive from the unique spatial location of borderlands. First, borderlands are located at a physical distance from the center zone of a sociopolitical unit. In this sense, they constitute a *periphery* whose existence and character are defined in relation to the center; simultaneously, the center defines itself in relation to the periphery. The periphery-center configuration is a *within* relation in the sense that it refers to the mutually constitutive and hierarchically articulated (Gupta and Ferguson 1997b:35) relation between spaces within a sociopolitical unit. Second and simultaneously, borderlands are located around the concrete, physical, and juridical boundary between two sociopolitical units (Donnan and Wilson 1994:4). In this respect, the territories on each side of the boundary form a border zone or *frontier* defined not just by their distance from the center but also by their proximity to each other and by the dynamic quality of social life arising from borderlanders' interactions with a politically spatial other, a social life that challenges the dominance of their respective centers. In this respect, borderlands in the frontier configuration are constituted by a *between* relation—between two sociopolitical units they simultaneously separate and join together; and they "serve as barriers of exclusion and protection marking 'home' from 'foreign'" (Donnan and Wilson 1994:3; see also Alverez 1995:450).

These two modes of borderland space are productive of processes of identity formation and emplacement in quite different ways.[14] Shields's work focuses on the margins or periphery that are juxtaposed to a core; together core and periphery form a single social entity, e.g., a nation-state. In this hierarchical configuration, peripheral spaces carry a negative connotation, a stigma (Shields 1991:3). Sheilds's analyses of Brighton in England, Niagara Falls in America, the Canadian north, and the north-south divide in Britain enshrine the view from the center of the periphery. If applied to places on the borders, his perspective would privilege only one spatial mode of borderlands as their essence. However, border regions look different from the perspective of those living in them. Heidegger and Bhabha emphasize that borderlands in a frontier configuration exist "in between" and are constitutive of two entities.

> A boundary is not that at which something stops but, as the Greeks recognized, the boundary is that from which something *begins its presencing* (Heidegger 1975:154, italic original)

> These "in between" spaces provide the terrain for elaborating strategies of selfhood—singular or communal—that initiate new signs of identity, and innovative sites of collaboration, and contestation, in the act of defining the idea of society itself … it is in the emergence of the interstices … that the intersubjective and collective experience of nationness, community interest, or cultural value are negotiated. (Bhabha 1994:1–2)

In this in-between mode, borderlands are dynamic and powerful sites for the positive construction of identities. Rather than being the stigmatized "ends of the earth" from the perspective of the center, they are for Borderers the beginnings of a deeply felt sense of place, self, and world. Further, the between relation does not make all borderlands "an interstitial zone of displacement and deterritorialization that shapes the identity of the *hybridized* subject" (Gupta and Ferguson 1997b:48, italics added). In the Scottish Borders, like the Shabe borders of Nigeria, "it is a local sense of deep placement instead of displacement, deep territorialization instead of deterritorialization, which forges strong feelings of rootedness in the borderland itself and creates a [nonhybridized] border identity" (Flynn 1997:312). The process by which contemporary hill sheep farmers forge such strong feelings of rootedness is the subject of the remaining chapters. Shifting focus from the Borders region to the rural community of Teviothead eight miles south of Hawick, I analyze the diverse range of farming practices and family relations through which hill sheep farming people cumulatively build their sense of place. I argue that what is distinctive about this sense of place is that family and farm, beings and place, are consubstantial; they partake of the same substance and are refractions of a single phenomenon—the family farm.

The process begins with the establishment of a singular relation between a farmer and a farm through one of the forms of land tenure that I describe in Chapter 4. More than just a legal relation, I show how tenure is not simply a material interdependence between a family and a hill sheep farm but also a relation in which a family comes to exist and have a distinct identity through its singular relation to a farm. In the following chapter I describe the two types of land and the sheep that make up a hill sheep farm. I highlight the way in which hill sheep bond to and embody a specific territory in the hills because this process of "hefting on" serves as a metaphor and mechanism for hill sheep people's consubstantial sense of place. Chapter 6 takes hill sheep's embodiment of land a step further by describing how, through herding ewes in the hills and breeding rams, the stockmanship and personhood of hill shepherds and farmers also becomes embodied in sheep. The cumulative result of tenure, sheep territoriality, and herding activities is that sheep both incarnate and mediate the relation between farming people and their farm.

The next two chapters follow lambs and rams to the auctions. In Chapter 7, I characterize the auctions of hill lambs as reflexive spectacles in which individualized hill sheep people create a shared experience of hill sheep farming as a way-of-life and the Borders as the place of hill sheep farming. I suggest that the cultural dimension of what appears to be an economic exchange is the result of the way sheep embody the personhood of those who herd them and of the common understanding that lambs are cultural objects whose value derives as much from their specific relation to particular shepherds and farms as from their exchange value as agricultural commodities. In Chapter 8, I analyze the annual ram sales at Lockerbie. I suggest that rams are presented as aesthetic objects that express breeders' personal value as hill sheep stockman and that ram sales are vehicles for status differentiation. I also point out how the annual ram sales are a mechanism for constituting a community of hill sheep people of the Borders through a redistribution of hill sheep farming skills and knowledge in the form of rams and their genetic make-up. Here again I highlight how sheep embody, suffuse, and mediate relations between a group of people defined by a form of life (hill sheep farming) and a place (the Borders) where it is lived.

Chapter 9 takes up class relations between farmers who own sheep and shepherds who are hired to care for them. While it is possible to locate class relations in large-scale historical, economic, and/or political processes, I instead follow how they are played out on hill sheep farms and how hill sheep farms inflected the way farmers and shepherds experience class. Based on the distinctive part-whole spatial organization of people on hill sheep farms that associates shepherds with a group of hill ewes and farmers with rams that mate with the whole flock, I explain farmers' and shepherds' differing views on the existence and importance of class in social life. The process of creating a consubstantial sense of place culminates in Chapter 10 where I identify the strategies hill sheep farming people adopt to keep the farm in the family. I point to hill sheep people's use of a genetic discourse, derived from their practical knowledge of how sheep acquire and biologically transmit their relationship to the land where they live, to transform the legal process of passing farm assets and management onto the next generation into a process of transmitting the consubstantial relation between farm and family. The consubstantial sense of place is thus both spatial and temporal: a family and a farm are experienced as refractions of a single phenomenon over time. In the concluding chapter, I explore how this notion of a consubstantial sense of place may be entailed in our concept of the rural.

Notes

1. Henry Scott Riddell (1798–1870) was the son of a shepherd who worked on several farms in and around Teviotdale. He, like James Hogg—*The Works of the Ettrick Shepherd* (1872)—composed poetry and ballads about Borders life.
2. Tim Douglas was until recently a hill sheep farmer on Gatehousecote Farm, Bonchester Bridge. He was kind enough to show me his poetical works consisting of more than two hundred items ranging over all aspects of life in the Borders.
3. For Borderers they are beautiful as the two poems of the epigraph express, but for most outsiders they are barren and foreboding (Fraser 1971:21)—somewhere only Borderers could feel at home.
4. For example, from the seventeenth to the mid-twentieth centuries, Hawick's growth and prosperity was as a mill town where wool from surrounding sheep farms was sold, distributed, and processed (see also Neville 1994:6).
5. See Smith (1995:152) for a listing of these Borders towns and their festivals.
6. Unlike the situation encountered by Nadel-Klein, there was not a class division in these "romantic and resisting" faces of localism. Farmers and hired shepherds adopted the romantic-resisting combination with respect to the European Community (1991:503).
7. Gupta and Ferguson all too easily assume that space is an a priori, meaningless form upon which humans bestow meaning as part of cultural life: "The idea that space is made meaningful is, of course, a familiar one to anthropologists; indeed there is hardly an older or better established anthropological truth" (1997b:40). Building on the work of Tilley (1994) and Casey (1996, 1997), I am refusing to take this for granted. Instead, I view space itself as humanly constructed. While in the modern era, as Casey shows, space is seen as universal and neutrally monolithic (1997:134), I instead treat space as a humanly constructed polythetic medium for place-making practices. Space is experienced as an a priori form but this is a mystification of the fact that someone else with power constructed the space in which we live and to which our place-making activity must adapt.
8. In order to maintain consistency of terminology in this discussion, I will substitute my usage of the terms *space* and *place* for de Certeau's usage of *place* and *space* respectively. This substitution of terms is marked by the use of italics.
9. Cultural geographers were also writing about the increase in importance of place (Agnew and Duncan 1989; Berdoulay 1989; Entrikin 1991; Relph 1976).
10. Despite these global processes of deterritorialization, Appadurai seems to imply that people and groups still create an identity by associating themselves with a place. The resources they use to imagine this place and their attachment to it are no longer themselves local but rather global.
11. Hansen traces this isomorphism to nineteenth–century German scholars who "developed the principle that national borders should coincide with linguistic and cultural boundaries" (1981:20).
12. Alverez concurs with this inverse relation between the experience of being-in-place and efforts at place–making: "Whereas at one time we conceptualized culture as territorially contained units and communities as likewise bounded entities, we now attempt to reconceptualize these notions from the perspective of a deterritorialized world, a world in which cultural and ethnic identities have in turn become deterritorialized and yet, stronger" (1995:449).
13. The concept of borderlands (see Adejuyigbe 1989; Donnan and Wilson 1994; Momoh 1989; Martinez 1994; P. Sahlins 1989) was developed to highlight what were seen to be common historical and cultural characteristics of the spaces

located around a geopolitical boundary. Its recent emergence as an anthropological genre (Alverez 1995) is one consequence of the parallel recognition of what I described earlier as the crisis of emplacement. Processes of globalization, deterritorialization, diaspora, and migration have rendered national boundaries less definitive of culture areas. Simultaneously, national or cultural identity and geopolitical territory have become disarticulated. Instead of spaces of national, ethnic, and/or other forms of social differentiation and political control, borders are now seen to be important sites for processes of identity formation characterized by juxtaposition, negotiation, political instability, paradox, irony, contestation—qualities that are central to a postcolonial anthropology of the late twentieth century. In this respect, borderlands are a prime site for the study of those cultural processes that have become mainstream issues in contemporary anthropology—hence the popularity of the genre (Alverez 1995).

14. Boundaries, margins, borders, and interstices, whether literal (geographical, political) or figurative, have long been objects of anthropological interest because they are recognized as powerful sites of symbolic death and rebirth and more recently of social contestation and creativity. The works of Mary Douglas (1966) on anomaly and Victor Turner (1967) on liminality analyzed the power of the ambiguity located on the margins. They both assumed a pre–existing social or conceptual structure of geographical separation, differentiated roles, and social states that were the condition for anomalous or liminal phenomena that spanned the boundaries of the structure. In this social location of transgressing and challenging boundaries, the "formlessness" (Douglas 1966:190) of these phenomena becomes a source of power that could be harnessed by ritual for the regeneration of society and the creation of new social phenomena.

REIVERS OF THE MARCHES
The Borders as Frontier

For people of the Anglo-Scottish borderlands, the fourteenth to sixteenth centuries remain a significant period
of their past for their contemporary identity.[1] It was a time of
feudal nobles with large landed estates extending over whole
river valleys and their dependants with small sheep farms nes-
tled in the Border hills. It was also a time when Scotland and
England were engaged in their protracted War of Independence, and "reiving" prevailed. Reiving strictly refers to acts
of robbery, raiding, marauding, and plundering. During the
three centuries of intermittent warfare between Scotland and
England, it became the central and defining feature of the
way of life of Borderers. Local land-owning lairds on both
sides of the border recruited raiding parties of twelve to
fifty—and sometimes nearly three hundred—men from
among their kin and feudal dependants to engage *en revanche*
in armed robbery, arson, kidnapping, blackmail, and occasionally murder against the enemy over the border as well as
against their neighbors. It was largely a practice of those living in the rural river valleys and bleak hills that characterized
the topography of the Border region. In a contemporary
description of Border life in the sixteenth century, Lesley,
Bishop of Ross, highlights several features of reiving, particularly how raiding parties used their intimate knowledge of
the terrain to avoid detection and evade capture.

Notes for this section begin on page 44.

They leave their frontiers in the night time in troops, going through impassable places, and through many bye paths. In the day time they refresh their horses, and recruit their own strength, in hiding places prepared before-hand, until the approach of night, when they advance to their place of destination. Having seized upon their booty, they in the same manner return by night, through circuits and bye-ways, to their own habitations. The more expert each leader is in making his way through these dreary places, windings, and precipices, in the darkest night, he is so much more accounted a person of superior ingenuity, and held in greater honor; and with such secrecy can they proceed, that they very rarely allow their prize to be recovered, unless they be sometimes tracked by their opponents, when discovered by keen scented dogs, who always follow them in the right path. (Lesley 1577, in Scott 1814, Vol. I, Appendix No. vi:lxvi)

The reivers' aim was rather prosaic and localized: to steal livestock and other goods as a means of subsistence. Fraser cites the results of two typical raids by Border families[2] and the extent to which reiving had become ubiquitous in the sixteenth century:

On 2 April 1581, Isabell Routledge, a widow, was visited by thirty Elliots, who ransacked her home, took her four oxen, her six cows, and her only horse, and made off with all her possessions … When the Elliots of Liddesdale were riding in the summer of 1581, they were moving in bands generally 100 strong. In June and July alone they stole in the West March of England 274 cattle and twelve horses, ransacked nine houses, "wounded and maimed" three men, and took one prisoner … The Elliots were one of many robber families; Liddesdale was one of many robber roosts, though admittedly the worst by far. According to a list of bills against Liddesdale, dated 30 April 1590, the reivers of that valley alone were riding an average of a raid a week through the winter of 1589–90. In that time they carried off more than 850 beasts, took sixty prisoners, wounded ten men, killed one, took insight of £200, and burned five houses. (Fraser 1971:75–76)

Once begun as a mode of subsistence, reiving took on a life of its own in the sense of its use being extended to a number of other ends, particularly when the practice reached its height in the sixteenth century. It was undertaken as retaliation in ongoing feuds between reiver families in the Borders, often initiated by the death of a kinsman during a raid. As an

example, in Teviotdale and Liddesdale a feud between the
Scotts and the Elliots began after a round of livestock thefts—
or accusations of livestock thefts, the murder of a Scott by the
Elliots in a raid, and, in retaliation, the execution of four
Elliots legally obtained by Scott of Buccleuch, the Keeper of
Liddesdale at the time. For over a year there was daily raiding
between the two clans. The parties settled the feud after the
Elliots, assisted by agents of the English government, ambushed
a large raiding party of Scotts (Fraser 1971:153). Such assistance in local feuds by national governments was another way
in which reiving became widespread. As the War of Independence between Scotland and England remained unsettled,
both governments used local animosities between families
(initiated and reproduced by reiving) and the reivers' ability
to attack by stealth to advance their national[3] interests in
times of peace. In the case of the Scott-Elliot feud, the English were able to keep "the Border Scotts at home" in order to
distract Buccleuch and his clan from their involvement in
Scotland's resistance to English domination (ibid.).

Commentators of the sixteenth century and historians of
the twentieth century explain the cause and pervasiveness of
reiving as a way for Border people to cope with the periodic
devastation of their land and livelihood during the three centuries of Scottish resistance against subjugation by England.

> Among all those provinces of Scotland, those which are situ-
> ated next to England assume to themselves the greatest habits
> of licence, in which they frequently indulge with impunity. For
> as, in time of war, they are readily reduced to extreme poverty
> by the almost daily inroads of the enemy, so, on restoration of
> peace they entirely neglect to cultivate their lands, though fer-
> tile, from fear of the fruits of their labour being immediately
> destroyed by a new war. Whence it happens that they seek their
> subsistence by robberies, or rather by plunder and rapine …
> nor do they much concern themselves whether it be from Scots
> or English that they rob and plunder and carry off their booty
> of horses, cattle, and sheep. (Lesley 1577, in Scott 1814, Vol. I,
> Appendix No. vi:lxii).

> What resulted was not only guerrilla warfare, but guerrilla liv-
> ing … to ordinary people, *war and peace were not very different.*
> The trouble with the Anglo-Scottish wars was that no one ever
> won them; they were always liable to break out again. There was
> no future for the Borderer in trying to lead a settled existence,

even in so-called peacetime ... So they lived as best they could ... The Border developed its system of existence ... It was a system of armed plunder, from neighbours as well as from subjects of the opposite realm. The astonishing thing about it was that, while both governments deplored what must be called the reiver economy, they exploited it quite cynically for their own ends. (Fraser 1971:16-17, emphasis added)

Whyte is skeptical of explanations that construct reiving as a pragmatic reaction to periodic devastation of war and suggests that endemic raiding was a response to pressure on resources due to overpopulation (1997:79-80). However, neither of these functional explanations explicitly accounts for why Borderers chose to be "lawless" and the particular ways they practiced that lawlessness.

Reiving was a discriminating response of Borderers sensitive to the marginal nature of the space that was being fabricated by the strategies and battles between England and Scotland to which they were subjected. Further, by engaging in lawless reiving, Borderers promoted a positive feedback process: they treated the Border region as the same kind of contested and marginal space as did the English and Scottish governments. Their reiving contributed to the process of creating and intensifying that marginality. This emergent parallelism between the spatiality produced by ongoing war between governments carried out by national armies and the spatiality produced by reiving carried out by local kin-based groups resulted in England and Scotland using the latter as a substitute for armed conflict to further their interests and pursue their war even in times of supposed peace. Thus, in both war and peace, the Borders was marginalized, a space where England carried out the strategies for its domination of Scotland and where Scotland carried on the defense of its independence from England.

My aim in this chapter is to analyze three aspects of reiving as a means to identifying the ways in which it continues to have significance for contemporary hill sheep farmers of the Borders. First, I describe the historical events that transformed the relations between Scotland and England. Second, I show how relations between Scotland and England in the fourteenth to sixteenth centuries redefined the Borders as a particular kind of space. These relations were largely

external to the Borders region in the sense that they originated outside the Borders in Edinburgh and London and
their strategic goals concerned territories that lay beyond but
encompassed the Borders. The paradoxical result was that
the Borders was constituted as a distinct and coherent space
in spite of the boundary. Third, I explain how reiving was
compatible with this kind of space and how it internally structured border space through the attachment of kin groups to
specific territories.

Stumbling Into Reiving

> Being delayed in crossing the Forth at Queen's Ferry until day-
> light was gone, and the night being dark, he [King Alexander
> III of Scotland] was advised by his attendants to spend it at
> Inverkeithing; but rejecting their counsel, he pushed on with
> all the speed he could to Kinghorn; when he was near the west
> end of that town, his horse stumbling in the sand, he fell, and
> his neck being dislocated by the fall, and no reasonable help
> given by his attendants, he expired. (Ridpath 1776:113§)

Foucault counseled that we should seek to identify "the accidents ... that gave birth to those things that continue to exist
and have value for us" (Foucault 1991b:81)—prophetic
words for the people of the Scottish-English borderlands. A
horse's stumble on a dark night in 1286 heralded a new era
of conflict between England and Scotland that continued
until the union of the crowns in 1603. In the context of
medieval European politics, Scotland's independence was
England's weakness. From England's perspective, Scotland
could ally itself with and provide a haven for the French, England's Continental enemy. In order to secure its own boundaries, England sought to bring Scotland under its authority in
the form of feudal homage to the English monarch. From
Scotland's perspective, England's policy of domination
threatened its sovereignty. The way the conflict was conducted changed the spatiality of the Borders so that it
became a different kind of space and Borderers came to have
a new sense of place.

Alexander's accidental death left the Scottish kingdom
with thirteen contenders but no direct heir to the crown.

King Edward I of England was invited to resolve the disputed succession. He saw this as an opportunity to gain control of Scotland and resolved the succession in favor of John de Baliol over Robert Bruce. Baliol's role was to be Edward's puppet in Scotland. In 1292 Baliol swore feudal fealty to the English king on behalf of the Scottish kingdom as a whole.[4] Edward also confiscated the English property of those Scottish nobles who resisted his domination of Scotland through Baliol. Three years later, the Scots attempted to reassert their independence by invading the border counties of England, retaking the town of Berwick and massacring English sailors garrisoned there. Edward retaliated in kind, marching an army of 35,000 through the Scottish borderlands, on to Edinburgh and north as far as Scone, "conquering and destroying wherever he went" (Oliver 1887:30). Oliver quotes the following verse from Boece's *Croniclis of Scotland* to give a sense of the devastation wrought on the people of the Scottish borders by Edward:

> This King Edward that furious wes and felloun,[5]
> With all his armie enterit in the toun.
> Within the toun that samin da war slane;
> Wemen and barnis also young and ald,
> War slane that day out of number on tald.
> Out throw the toun abundantlie the blude
> Of tha slane men ran in so greit ane flude,
> Baith deip and wyde that large was and lang,
> Wes sufficient to gar one corne myln gang.[6]

For the next several years, there were periodic battles between English and Scottish armies in the Borders region. Robert Bruce's grandson, the Earl of Carrick, carried on the Scottish resistance and achieved the throne and a period of independence for Scotland after his decisive victory at Bannockburn in 1314. His military tactics included starving the enemy by destroying all potential food sources on the Scottish side of the border through which the English army would have to pass in carrying out its campaign. The effects of these tactics on the people of his own Border region were not much different from those of Edward's campaign. "The inhabitants, with their cattle and sheep, were all securely hid in the recesses of the hills, the barns and houses all burned, the fields laid waste, and the country left a black and desolate wilderness" (Oliver 1887:32). In their military campaigns, and, as we will see later, during periods of peace, Borders people and land were expendable for nationalist goals.

The events of the late thirteenth and early fourteenth centuries established a pattern of how England and Scotland pursued their national interests in the Borders over the next three hundred years. The actions of both governments produced and reflected their view of the Borders as a marginal space of a particular kind. The Border region was subjected to devastation, its social and political boundaries violated and its people reduced to poverty by armies during periods of war and by reiving parties of local families during periods of peace. Despite the English and Scottish governments' differing views of the sovereign status of Scotland in international relations, the way the conflict was conducted and the way it shaped the social life of the Borders was based upon a view common to both governments about the nature of Border space. In the following discussion, I identify several dimensions of this common view of border space and how the conduct of the conflict produced a spatialization of the Borders that simultaneously was the product of the governments' strategies and set conditions for the emergence of reiving and its incorporation into the War of Independence.

The Border Frontier

The Border region was a frontier.[7] Initially, I was tempted to continue using the concept of marginal or peripheral to describe how Border space was constructed in the War of Independence between Scotland and England. Both frontier and margin include a similar set of central ideas: distance, boundary, separation, subordination, and distinctiveness. Moreover, Tsing's (1993) penetrating treatment of Dyak marginality in Indonesia contained several similarities with the historical situation of the Borders during the War of Independence. Like the Dyak, Border people occupied land that was considered to have low agricultural productivity, but this was less important in the definition of Border marginality than of Dyak marginality. Both peoples were in a subordinate position in relation to governments that defined them as politically and socially unimportant through their military tactics. By engaging in reiving, Borderers, like the Dyak, participated in the process of producing their own marginality.[8] This marginality enabled governments—Indonesian, Scottish, and English—to construct a discourse of "otherness" and primitivism that legitimated subordination and violent subjugation as well as their reflexive imagining of the self through the marginalized other, Dyaks and Borderers respectively (Torgovnick 1990:18).

But I decided not to use marginality because the concept has been applied to otherness and subordination without the geographic locational reference that the notion of frontier retains. Adopting a center-periphery model, Shields (1991), for example, argues that the marginalities of Brighton, Niagara Falls, the Canadian north, and the north-south divide in the United Kingdom emerge not so much from their geographically distant locations but rather from their exclusion from and subordination to moral and political centers. Spatiality in this figurative sense refers to a social and political distance independent of geographical location. The margin can be sited spatially anywhere as long as it is in a social relationship of exclusion and subordination and as long as it acts as a "signifier[s] of everything powerful 'centers' deny or repress" (Shields 1991:276). I use the concept of frontier because, while including the figurative spatiality of political and social exclusion, subordination, otherness, and/or primitivism of marginality, it also retains geographical locatedness around a tangible national boundary as a crucial dimension of spatiality (Donnan and Wilson 1994, Wilson and Donnan 1998).

The Borders region was distant from the seats of both governments geographically and politically, but in different ways. England had a comparatively strong central government but the geographic distance of the border with Scotland in the north from London in the south (over 550 kilometers) created logistic difficulties in exerting political control. In this sense, geographic distance created a sense of political distance from the center of English government. Conversely, while the Borders were geographically closer to Edinburgh with consequent easier access for control, the region was politically distant because the Scottish govern-

ment's authority was spread too thin in the troublesome
Highlands and Borders to control either region effectively.
Thus, for the Scottish government, political weakness had
the effect of creating a sense of geographic distance between
Edinburgh and the Borders region that was exacerbated by
the rugged terrain.

The frontier nature of Border space more fundamentally
derived from its geographical location on the boundary separating two states. From the perspective of the governments
in Edinburgh and London, the region was located on an
explicit border with another state and social world. It is the
combination of the distance from the political, social, and
moral center of each kingdom and the closeness to another
state and form of social life that characterized the Border
frontier. A frontier space of distance and otherness autho-
rized a discourse of primitivism in both its romantic and
menacing incarnations that reflected the contemporary
political goals of each state in the War of Independence (see
Torgovnick 1990 and Tsing 1993). Confirming Torgovnick's
insight that "the needs of the present determine the value
and nature of the primitive" (1990:9), Border reivers represented what was most cherished and feared:[9] they were seen
both as the pure embodiment of the ideal attributes of
humanity and as a lawless horde confusing the boundaries
between "us" and "them." Sir Walter Scott's *Minstrelsy of the
Scottish Borders* is a testament to the romantic evocation of the
Borders and its people. He called the Douglas clan "this race
of heroes" (Scott 1932:57); he applauded the gallant resistance of the Earl of Angus to the unworthy monarch, James
III, and of other Border chieftains to tyranny (61, 102); he
attributed to them honor and moderation even in their rap-
ine (110, 120), "fidelity to their word" (122), simplicity and
classlessness in demeanor (128), and a "natural pathos" and
"rude energy" (160).

Bishop Lesley, Camden, and other near contemporaries
present the menacing image of the primitive. The Borders
are located on the edge of civilization, and its reivers threaten
social order with the dissolution of boundaries of all kinds.
For Lesley, lawless Border reivers ignore the social distinctions
of ownership, "for they have the persuasion that all property
is common by law" (Lesley 1577, in Scott 1814, Vol. i, Appen-

dix No. vi.:lxv). Fraser makes reference to English and Scottish travelers' accounts in which Borderers are described as "barbarous, crafty, vengeful, crooked, quarrelsome, ... wild and ill to tame" (Fraser 1971:28-29). He also quotes Camden's parallelism between border landscape, animals, and people: "In the wastes ... you may see as it were the ancient nomads, a martial kind of men who, from the month of April into August, lie out scattering and summering with their cattle in little cottages here and there ...'(29). For both governments, these images of the border reivers actively resisting their disciplines of ownership, residence, and human-ness established the grounds for subordination and violent subjugation.

A similar frontier-space ambivalence pervades the way Border topography was depicted in verbal landscapes. While the region includes fertile plains in the coastal districts, "It is the hills that people remember" writes Fraser (1971:21) summarizing contemporary description of Border landscape. Again, Scott's romantic vision of Border people pervades the composed illustrations that accompany the ballads in *The Minstrelsy of the Scottish Borders* and the written landscapes in *The Border Antiquities of England and Scotland*. But more typical were descriptions of Border topography as bleak and ominous in which the hills were the most potent symbol. In the sixteenth century, Camden described the hills as "Lean, hungry and waste"(Camden 1695, quoted in Fraser 1971:21). Fraser's own contemporary description echoes the same vision of Border landscape.

> Along the central part of the frontier line itself is the great tangled ridge of the Cheviot, a rough barrier of desolate treeless tops and moorland with little valleys and gullies running every way ... they are melancholy mountains; probably only the Border people feel at home in them ... but for the most part the Border is mountain. (Fraser 1971:20-21)

Watson similarly portrays the area in which Teviothead is located: "In the middle of the Cheviot country ... lies a stretch of upland so stark and empty that the Romans are alleged to have christened it *Ad Fines*—the End of the World" (1985:24).

Thus to outsiders (i.e., the Scottish and English governments), the sparsely populated mountainous topography of the Borders appeared desolate, foreboding, and—like the people who lived there—untamed. The wild, uncivilized image contributed to the apparent moral and political distance of the Borders from London and Edinburgh and constituted it as a distinct region. In addition, as we saw previously in Bishop Lesley's account, both Scottish and English reivers used their intimate knowledge of the hills to avoid control by governments. Thus the topography and reivers' use of it also contributed to the region's coherence as a single, distant, inaccessible and strange landscape that mocked the international boundary)see Figure 1.1).

Figure 1.1   Border Hills, Teviothead

The ambivalent nature of these fourteenth- to sixteenth-century Border landscapes, and the foreboding images included in them, suggests a reconsideration of the landscape concept. Landscapes are a particular form of "scaping," a concept that highlights an idea prevalent in Western society about a mode of seeing and representing nature (see Cosgrove 1984; Porteous 1990; Relph 1985). There are three dimensions to the act of scaping. First, it is a mode of seeing that gathers the things, elements, and phenomena enclosed by it into a coherent whole, a unity. In Western society, when the entities which are gathered together are predominantly of "nature," then we have a landscape. Second, the source of this unity derives from human involvement in the world and the experience and knowledge formulated through such involvement. In this sense, a scape is "a projection of human consciousness, an image received" (Erlich 1987:24, quoted in Porteous 1990:4). Third, the relation between seer and scape is external. That is, the mode of seeing that constitutes scapes also constitutes the person perceiving the scape as an observer who is removed from it. Scapes "cannot be embraced, nor touched, nor walked around. As we move so the landscape moves, always there, in sight but out of reach" (Relph 1985:23). It is in this latter respect that the concept scape, and the particular form landscape, differs from but complements Hirsch's (1995). For Hirsch, landscape is a cultural process in which the foreground actualities of social life are brought into juxtaposition to the background ideal potentialities of social life:

> There is a relationship here between an ordinary, workaday life and an *ideal*, imagined existence, vaguely connected to, but still *separate* from, that of the everyday ... Foreground actuality and background potentiality exist in a process of mutual implication, and as such everyday life can never attain the *idealized* features of a representation. (Hirsch 1995:4, 23, italics added)

Note that while Hirsch privileges the relation between foreground actuality and background potentiality, the relationship's existence and the landscape's ability to present another representation of social life depends upon there being a moral distance between them. Further, Hirsh implies that the background potentiality of social life represented and brought into focus by the landscape—whether written or pictorial—is a "good." This is a one-sided vision of landscape. The bleak and ominous Borders landscape described by the contemporaries of the time represents a background potentiality that is the nightmare of both governments. The Border hills that the reivers used so effectively in their exploits also came to symbolize those exploits—real acts of resistance to and flaunting the authority and control of both governments.

But for London and Edinburgh the most ominous feature of the Border frontier, its people, and their endemic reiving was the confounding of what their War of Independence was about: national boundaries. This occurred in a number of ways, some of which were self-inflicted. The region on both sides was treated by London and Edinburgh as a single, separate and coherent space with its own character despite the fact that it lay within two kingdoms and societies. England and Scotland initiated this paradoxical spatialization of the borders through the institution of the Law of the Marches.[10] The *Leges Marchiarum* was an accretion of customary procedures and formal agreements about administering laws and penalties that began with a conference in 1248 between knights from England and Scotland. The Law de-emphasized the significance of the national border between England and Scotland because it applied only to and thus defined the zone on both sides of the border as a separate legal space. In administering the Law, the border zone was divided into six regions, three on each side of the border but arranged and labeled in mirror image. The Scottish West March lay across the boundary from the English West March; the Scottish Middle March (where Teviotdale was located) across from the English Middle March; and the Scottish East March across from the English East March.[11] Each government appointed a Warden for the three Marches within its national boundaries. The Warden was the "monarch's man" (Fraser 1971:102) acting on his king's behalf to govern for the benefit of the Borderers by guarding the frontier from incursion, investigating and punishing crimes within his March, pursuing criminal raiding parties across the border, and cooperating with the Warden on the opposite March in keeping the peace.

However, Wardens were subjected to the same self-inflicted paradox as the frontier space they governed; the model for their confounding practices was the actions of their kings. As described above, in the early stages of the War of Independence the military tactic of laying waste to the region used by Edward III and Robert Bruce made no distinction between one's citizens and one's enemy or between English and Scottish territory. Wardens, likewise, blurred this distinction as well a number of others that were constitutive of the political, legal, and moral authority of each state and its responsibility to protect its citizens. They confounded the boundary between government authority and resistance to that authority, or between law-enforcer and law-breaker.

According to the Law of the Marches, a Warden was supposed to cooperate with the Warden of the opposite March
in capturing and punishing reivers. This was a mechanism for
unifying and pacifying the Borders. Yet each government
strategically directed its Wardens to spy, incite feuds between
reiver families, or ignore raids on enemies, thereby exacer-
bating the disputes that they were supposed to stop. Perhaps
the most successful of these "stirrer" Wardens was Thomas,
Lord Dacre who was Warden of the English West March from
1509 to 1525. Under the direction of Henry VIII, whose tactic for settling the "Scottish" problem was to incite turmoil in
the Borders, Lord Dacre conducted "undercover work
among the Scottish nobility" and "continued to wreak havoc
by employing Scottish riders to plunder north of the Border.
'I have … four hundredth outlaws, and giveth them rewards
that burneth and destroyeth dayly in Scotlande, all being
Scottsmen whiche shuld be under the obeysaunce of Scotlande'" (Fraser 1971:183). As a result, like the national borders they watched and raided, the boundary between Warden
and reiver was often ignored by Wardens themselves at the
direction of the national government. In a letter, Dacre
describes his own exploits, which are difficult to distinguish
from those of the reivers he was appointed to capture and
punish: "I have caused to be burnt six times more townys and
howsys within the west and middill marshes of Scotland in
the same season than is done to us … The head of Tevyot,
Borthwick, and Ale, lyes all every one of them waste now, no
corne sawne upon none of the said grounds" (quoted by
Oliver 1887:100). On the Scottish side, there were similar
examples of Wardens crossing the boundaries between law-
enforcer and raider. The most pertinent example is Scott of
Buccleuch in Teviotdale, who was both an accomplished
reiver and the government's Keeper of Liddesdale. In 1596
Buccleuch led one of the most daring raids of the period that
freed the notorious reiver Kinmont Willie Armstrong, who
had been arrested and imprisoned in the English garrison at
Carlisle. The raiding party included both reivers and March
officials from the English and Scottish sides of the border.

War and peace were also confounded on the frontier.
These peacetime exploits of Dacre, Buccleuch, and other
Wardens were no different from the wartime military modus

operandi developed by Edward III and Robert Bruce to lay waste the region with little regard for the existence of the border. These tactics carried the import that the people and production on both sides of the frontier were of marginal importance to their governments. Further, in a metaphor of the political nature of the Border frontier, the governments confused the effect of their tactics—setting the conditions that resulted in the emergence of reiving as a means of coping with them—with their cause. What was a consequence of the governments' actions in both war and peace on the Border became the cause of the same action because it suited the spatial character of the Borders produced by the governments. Thus from the governments' perspective, precisely *because* the Borders was lawless and populated by unruly, crooked, and wild people who raided rather than reaped (an *effect* of their policies and strategies in the War of Independence), it was an expendable space where England and Scotland could carry out their warfare by laying waste to the region without plundering the more central regions and population of each kingdom. Thus it was the governments' actions that produced the very conditions for people to resort to lawlessness as a means of coping with periodic devastation or overpopulation.

Reiving and Border Space

In the previous section I described the way in which the Borders was constructed as a single and coherent frontier space by authorities "external" to the region, i.e., the governments and their agents. In this section I describe the social relations of reiving and how they internally divided up the Borders frontier by associating raiding families with particular territories.

Reiving practices that occurred on a local scale and for local reasons assumed and reproduced the same spatial qualities in the Borders region that the War of Independence produced. Reivers treated the Borders as a separate and coherent social space in which externally instituted political and moral boundaries were ignored. Reivers recruited on the Scottish side of the national boundary carried out raids in both England and Scotland, thereby confounding the state-based distinction between enemy and neighbor—the local equivalent of the scorched-earth military tactics of both governments that blurred the distinction between their own citizens and those of their enemy. Even more, as we saw with Buccleuch's raid on Carlisle to free Kinmont Willie Armstrong, Scottish and English reivers could cooperate.

> Border families from both sides were quite happy to gang up to help in each other's feuds, an English surname joining a Scottish surname against another Scottish or English family as occasion required. As Borderers they all had more in common with one another than with the tiresome governments in Edinburgh and London who inexplicably required them to be obedient and peaceful subjects. (Smout 1985:97) [12]

In addition to mutual raiding and cooperation between English and Scottish Borderer there was frequent intermarriage between reiving families. The irony here is that while the governments were willing to confound the boundary for their nationalist goals, they found similar actions by the Borderers to be unsettling. Fraser (1971:49) quotes a letter to the Privy Council from John Carey, a Warden of the English East March: "There is too great familiarity and intercourse between our English and Scottish borders, the gentlemen of both countries crossing into either at their pleasure, feasting and making merry with their friends, overthrowing the Wardens' authority and all Border law". The governments wanted to control the contexts in which such national boundary-blurring occurred. To this end, London and Edinburgh passed laws that required a license or a Warden's permission to marry across the border in a futile attempt to prevent kinship alliances becoming so dense and complex that it was difficult for each government to know who was friend and who was foe. Thus in both raiding and marriage, Borderers treated the region as a single social space.

If reiving constructed the Borders as a distinct and coherent space, its social organization internally divided that space through the distinctive way it associated people with specific areas of land and thus defined discrete territories within the region. During this period, the Borders region was partitioned into "surname" areas where reiving "families" dominated (see Map 3). This spatialization, which consisted of associating a kin group with a specific territory, was the result of two forms of social relations between people whose combination determined their relations to land.[13] The first was agnatic kinship which formed the basis of Border clans or families, and the second was the political relation of feudal fealty, subordination and dependency.

Map 3   Border Marches and Surnames

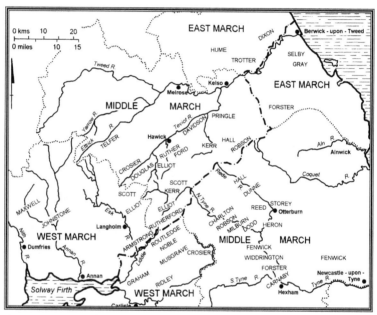

Source: Reed 1973:46–47

Kinship reckoning in late-medieval Scotland was agnatic with clan membership and identifying surnames passing in the male line. All people with the same surname formed a distinct "clan," though, as we will see shortly, there was a territorial dimension to the formation of the Border kin groups and the "families" that engaged in reiving (see Whyte 1997:6). Interpenetrating kinship was Norman feudalism, in which people gained access to land though expression of subordination to a superior. It was a relation creating noble persons and political spaces. The authority of the monarch was delegated to tiers of subordinates (vassals) in the form of fiefs which were the specific territories where they exercised authority on his behalf. Robson lists some of the noble families of the Borders who held their property by direct royal gift: Douglas, Maxwell, Hepburn, Hume, Murray (1977:47). The political center of each fief was the noble's castle from which he had the duty of maintaining order and protecting those living in the fief, and the right of collecting rents from tenants. In return, vassals swore loyalty and provided military support to the monarch. At the local and lower level of the feudal hierarchy were lairds who had been granted fiefs, often hereditary, by these Scottish nobles. These fiefs became the political bases for the formation of reiving families by local lairds.

In the Borders, local lairds combined their kinship relations with their territorial feudal rights to recruit a set of dependants who could be called upon for raiding others and for defending their lands. There were three ways in which lairds recruited dependants and established a territory of influence and followers. One was granting tenancies to peasants for sheep farming in return for rent, loyalty, and military service, i.e., raiding. Second, and most important for the system of reiving, rights of heritable tenure could be granted at "moderate rents" (Smout 1985:137) to "younger sons, nephews, cousins" of the laird, that is, men of the same clan or surname. They "were in effect minor lairds [gentlemen] who used their property as a sort of title" (Robson 1977:49). Combining kinship and feudal dependence, these "kindly tenants" also had the duty to return loyalty and military service, usually in the form of joining raiding parties organized and led by the laird. They were the mainstay of a laird's strength. "Every nobleman surrounded himself by a net of lesser gentlemen who bore his surname and gave him unquestioning devotion ..."(Smout 1985:35). Third were bonds of "manrent" between lairds of nearby territories that promised mutual allegiance and military support, again often in the mounting of defense against raids. Whyte aptly summarizes how the interpenetration of kinship relations and feudal rights effected an association between kin and particular territories that constituted "families."

> The [manrent] relationships were the same as those which were expected within a framework of kinship and involved the extension of values based on kinship to people who were not

related. This emphasizes the importance of kinship in late-medieval Scottish society and stresses how kinship and lordship supported each other. The possession of clearly defined regional spheres of influence buttressed by lordship, kinship and kinship-type ties ... was one of the most distinctive features of late-medieval Scotland, a system of regionalized power structures ..." (Whyte 1995:81)

Internal Border spatialization was produced by reiving and the necessity of lairds to recruit raiding parties and to defend against raiding parties of other lairds. At the spatial center of their sphere of influence, local lairds built defensive peel towers (see Figure 1.2). Often surrounded by a large wall that provided refuge for the laird's dependants and their stock during raids, these were structures of three to four stories with extremely thick walls and a narrow spiral staircase that enhanced the defender's position and (Fraser 1971:37).

> With his fortified home [peel tower] behind him, the laird who wished to increase or replace his stock and other goods would organize and himself lead a raid over the Border or into a neighbouring district. Then tenants-at-will might compose the raiding band; and, since they were suppliers of produce, they were the people who suffered most immediately if their ground was raided. (Robson 1977:50)

The tower formed the center of a pulsating space of influence. In times of peace, dependants spread out over the territory of the laird, and in times of war or raids they congregated around the peel tower for defense or rallied to form raiding bands. As a result of reiving, then, particular Border families became dominant in and associated with specific river valleys. Robson (1977:53ff) places the Douglases in Ettrick in the mid-sixteenth century; the Elliots followed by Scotts of Buccleuch in Teviotdale; the Douglases (fourteenth century) followed by Armstrongs and Elliots (sixteenth century) in Liddesdale; the Scotts of Buccleuch in Borthwick; the Armstrongs in Ewesdale; and the Beatties in Eskdalemuir. This association of families—centered upon a laird skilled in reiving—and territory is what the fifteenth- and sixteenth-century "family maps" of the Borders represent.[14]

This same process of associating particular persons with a specific place in constituting kin groups or families also oper-

Figure 1.2   Gilnockie Tower, Canonbie

ated in identifying individuals. I am referring here to one of the common nicknaming practices used in the Borders. The necessity of nicknames arose because there were a large number of people with the same surname but there was a limited set of given-names resulting in many people with the same name. Fraser reports that in the Borders there "were no fewer than twelve Hob Elliots, and there were an abundance of Jock Armstrongs, Walter Scotts, Richard Grahams, Andrew

Fosters, and so on" (1971:56). Thus Borderers developed several types of nicknames to uniquely identify individuals. Some appended the father's given-name to a person's given-name, e.g., Eckie's Thom (Armstrong) (Watson 1985:184); others alluded to physical appearance, e.g., Fingerless Will (Nixon) (Fraser 1971:57), or quirks of dress, e.g., Whitesarke (white shirt) Willie (Elliot) (Watson 1985:185). But the form of nicknaming that has particular relevance to contemporary hill sheep farmers in Teviothead combined a man's given-name with his farm or place, e.g., Jock o' the Side (Armstrong). This association of person and place went so far as the practice of referring to family leaders "not by their given names, but by [the name of] their estates" (Fraser 1971:57).

Conclusion

This chapter presents a fourteenth- to sixteenth-century time-slice from the history of the Borders to introduce several aspects of social life that, to paraphrase Foucault's words quoted previously, continue to exist and have value for Borderers. First, it was during this period that sheep farming in the hills became established. While there has been much consolidation of these small farms over the past centuries, contemporary hill sheep farms in the Borders still spatially follow the topography, lying in valleys and with their boundaries defined by ridge tops; and through their sheep farming, Border people continue to gain an intimate knowledge of the hills and feel at home in a landscape that to outsiders appears bleak and barren. Second, the rural territory on both sides of the Anglo-Scottish border remains a separate and coherent place with people recognizing a commonality of interests and culture based upon sheep farming and an identity linked to reiving that spans the artificial divide created by the governments in London and Edinburgh. One day while walking around the hills of Teviotdale with a sheep farmer, we were talking about Border people. He told me that the national border between England and Scotland should be redrawn from Carlisle to Newcastle-upon-Tyne because all the English people north of that line to the current national boundary were "Borderers just like me." Third, it was in the formation of reiving families located and identified by the place where they lived that persons and place became refractions of a single phenomenon—a theme I develop throughout the rest of the book.

Reiving has current significance in yet another way. It has become a historical image linking hill sheep farming people of Teviothead into wider Borders regional processes of identity-making. In the Introduction, I argue that contemporary people of Border towns and countryside recall different events—the Battle of Flodden and reiving—in constructing the Borders as a separate place. Both, however, refer to the same historical period, thereby providing a common place and time to build a regional identity even if through quite different events. The Battle of Flodden and reiving happened in the Borders during the three-hundred-year War of Independence between Scotland and England, and each is now used to represent the particular way town people and country people of the Borders were part of it. Further, during a recent period of fieldwork in the Borders, I was struck by two tangible indications that reivers were becoming a prominent symbol of a distinctive Borders regional identity. First, The Borders Regional Council—representing Borderers of town and country—has erected signposts on all the main roads leading into the region announcing to travelers that they are entering "The Borders." These signposts contain a striking logo depicting the distinctive "steel bonnets" of the reivers. Second, in Teviothead on the main A7 road from Edinburgh to Carlisle that runs through the major Border towns of Galashiels, Selkirk, Hawick, and Langholm, a small commercial museum recently opened. Its name is The Johnnie Armstrong Museum and it portrays the exploits of this most (in)famous of Border reivers, who was betrayed, captured, and hung, "tradition has it" (Watson 1985:94) at Caerlanrig Farm in Teviothead and buried in the nearby churchyard.

Notes

1. The material upon which this chapter is based is mostly drawn from a limited set of historical sources: two twentieth-century accounts of the Borders mainly concerned with reivers (Fraser 1971; Watson 1985); one nineteenth-century history of Teviotdale, the locality of my own ethnographic fieldwork, that gives prominence to a Border clan, the Scotts of Buccleuch, who were intimately involved in reiving as well as in the restructuring of agriculture along capitalist lines in the eighteenth and nineteenth centuries (Oliver 1877); an eighteenth-century political history of the Borders region (Ridpath 1776); Sir Walter Scott's seventeenth-century (1802) historical introduction to his collection of Border ballads (Scott 1932); and a sixteenth-century contemporary description of the Borders focusing on the reivers (Lesley 1577, quoted in Scott 1814).

2. Historians (for example, Fraser 1971; Smout 1985; Whyte 1997) tend to use the terms "family", "clan", and "surname" interchangeably to refer to relatively large kinship groups based upon agnatic-descent reckoning and associated with particular localities in the Borders. I will retain this usage throughout the chapter.

3. The period of the War of Independence between Scotland and England was not just about the status of Scotland as an independent kingdom but also about the emergence of English and Scottish national sentiment and territorial sovereignty as feudal relations disintegrated. I use the terms "nation" and "national" throughout this chapter to refer to this emerging sense of common identity and territorial integrity in Scotland and in England that preceded the imposition of political authority of a nation-state. Thus, I do not use the term "nation" in its more technical sense of the modern nation-state that developed after the French Revolution but in the pre-modern sense of the "idea of national territorial sovereignty" (Sahlins 1989:3).

4. Previous Scottish monarchs had paid homage to kings of England only in relation to the land they held at the kings' pleasure. Baliol acknowledged the king of England as Lord Superior of Scotland.

5. Fierce, cruel (see Robinson 1985:193).

6. "Gar": to make or fill; "corne myln gang": the five- or six-sided building that housed the driving apparatus of a horse-driven threshing mill. Thus the line means that there was sufficient blood to fill a building housing the apparatus for a horse-driven threshing mill.

7. Martinez (1994:5) and Donnan and Wilson (1994: 4, 7-8, 10) tend to use the terms "borders" and "frontier" interchangeably to denote the zone distance from political centers lying on both sides of the boundary separating them. Others, such as Adejuyigbe (1989) reserve the term "frontier" for the zones where expansion from a core area of a political entity takes place prior to the establishment of a formal, juridical boundary between two political entities. Lightfoot and Martinez (1995) adopt a similar terminology, placing the frontier on the periphery of an expanding colonialist political center. Sahlins (1989:4) is critical of the latter usage. My use of the frontier concept for the Anglo-Scottish Borders in the fourteenth to sixteenth centuries more closely follows that of Sahlins whose description of the French-Spanish frontier is not dissimilar to the Anglo-Scottish frontier: "Only in the later thirteenth century did the two [boundary and frontier] become different. The word 'frontier' dates precisely from the moment when a new insistence on royal territory gave to the boundary a political, fiscal, and military significance different from its internal limits. The 'frontier' was that which 'stood face to' an enemy" (1989:6).

8. In this respect, Tsing's core-periphery model of Dyak marginality does not suffer from the problem of treating the periphery "as passive recipient[s] of core innovations" (Lightfoot and Martinez 1995:472).

9. Geertz (1975) found Balinese cocks had the same ambivalence for Balinese men. He suggested that the fascination with cocks derived from this ambivalence. The same could probably be said for the Scottish and English governments' fascination/obsession with the Borders.

10. The label "march" was used at that time for a frontier region that was the subject of dispute between two countries.

11. In addition, there was a separate warden-like Keeper of Liddesdale because it was a particularly notorious region of reivers called "The Debatable Land" (see Fraser 1971:236ff).

12. In this respect, the "oppositional model of national identity formation", "the sense of difference—of 'us' and 'them'—which was so critical in defining an identity" (Sahlins 1989:9), is not quite accurate for the situation in the Anglo-Scottish frontier. Fraser (1971:32) also argues that there was not an overriding opposition between Scottish and English Borderer, rather there was an opposition between the Borders and the governments in Edinburgh and London that unified Scottish and English Borderers.

13. I am alluding here to a distinction made by Dumont (1977) between two systems of relating people and land in the formation of territorially based groups such as villages. In one system, which he argues is typical of "traditional" societies, it is the relations between people that determine the individuals' relations to land. In the other, which he maintains is typical of "modern" society, it is the relations between people and land that determine the relations between people.

14. Recognizing the interpenetration of kinship and territory in their formation, Whyte calls these groups "family communities in which particular localities were dominated by one or more landed families tied together by kinship and feudal relations" (1997:69).

Chapter 2

TENANTS ON LANDED ESTATES
Capitalist Agriculture in the Middle Shires

We have thot good to discontinue the divided name of England and Scotland out of our royal style, and do intend and
resolve to take and assume to us ... the name and style of King
of Great Britain.
                                Proclamation of King James VI and I

Queen Elizabeth I's lack of issue is another of those "accidents" (Foucault 1991b:81) changing the course of Border social life.[1] Upon her death in 1603, the English mon-
archy passed to James VI of Scotland. In proclaiming Great
Britain, he annulled the international boundary and thus the
frontier separating England and Scotland that were conditions for the three-hundred-year War of Independence.
Almost overnight, the Borders was a different space. No one
embodied this historical rupture more than Sir Walter Scott
of Buccleuch. In the last decades of the sixteenth century
"Bold Buccleuch" (Oliver 1887:252) was one of the most
"daring and energetic leaders on the frontier" as well as a
"murderous, plundering ruffian" (Fraser 1971:286) (in)famous
for leading the 1596 raid on the English stronghold in
Carlisle to free another notorious reiver, Kinmont Willie
Armstrong. Hardly more than a decade later, he became an
agent of discipline in two ways. First, he acted on behalf of
the government of James I to pacify the Borders by capturing
and punishing his former fellow reivers. Second, he and his
ancestors became owners of more properties throughout the

Notes for this section begin on page 62.

Borders than any other landowner. Over the next two centuries they introduced administrative reforms into the management of the Buccleuch Estate. The intent of these reforms was to transform the estate from the pre-seventeenth-century order of political domination in which the feudal relations of loyalty and service between a laird and his subordinate kin were paramount and determined the latter's access to land to a modern economic order in which capitalist relations of ownership were paramount and determined tenants' relations with the landlord in loyally paying rent.[2]

In the following, I examine this shift from feudal to capitalist relations between landlord and tenant and the concomitant shift from reiving and subsistence agriculture to the production of sheep for sale and profit. I use some of Foucault's (1977) concepts to describe how Buccleuch and his descendants applied "punishment" and "discipline" to create a new spatialization of the Borders into large landed estates made up of individualized farms that were "functional sites" for sheep production by industrious tenants and their families. One result of this process was a metamorphosis of the earlier person-place association between reiving families and feudal territories to an association between tenant farming families and profitable sheep farms. In creating a new person-place association based upon commercial relations, the administrative reforms introduced by the Buccleuch Estate transformed both the family and the farm-place to which it was attached.[3]

Preparing the Ground for Capitalist Agriculture in the Middle Shires (Seventeenth Century)

Two changes in the nature of Border space were brought about by the unification of the kingdom and the pacification of the Borders. First, the Borders moved from the periphery to the center of the kingdom. Second, the region was no longer partitioned into political territories of reiving families. As I described in the last chapter, what historians label a "clan" or "reiving family" was the confluence of kinship and spatial relations. The territorial concentration of clan members in a river valley was the result of asymmetrical feudal relations of loyalty to a laird and the duty of providing military service for raiding and defense by subordinates who were for the most part kin of the laird. Over the next one hundred years, the Scottish Borders region was ordered by a different form of asymmetrical relations based on the consolidation of large tracts of land into capitalist estates with dependent, rent-paying tenants who were not kin of the landowner (Whyte 1995:153).

When James VI of Scotland assumed the English crown, he proclaimed a new nation, Great Britain. Displaying an acute spatial sense, James renamed and respatialized the international frontiers of England and Scotland as the domestic center of the kingdom of Great Britain: "The King, in pursuance of his favourite purpose of extinguishing all memory of past hostilities between his kingdoms, and, if possible, of the places that had been the principal scenes of these hostilities, prohibited the name of *borders* any longer be used, substituting in its place that of the *middle shires*" (Ridpath 1776:484, italics original). The scorched-earth military tactics and reiving (for strategic and subsistence purposes) that were appropriate on the distant and wild Borders frontier between two kingdoms now became detrimental to the interests of peace in the middle of the unified kingdom. One of King James I's first priorities was to pacify the region and integrate it into the kingdom. To this end, he abandoned the Laws of the Marches and the system of Wardens that had made the Borders a separate space. He established a ten-member commission and issued ordinances aimed at subduing the region by subjecting it "to the same laws and discipline as the rest of the Kingdom" (Fraser 1971:316).

One of the primary ingredients of his view of pacification was to transfer the energies of the Border people from the political disobedience of reiving to the economic utility of agriculture. The methods he used in doing so combined sovereign techniques of acting directly upon the body and modern techniques of producing "docile bodies" for capitalist agriculture through "disciplines of space" (Foucault 1977). The sovereign techniques were first applied during the first decade of the new kingdom. Shortly after assuming the throne, King James I empowered the commissioners and lairds to bring about political obedience by hunting down criminals and meting out harsh corporeal punishment. Thieves were to be hanged. The remaining members of territorially based reiving families were spatially dispersed; some, like the Grahams of Esk Valley were transported to Ireland (Fraser 1971:318ff). In addition, lairds like Sir Walter Scott of Buccleuch, who previously had been leaders of reiving clans inciting their tenants to unlawfulness, became disciplinary agents for the government. They were made responsible for the actions of their tenants and charged with meticulous surveillance. They were ordered to give the names and trades of all people living on their estates to the justice courts. All weapons that could be used for criminal acts were to be surrendered. The other instruments of reiving were transformed into productive tools of agriculture. Thus, people were permitted to own only workhorses that could be used for "the labouring of the ground" (Register of the Privy Council, Vol. VII:703; quoted in Robson 1977:91), and "…all the places of strength [peel towers] in these parts [were] to be demolished, except the habitations of noblemen and barons; their iron gates to be converted into plough-shares, and the inhabitants to betake themselves to agriculture, and other works of peace" (Ridpath 1776:484).

These actions annulled the nature and divisions of frontier Border space. Clans, as constituted by lairds and their loyal tenant kin occupying contiguous stretches of land, ceased to be the primary spatial divisions in the region.[4] The region became politically and spatially stable. Landlords and tenant farmers could now expect a more enduring relation to the land they occupied. During the Wars of Independence, a Scottish laird might lose his royal land because it was located in territory lost to the English as a result of war and granted to an English noble, only to regain it later when the Scots were victorious; and, as Bishop Lesley recounted, tenants were not motivated to intensive farming given the likelihood of the produce being taken by reivers. Further, peace and stability opened the region to local, national, and international markets for agricultural produce. As early as the 1630s, tenant farmers of the Buccleuch Estate were selling sheep for fattening to English farmers in Northumberland; and by the 1650s they were selling wool to dealers in Carlisle. The Baltic countries were the chief buyers of coarse cloth manufactured in Scotland from the wool of Border sheep (Robson 1977:411ff; Whyte 1995:271ff); the rapid growth of towns in the seventeenth century generated increasing demand for agricultural produce sold at local markets (Whyte 1997:122, 172ff); and in the eighteenth century the coarse wool of hill sheep was sold to the developing cloth industry in Scotland and northern England.

As a result of the pacification, the Middle Shires were open to a new spatialization into large landed estates and a new type of relation with tenants. Lairds, like Scott of Buccleuch who facilitated and benefited from the process, became landlords of commercially oriented estates through accumulating extensive tracts of land. From the center of his domain in Teviothead, Buccleuch took over from Lord Bothwell the forfeited succession to Liddesdale (Oliver 1887: 248-251); forced out the kindly tenants of Eskdalemuir; purchased land in Teviothead from minor lairds, such as Elliot of Redheugh, who found themselves in debt; obtained land through reversionary mortgaging arrangements ("wadset"); and was given other lands by a king grateful for Buccleuch's efforts in pacifying the Borders (Robson 1977:52ff). Within pacified estates such as Buccleuch's, landlords no longer needed to grant land to kin in return for fealty and military service; instead, they sought to engage tenants in relations of economic dependence for profit. This involved replacing heritable tenancies granted to loyal kin with ordinary tenancies granted to farmers who could pay rent, so it did not matter if the tenants were kin. Over the next two centuries, landlords transformed the character of their relations with their new type of tenants and further normalized the region largely through disciplines of space: enclosing farms, partitioning the estate into enough farms for each tenant, and creating functional farm sites.

The Production of Capitalist Agriculture and Family Farms (Eighteenth to Nineteenth Centuries)

By the beginning of the eighteenth century, the Middle Shires was divided into large landed estates whose aim was to develop capitalist tenant farming as a means of creating

Map 4   Buccleuch Estate Lands, Seventeenth and
Eighteenth Centuries

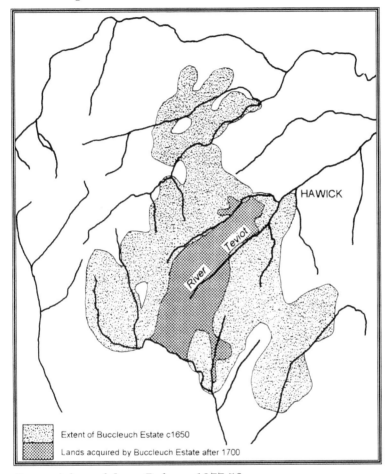

Source: Adapted from Robson 1977:53

rents. Robson (1977) highlights the way in which the large
estates, like those of Buccleuch, focused on administrative
and management reforms in order to turn the estates into
commercial enterprises. Two dimensions of these reforms
were the way they delineated the nature and use of the spaces
that constituted the estate and the way they associated people
with particular spaces. In this section I describe these administrative changes that Buccleuch landlords made to their
estate after the pacification of the Borders. The main object

of these changes was to transform the Estate's farms into capitalist agricultural enterprises through the use of spatial disciplines to produce tenants who would maximize production for and obedience to the landlord. In order to achieve this (and to extract maximum surplus value from the tenants' labor), the estate needed to: delineate individual farms; attract hardworking and efficient tenants who would push their farming activities to the limits of the land and thus be able to pay rents regularly to the estate; create functional sites integrating industrious tenants and specific tracts of land into units called farms; and foster a long-term association between a farm family and a farm, between person/s and place, so that their mutual well-being was intertwined. This period of administrative reforms saw the second phase in the transformation of the nature of family on Border hill farms. If the pacifications of the seventeenth century broke the collateral kinship linkages of large reiving families dependent upon a laird, the spatial disciplines of the eighteenth- and nineteenth-century landed estates established the individual farmer and his nuclear family as the preferred tenant paying rent to the landlord.[5]

Industrious Tenants

In order to create a profitable estate, the Buccleuchs and their administrators (chamberlains and factors who advised the landlord and managed the estate) sought to attract suitable tenants for the farms. A forthright description of what constituted a suitable tenant was made by the Duchess of Buccleuch in 1713: "...lett them [tenants] be assured, that whoever does not exert his outtmost to Serve me on this occasion, Noe plea of past service or merit, or anything else Shall prevaill with me to continue him in his office, for I am in earnest, and will execute what I threaten. Money I must have" (Buccleuch Muniments 935/4 12 December 1713, quoted in Robson 1977:117). The new regime is clear. In the past when feudal dependence organized relations between laird and tenant, loyalty to the laird (whose aim was more political control of a territory rather than economic gain from the land) in terms of military service was more important than payment of rent.[6] Now relations were to be organized by economic aims of profit, and loyalty to the landlord was shown by the regular payment of rent. As the following extract from the Buccleuch Estate illustrates, the suitable tenant was industrious, knowledgeable, and skilled in farming ("country affairs"), for these were the qualities necessary to enable him to pay rent:

> It is the part of the Grandure of a great Man to have a Substantial Tennandrie living and thriving under his Protection and who so fit to Compound and make out such a sett of People as those who nature seems to have ordained for that very end and who from their youth are train'd up as course of Labour and Industry and by degrees Lett into the knowledge of Country Affairs which is a study of its own kind and not to be come by at one jump. (Buccleuch Muniments, 307, quoted in Robson 1977:118)

The issue for the Buccleuchs and their administrators was to set the conditions for (1) attracting such industrious tenants and inducing them to extend the productivity of the farm and thus the amount of the rents that could be assessed, and (2) inhibiting acts of resistance by tenants. The means of doing this were largely spatial and disciplinary. Through acts of enclosing and partitioning land within their estate, the Buccleuch landlords delineated individual farms and linked them to individual tenants in space and over time through lease arrangements. The result was that on the Buccleuch Estate each individual tenant had his own farm, and each farm had its individual tenant.

Enclosing and Partitioning: Individual Farms and Farmers

Two types of administrative reforms instituted by the Buccleuch Estate addressed the issues of attracting industrious tenants and inhibiting resistance. One defined individual farms through organizing the distribution of farms and farmers in space, and the other individualized farmers and knowledge of farms through methods of setting rents. The success of these reforms can be measured by the change they brought about in the number of tenants holding rights in a farm. In the period prior to pacification, the tenancy of farms was usually held by groups of tenants or subtenants and their families, these groups often being listed as "neighbours" (Robson 1977:93-94). For example, in 1569 a group consisting of "Will

Grief, Thome Grief and twenty-one others were described as tenants to Sir Walter Scott of Howpasley in Outtersiderig [farm]" (Robson 1977:88). But by the early eighteenth century there were single tenants and their (nuclear) families on all Buccleuch Estate farms (Robson 1977:144, 166).[7]

One of the major reforms carried out by the Buccleuch Estate was to precisely define the boundaries of its farms. Robson writes that prior to the mid-seventeenth century "the outer parts of farms were previously little used" in the hill country (1977:42), thus resulting in the relative unimportance of marking farm boundaries. The reason for this lack of concern for the boundaries of farms appears to be the prevalence of reiving. Reiving engendered a centripetal tendency in the social use of space. We saw in the last chapter how the peel tower of the local laird acted as a center of social gravity and defense to which kin and dependants gathered in times of raiding. Further, because of the raiding and plundering, farmers were not motivated to extensive farming. Instead they limited their productive activity to subsistence and concentrated their farming spatially so that it did not extend to the boundaries of their allotted land where they were vulnerable to reiving. As a result, there were few boundary disputes. However, in the early eighteenth century, after a series of disputes,[8] the Buccleuch Estate embarked on a program of defining the boundaries of its property and of the farms within it. In 1714, the Duchess of Buccleuch engaged a surveyor to "make an exact plan of every farm that must 'distinguish each piece of ground how it lyes, what quantity of acres it containes, and what is the nature of the quality of it' and be especially accurate in setting out the marches...." (Robson 1977:43). The boundaries of most farms were determined by topographical features, principally by sykes (small streams or water courses; clefts in the ground), burns (brooks or streams), and rigs (hillcrests). One effect of instituting a survey was to partition the entire estate into clearly differentiated farm units.

A second set of reforms was instituted to regularize the fixing of rents so that they were at a level sufficient for running the Buccleuch Estate but not so high as to bankrupt tenants. As one Estate factor advised the Duke in 1777: "a moderate well paid rent is better to your Grace than a high rent ill paid" (Buccleuch Muniments:657, quoted in Robson 1977:121). The problem was deciding what methods to use in determining such a "moderate" rent. Prior to the unification of the crowns, when feudal relations prevailed, tenants were usually kin of the laird who were given hereditary tenure in return for military service—moneyed rents were less important. As a result, the estate had little experience in setting commercial rents.

The Buccleuch Estate experimented with two methods. The first involved competition. Each prospective tenant submitted a bid in the form of the yearly rent that would be paid to the Estate. Such a system was founded upon the assumption that a good farmer, and thus a good tenant, would have knowledge of the farm's productive capacity but that such knowledge "remains a secrett with himself" (Buccleuch Muniments:307, quoted in Robson 1977:120). In adopting this rent-setting method, the Estate fostered a farmer's individual knowledge of a farm. It also implied that the Estate did not possess such knowledge; if it did, it would be able to assess both the productive capacity of the farm and the rent that could be assessed. It was precisely this recognition of the importance of detailed knowledge of its farms for exercising control in assessing rents that led the Buccleuch Estate to increase its administrative surveillance of tenant farmers and their farms.

The second method of determining rents was based upon the number and quality of sheep a farm could carry, since this established the amount of income a farmer would get from selling his sheep on the market. This method, adopted on the Buccleuch Estate after 1750, necessitated not only that the farmer had knowledge of the farm's productive capacity but also that the estate did so as well. It was under these conditions that the estate turned its gaze firmly on its farms. In 1791 and again in 1857, the chamberlains of the Buccleuch Estate, Keir and Asquith respectively, carried out a formal Estate-wide collection of detailed information about the conditions of each farm. The aim was to determine the value of every farm based upon its particular conditions: the amount of land, the quality and types of fields and areas of hill pasturage, the condition of the buildings, and the number of sheep it could carry (Robson 1977:124) The administrator of the latter review told the tenants that each farm should have an individual valuation that recognized its unique features and capacity to produce income for the tenant and for the estate. As a result of these surveys, each farm on the Buccleuch Estate became a distinct spatial cell—an objectified individual case—with its own specific characteristics that determined the rent that could be assessed.

The strategic nature of this method was that it disenabled comparison by tenants of their rents and thus the ability of each to argue against the rent set on their individual farms by comparison with other farms' rents. In other words, through this knowledge the Estate was able to establish a singular relation with each individual tenant that was based upon the unique characteristics of the tenant's farm rather than a shared relation with a group of tenants. This method of setting rents inhibited the formation of "collective dispositions" (Foucault 1977:143) of tenants. In Marxist terms, it hindered the formation of class consciousness on the part of the tenants and was used by the Estate to discourage tenants from acting in groups for their mutual benefit. The Estate wanted to deal from its ownership position of strength only with structurally lone tenants in setting conditions of tenure. Robson describes a consequence of Asquith's 1857 survey and his recommendation to raise rents significantly. There was an explicit attempt on the part of Buccleuch Estate tenants to enter into a "combination" as a means of forcing the Estate to reduce the rents.

> With slight modifications only, these [rent] increases were made, and provoked another "Liddesdale rebellion" in Teviotdale. The chamberlain, William Ogilvie, called it "a sad commotion in the Camp." Three leading farmers, Aitchison in Linhope, Moffat in Craik, and Grieve in Skelfhill delivered to Ogilvie a memorial of complaint upon which the latter enquired "whether they came … in the character of a Deputation." They said they did. Ogilvie told them how the new rents had been fixed, and added his opinion: "I do think you are placing yourselves in a very awkward position with the Duke. Here you are approaching His Grace *collectively*, in a body, telling him, that he must repudiate this Mr. Asquith's valuation altogether, as a person who knows nothing about the value of these lands, and in short, that we are the men who are to be the valuators of your Grace's Estate." He observed that it was

absurd of them to want the same percentage of increase as was added in Eskdale, and that each tenant's farm deserved an individual valuation. He objected to their coming "in a body," and thought the whole affair to be "a very unpleasant business with no easy solution." In reporting to the Duke he wrote: "We have come, as it were, into collision with the Tenants, men who for generations have been holding their Farms, under indulgences and at Rents which no other Landlord would have granted, and now that an attempt is made to raise their Rents to proper value, they *rebel*." (Robson 1977:124-125,emphasis added)

In this case, we see how the Estate drew upon its detailed knowledge of each farm to form a separate relation with each tenant farmer and his farm as a technique for exercising control, maximizing political obedience, and breaking up any collective actions by tenants. It demonstrates the importance that Foucault attributed to the way disciplinary space tends to be divided into as many sections as there are bodies or elements to be distributed (1977:143). The exercise of this control by the Estate to punish tenants forming such combinations to resist rising rents is evident in another case:

The sons of John Elliot of Thorlieshope, who was reputed to have made "very great profite" from his lands before his death in 1698, suffered from a severe fall in sheep prices during 1704 and 1705. They therefore *banded together* and persuaded others to join them in a plan to secure reductions of rent. In March 1706 they all resolved to resign their farms. But a month later the Duchess of Buccleuch ordered the seizure of their goods as security and their removal at Whitsunday. Immediately the brothers were deserted by their supporters, who sought to be reinstated. This the Duchess allowed, and so the leading rebels were forced to petition abjectly for their farms. The Duchess was not inclined to be merciful to the ringleaders, so, though she accepted their plea, she imposed increases of rent "as a punishment to prevent their combineing for the future."

The Elliots were not content with defeat, and in March 1709 they assembled a number of the Liddesdale tenants at Castleton, "where they amused them with a false story of the haill Tennants in Ettrick Forrest gieving up their grounds." They urged the others to keep firm and declared that they now had a chance of both an abatement of arrears and an easy rent. Perhaps the severe winter of 1708-9 led them all to believe that few would be able to step in if they were to be evicted from their farms, but it seems that the latter years of the seventeenth century had been prosperous ones for the sheepfarmer and there were evidently more tenants of means about. In any case, those that had been "innocently led into this Combination" again melted away, and after apologising were readmitted as tenants. As an example to the rest, Henry Elliot was removed from Hudshouse, while the others were allowed to continue after publicly "acknowledging their folly and misdeamanor." (Robson 1977:114-115, emphasis added)

Leases: Creating Functional Sites

A third administrative reform and spatial discipline instituted by the Buccleuch Estate concerned the conditions of leases. By tactically devising its leases, the Estate created what Foucault called "functional sites" (1977:143), that is, the leases defined the useful spaces on farms. This was another technique for regulating farming and articulating the relations between tenants and the farm's resources in such a way as to maximize production and minimize resistance. Again the Estate-wide surveys of Keir and Asquith were central. They incorporated the information on each farm into the leases, which identified the various types of land on hill sheep farms based upon their productive potential and limited the kind of agricultural activity that could take place upon them. These leases also fostered a singular relation between a tenant and a farm over time. Three conditions of the leases were crucial to these spatial disciplines: length of leases, security and continuation of tenure, and improvements to the farm.

Throughout the seventeenth century when commercially oriented sheep farming was just beginning and when tenants still had relatively little knowledge, capital, or resources to withstand bad years, the Buccleuch Estate set one-year leases with minimal terms other than the payment of rent and maintenance of houses. Such leases were not ideal for the Estate's aim of receiving a regular rental income over time. They did, however, ensure an income from cautious tenants who saw longer leases as risky. Rents set in average or good years were problems because bad weather could destroy the lambing, leaving tenants unable to pay the rent. They could end up losing their lease and their possessions.

By the eighteenth century, successful tenants and their descendants had built up enough knowledge and capital not only to withstand bad years but also to improve their farms in order to increase their production and income. In these circumstances, the idea of the "improving lease" became attractive to both tenants and landlord. Both saw short leases as a hindrance to the tenant making improvements on his leased farm: since most improvements involve a capital outlay, a tenant under a short-term lease might not realize the financial rewards of making them; and landlords saw regular and increased income accruing from longer leases that encouraged and/or required improvements. By the beginning of the nineteenth century, the Buccleuch Estate normally set leases between nine and nineteen years. These "improving leases" further partitioned the farm into discrete spaces and defined the activities that could take place within them. The tenant was required to erect fencing or dykes to separate arable fields from grazing areas and to exclude cattle and horses from grazing in sheep pastures, and was forbidden from plowing land in sheep grazing areas. In return, the Estate often undertook to improve the farmhouse and other buildings.[9]

Further conditions were aimed at giving the tenant security of tenure so that he would be assured of reaping the financial benefits of the improvements the lease required him to make. In 1768, the Duke of Buccleuch indemnified the improvements with security of tenure: "while they [the tenants] use their possessions well, and duly pay up their rents, they may depend upon my favour and protection … the indolent and slothful tenant can expect no indulgence, whatever length of time he, or his *ancestors*, may have been in possession" (quoted in Robson 1977:140,emphasis added). Robson (140) interprets this as a statement of intention to reward tenants who made improvements with security of tenure, or, if a tenant had to leave before realizing the rewards of the improvements, to ensure the incoming tenant paid the equivalent of the remaining value of the improvements to the outgoing tenant. In addition, he emphasizes several times that a continuing principle of the Buccleuch Estate was to enhance security of tenure by setting conditions for tenant families to remain on farms over generations (92, 98, 129, 140, 142). Thus it was customary in leases that a son automatically succeeded his father's tenancy.

The agnatic reckoning of reiving clans resurfaces here in another form as a means of extending over time the spatial association of a unique farm with an individual farmer. The Grieve (descent) family of Teviothead is a good example of the way leases with such a provision encouraged generations of a family to remain tenants on a farm (see Robson 1977:152ff). After four generations of Grieves on Branxholm Park from 1684 to 1799, when Walter Grieve died the Buccleuch chamberlain described him to the Duke as "the oldest Tenant upon your Estate, of the oldest 'family' of Tenants upon it, and perhaps the oldest man ..." (154).[10] The notion of "farming family" thus came to have a spatial and temporal existence through its association with a particular farm. This constitutive person-place relation was entailed by the administrative reforms implemented by the Buccleuch Estate. It was perhaps the ultimate aim and effect of the disciplinary techniques, for they ensured a spatio-temporal distribution of people through which, paraphrasing Foucault (1977:143), each individual tenant had his own farm over time; each farm had its individual farmer over time; and each farmer had a separate relation with the Estate over time. A description of the resulting industrious tenant sheep farmer of the late eighteenth century is quoted by Robson:

> Having to acquire, not to enjoy, a fortune, his faculties are sharpened by necessity, his whole energy is called forth, as he must either do or die; his attention is ever alive to the most minute details, that can contribute, in any way, to his purpose. In this manner ... he acquires more perfect practical skills in the business of his profession; his plans are laid down with judgment, conducted with accuracy, and with the most minute attention to the oeconomy in expence. Subjected to almost no public duties, his attention is not distracted from the peculiar business of his profession; he can personally oversee every operation, and attend to the whole detail of practical oeconomy (Findlater 1802:314-315, quoted in Robson 1977:156-157)

Conclusion

There are several developments of this period that remain inscribed in contemporary hill sheep farms and Border landscape. First, the Buccleuch Estate is still the major landowner in the Borders. Of the fifteen farms in the locality of Teviothead, ten are presently owned by the Buccleuch Estate, and another three were sold to their present owner-occupiers by the Buccleuch Estate. Further, while there has been some selling and consolidation of farms by the Estate, most of the existing farms in Teviothead are mentioned in sixteenth- and seventeenth-century records of the Estate (see Robson 1977, passim). Thus the spatialization of the Borders brought about by the Buccleuch Estate in the seventeenth and eighteenth centuries and the unique, individualized farms they marked out are largely intact.

Second, there is still an emphasis on a patri-line of loyal tenant families. In contemporary practice, the son of a Buccleuch Estate tenant has the first right to take up his father's tenancy. It remains a mechanism for ensuring security of tenure over generations that fosters a relation of mutual benefit between landlord and tenant and of mutual well-being between farmer and farm. Over the past fifteen years, five tenancies in Teviothead have been taken over by a son of the former tenant.[11] Security of tenure benefits the Buccleuch Estate because, as several contemporary farmers in Teviothead emphasized to me, it motivates tenants to make improvements that increase the productivity, capital value, and rental of their farms. As well, tenant farmers in Teviothead usually want their sons to take over their tenancies in order to reap the benefits of any improvements and to continue the relation between the family and the farm.

Third, current procedures used by the Buccleuch Estate for leasing farms and setting rents combine the competitive and calculative (i.e., rent based upon amount of land and/or number of sheep carried) methods. Lease contracts still contain detailed knowledge of the farm, including maps of each field and type of pasture, an inventory of buildings and Estate property, and conditions for the use of the various types of land. They also include further surveillance rights for the Estate, such as periodic inspections of the farm and its account books. Many tenant farmers in Teviothead told me that they felt the Estate was more domineering now in the way it treats tenants. In this respect, at least, its disciplinary techniques of knowledge and surveillance rights are still being exercised with a similar effect.

Fourth, the singular and genealogically enduring association of an individual farmer and his (nuclear) family with a specific, unique farm—fostered by administrative reforms and capitalist farming—is still the basis of Teviothead farmers' sense of place. One of the themes I will be developing throughout the book is the way in which this person/s-place relation is a fundamental dimension of the way hill sheep people understand their family farms and more generally experience living in a rural space.

Notes

1. Like the previous chapter, the analysis draws upon a limited set of historical material (Whyte 1995, 1997 and Robson 1977). Robson's work is particularly important because he brings together a wide range of primary sources about Borders sheep farming and estates in this period.

2. Dumont (1977:5) characterized this transformation from "traditional societies" in which "the relations between men are more important, more highly valued, than relations between men and things [e.g. land]" to "modern [capitalist] societies" in which "relations between men are subordinated to relations between men and things."

3. The term "family" has been used in multiple ways by several historians of the period (e.g. Robson 1977; Fraser 1971; Whyte 1995, 1997). When discussing the reiving families of the sixteenth century, the term refers to the group of agnatically related kin with the same surname recruited by a local laird through feudal relations of dependence. We saw in the last chapter that these reiving families were relatively large—the raid on Isabell Routledge had thirty Elliots—because the local laird could recruit widely among collateral members of the clan. In accounts of the seventeenth century onward, the term conflates the nuclear family of a tenant farmer on a capitalist estate and the patri-line of descendants of a tenant farmer who continued to rent the same farm. When it is necessary to distinguish these two usages in the text, I will call the former "(nuclear) family" and the latter "(descent) family".

4. This is a particular instance of what Whyte describes as a widespread change in the importance of kinship: "By the later seventeenth century kinship was probably as unimportant as a framework for economic, social and cultural relationships as it was in England at the same period" (1995:153).

5. "A range of [kin] relations were sometimes found in gentry households but at lower levels the two-generation family without any other resident kin [i.e., the nuclear family] was normal" (Whyte 1995:153).

6. From Robson's account, it appears that kindly tenants had the obligation to be loyal and provide military service to the laird who granted the heritable tenure; the kindly tenants did in turn let the land to subtenants who paid rent to them and who were the men recruited by them when they were obliged to provide military service to the laird (1977:48-49).

7. What is missing from accounts of Border farms during this period is a detailed description of the tenant farming families in the sense of the kin and relatives that lived with and worked on the farms. Robson (1977:255-257) does give some indications of the make-up of tenant farm families. In a description of a visit of the Duke to the farm of one of his tenants, the farm family appears to be nuclear, consisting of the "old man" (the tenant), his "gude wife", and his "lads and lassies", with "farm servants" making up the rest of the household.

8. It is probably not a coincidence that boundary disputes arose after pacification when farmers were able to push their farming activities to the productive and spatial limits of the farms in search of increased incomes.

9. It is clear from Robson's description of eighteenth-century farmhouses on the Buccleuch Estate that the architecture assumed that the resident tenant was part of a nuclear family: "The fine new residences had a central front door leading into a small lobby or hall and a staircase, with the kitchen, scullery and servant's bedroom on one side and the 'best room' on the other. Upstairs were two small bedrooms over the kitchen, the drawing room and a small 'sleeping closet'" (1977:246).

10. I use this example because by the mid-1980s in Teviothead, a Grieve family was still the longest tenant on a Buccleuch Estate with a two-hundred-year period of continuous tenancy on Southfield Farm.

11. There were four other farms that came up for letting during this period. However, in all these cases the tenants either died without a son to take over, came out of the farm for financial reasons, or voluntarily terminated the lease.

CR Chapter 3 ℘

SHEEP FARMING IN THE COMMUNITY

The Borders as Rural

In 1973 Britain joined the European Community, and British agriculture became subject to the Common Agricultural Policy. In a figurative sense, perhaps, it was another of those "accidents" (an unfortunate and literal one, argue the "Euro-sceptics"[1]) that transformed Britain. It certainly made the Borders a different space because under the Common Agricultural Policy, the region, along with others in Scotland and the Community, was classified as a "Less Favoured Area." In this spatial regime, the peripherality of the Borders again re-emerges as a dominant attribute of its location but now with quite a different significance that is portrayed in the European Community's discourse of rurality. During the fourteenth to sixteenth centuries when reiving prevailed, the peripheral nature of the Borders was the result of its frontier location on national boundaries and its antisocial lawlessness. In the late twentieth century its marginality is the result of the region's *rural* location, a type of space produced by European Community agricultural policy and characterized by remoteness, depopulation, and minimal economic potential on the edge of financial and social viability.[2] Paradoxically, the region's position as the Middle Shires also re-emerges, likewise in a transformed state. Now, precisely because of the economic marginality entailed by its Less Favoured Area classification, the Borders is, like rural areas throughout the Community, the space for "the family,"

Notes for this section begin on page 81.

relaxation and leisure, and an ecological buffer zone (European Communities Commission 1988:5, 15-16). Rather than providing for material reproduction through agriculture, rural space provides for the moral and environmental reproduction of society as a whole.

My aim in this chapter is to draw out the spatial consequences for the Borders region of the Common Agricultural Policy, the Less Favoured Area Directive, and the European Community Commission's report on *The Future of Rural Society* (1988) in the 1980s and early 1990s before the MacSharry reforms were implemented between 1993 and 1995. The issues I address are how these policies respatialized the Borders region as part of the process of European integration, how they reformulated the image and nature of rural space in the Community, and how Teviothead hill sheep farmers practiced this rural space to reconfigure their farms and their sense of place in the European Community.

Two Modes of Rural

In reflecting upon the myriad analytic definitions of the "rural," Halfacree identifies a distinction between rural as locality and rural as social representation (1993:32). In the former, rurality is treated as a specific type of space that has a concrete geographic location where its character is objectified in the physical and social attributes of that location. In this mode, rural locations can be observed and analyzed in various terms: topographic attributes, social composition of the people living and/or working there, forms of activity, nature of social relations, and relations with other spaces of similar or different type in other geographic locations. In the mode of social representation, rurality is a cultural concept that has a "disembodied and virtual character" because it is not linked to a concrete geographical location and thus it "lacks empirical clarity" (Halfacree 1993:32). Instead it is a discourse about a type of space that is usually morally charged and about the kind of social life that occurs in it. Often it includes landscape images, either visual or verbal, placing the rural at a distance and thereby presenting idealized pictures of society that are implied by but can never be attained in everyday life (see Hirsch 1995:9, 23). In this mode, the rural is something expressed rather than observed, interpreted rather than studied. It is related culturally (by meaningful contrast and similarity of image) to other representations of other types of spaces, particularly those of urban space (see Creed and Ching 1997; Murdoch and Pratt 1993; Williams 1975).

The people who constructed the Common Agricultural Policy[3]—including its objectives, guiding principles, and policy mechanisms for achieving them—do not appear to have appreciated Halfacree's distinction between rural as locality and rural as social representation. Instead, over the first three decades of its development and operation, the Common Agricultural Policy conflated and alternately adopted these two modes of conceiving the rural in a process that transformed the image of rural space and produced the concrete spaces which objectified the image. This process occurred in three phases

Phase 1: Rural as Social Representation in the Construction of the Common Agricultural Policy

The first phase occurred during the formation of the Community and the original formulation of the Common Agricultural Policy in the late 1950s and early 1960s. The realization of a unified European Community from a spatial context of national boundaries, wars, and political fragmentation required a communal space and common meanings for integration. For a number of economic and political reasons—the strategic goal of self-sufficiency, the effects of food prices on costs of industrial production, and the political power of the rural vote—agriculture was a linchpin for the process of integration (Bowler 1985:10-12). The Common Agricultural Policy became the major vehicle for the construction of European communal space and the codification of European common meanings about agriculture and rural society that could be agreed to by people representing different member states.[4] By codification I am referring to Bourdieu's (1990a:80) description of the practices that effect an ontological change in the nature of a phenomenon. Paraphrasing that description for the present discussion, the Common Agricultural Policy changed the image of the rural from a vague, indeterminate, national context-specific, improvised sociolinguistic practice to an objectified, publicly visible, formalized and generalized Community-wide representation of the rural that has the political advantage of enabling each member state to interpret it in terms of its national interest. In this respect, Charles Taylor's distinction between common and shared meanings provides a clear statement of the nature and function of the "commonality" sought in the Common Agricultural Policy:

> Common meanings are the basis of community. Intersubjective meaning gives people a common language to talk about social reality ... what is meant here is something more than convergence. Convergence is what happens when our values are shared ... But we could also say that common meanings are quite other than consensus, for they can subsist with a high degree of cleavage; this is what happens when common meaning comes to be lived and understood differently by different groups. (Taylor 1979:51)

Common Space

The nature and degree of integration of member states envisioned by the Common Agricultural Policy (CAP) was spelled out in its three guiding principles: (1) a single market, with no internal tariff protection imposed by member states, that allows labor, capital, and agricultural products to circulate freely throughout the Community at comparable costs; (2) a Community preference for agricultural goods backed by an external tariff on products imported into the Community; and (3) a sharing of the financial burdens and benefits of the CAP by the Community as a distinct entity, rather than by distributional procedures to and from member states.[5] While these principles were overtly economic in character, they also identified the types of practices that would determine the nature and geographical limits of a distinct European space that transcends the collection of member states. Thus, the unified market, free internal movement of agricultural products and common prices, and common financial responsibility partially neutralized the national partitioning of European space epitomized by the import levies of member states to protect their agricultural industry and by their separate financial responsibility for their national agricultural sectors. Simultaneously, the uniform external tariff and the sharing of the financial burden of the CAP was the boundary that marked the limits of the Community.

Common Meanings

Within this European space, a major difficulty in formulating an agricultural policy was the diversity of farming in member states in terms of resource endowment, the range and average size of farms, the density of population, the level of food self-sufficiency, and the importance of agriculture in national politics. Despite this diversity, there were two similarities in the agricultural sectors of member states that formed centers of gravity for the "commonness" of a European agricultural policy. Both derived from the extensive government intervention in the agricultural sectors. First, all prospective member states had established tariffs mechanisms to protect their farmers' incomes and their agricultural sectors from cheaper imported agricultural products and, remembering the privations during and following World War II, to maintain strategic self-sufficiency in food supplies. Second, in all member states a "romantic" image of rural society portraying people and their agricultural way of life in the countryside had cultural value and rural interests had political significance (Bowler 1985; see also Gray 1996b; Newby 1979). The Community's agricultural policy that emerged from these two points of convergence was multidimensional. Its five objectives addressed economic issues of efficiency of the agricultural sector and stability of prices, political issues of national self-sufficiency of food supplies and reasonable prices for consumers, and social issues of the equitable distribution of income to farmers. In the following analysis I particularly highlight the association of agriculture with rural locations that became a primary concern in developing a European-wide agricultural policy (Folmer et al. 1995:48; Kearney 1991:126; Pearce 1981:36).[6]

The original formulation of the Common Agricultural Policy combined two conflicting aims at different levels of society: (1) achieving social equity at the level of individual farmers and (2) promoting economic efficiency at the abstract level of the agricultural sector. With respect to the former, the Treaty of Rome set as an explicit objective for the Common Agricultural Policy "to ensure a fair standard of living for the agricultural population, particularly by increasing the individual earnings of persons engaged in agriculture" (Article 39[1b]). With respect to the economic efficiency of farming, the Treaty of Rome set the objective of increasing "agricultural productivity by promoting technical progress and by ensuring the rational development of agricultural production and the optimum utilization of all factors of production, particularly labour" (Article 39[1a]).[7]

The social objective of maintaining farmers' standard of living was vital to an abiding goal of the Common Agricultural Policy to preserve the family farm as a major feature of agriculture and rural society even if this inhibited the process of increasing efficiency. At the Stresa Conference in 1958 where the Community's objectives for agricultural policy were defined, it was explicitly stated that "the structures of European agriculture were to be reformed and become more competitive, without any threat to family farms" (CEC [1958], quoted by Folmer et al. 1995:12; see also Pearce 1981:7). The implied causal link between family farming and the preservation of rural society was later made explicit in the 1987 Green Paper, *Perspective for the Common Agricultural Policy*, which states that its aim is "to maintain the social tissue in the rural regions" by ensuring continued employment opportunities in agriculture. Moreover, the paper presents the Community's image of rural space: "An agriculture on the model of the USA, with vast spaces of land and few farmers, is neither possible nor desirable in European conditions in which the basic concept remains the family farm" (quoted in Kearney 1991:135). The same aim and image of rural space was reaffirmed a year later in the European Community Commission's paper, *The Future of Rural Society*: "This communication … reflects the Commission's concern to avoid serious economic and social disruption [caused by structural measures] and to preserve a European rural development model based on the promotion of family farms …" (CEC 1988:67). These statements codified a conception of rural space that consists of farming, family-based production units, and a form of social life. While there was little specification of the attributes of farm, family, and social life, they do make family-based agriculture and society mutually constitutive: rural space is the condition for family farming, and farming carried out by family production units is the condition for the kind of social life characteristic of rural space (Marsh 1991:16).

Bowler's account of the origins of the Common Agricultural Policy provides some insight into the nature of this image of society nurtured in rural space by family farming. He argues that the Common Agricultural Policy appropriated "rural fundamentalism", an urban-based and edifying image of agrarian society pervasive in the member states of the Community at the time: "farm people … were thought to make a special contribution to political, economic and social stability, economic growth and social justice," and the ownership of small parcels of land characteristic of the family-size farm was considered to be "the basis of a vigorous democracy" (1985:16).[8]

In this image, rural space and society are relatively homogeneous—agriculture is carried out predominantly on small-size farms managed by families. In addition, there is a causal relation between a specific form of agricultural production and exemplary society. Family farming creates the kind of space where rural society can flourish and where the ideals of wider society are nurtured and preserved. Family farming sustains not just rural society, but society as a whole characterized by the ideals of stability, justice and equality. Thus, despite the claimed academic marginality of such romantic representations of peripheral rural farming communities (S. Macdonald 1993:10-11), it was this morally charged image of rurality that was codified in the Common Agricultural Policy. The link between material production and moral reproduction that is characteristic of this image of rural space continues through the transformations wrought upon it by the ongoing development of the Common Agricultural Policy.

Phase 2: Rural as Locality in the Implementation of the Common Agricultural Policy

In order to devise and implement mechanisms to preserve the rural fundamentalist image of farming, family, and rural society, there had to be tangible places within the Community's boundaries where it was manifest in geographical attributes of landscape, topography, and spatial relations and in social attributes of farm size, family personnel, and interpersonal relations. The Common Agricultural Policy thus required a bureaucracy to locate and analyze rural society and agriculture in various member states. Through these theoretical practices (Bourdieu 1990a:60), the Common Agricultural Policy transposed rural as social representation into rural as locality. Its policies then transformed the nature of those localities.

Analyzing Rural Localities and Their Problems

In *The Regions of the Enlarged Community: Third Periodic Report on the Social and Economic Situation and Development of the Regions of the Community* (CEC 1987), a new spatial regime was formulated and new kinds of spaces were produced. Regions were geographically marked and their attributes described in terms of income, employment, and dependence on agriculture. Instead of national boundaries partitioning Europe, it was regional boundaries demarcating spaces within the Community. Continuing the concern with the link between family farm production and society reproduction, the developing Common Agricultural Policy in the 1970s and 1980s addressed two interrelated predicaments of agriculture in rural regions. These predicaments derived from and paradoxically were intensified by the CAP's conflicting aims of social equity and economic efficiency. The predicaments were known as "the farm problem" (Bowler 1985:46-48) and "the rural problem" (Kearney 1991:126). The farm problem refers to the effects of general economic processes on the agricultural sector, in particular the accelerating inverse relation between increasing agricultural production by farmers and slackening demand for food by consumers. On the one hand, as national economies in Europe develop in a context of slow population growth, consumers spend less of their increasing income on food. Thus growth of demand for agricultural products is less than growth in income. On the other hand, as farmers use more and more technology to increase agricultural production, the supply of food expands faster than consumer demand. This process suppresses the prices of agricultural commodities and the income of farmers. Low farm income, which threatens the viability of rural society, is one of the two central issues of the farm problem specifically addressed by the Common Agricultural Policy. Since one of its goals is to ensure a fair standard of living for farmers by maintaining income equity with other sectors of the economy, market intervention mechanisms were developed to prop up the prices farmers received for their products.[9] However, because support prices were above those of the world market, there was a need to protect them by erecting a clear boundary around the European agricultural market with import duties. Thus a space was created where family farms and rural society could flourish, even if "artificially" in economic terms.

Since Community analysts defined the essence of the farm problem as overproduction, the second and more fundamental solution to both the farm problem and the increasing financial burden of price support mechanisms was to decrease the size of the agricultural sector. This was the central point of the review of the Common Agricultural Policy carried out by Sicco Mansholt in 1968. He suggested decreasing the amount of land in production and decreasing the numbers of people engaged in farming. Such "structural" changes would force small, economically inefficient farms (i.e., family farms) to go out of business and allow their consolidation into larger production units. As a result, there would be fewer farmers with larger farms producing a greater share of food required in the Community and thus increasing their incomes. This type of "resource-adjustment" (Bowler 1985:47) requires people leaving the agricultural sector to look for employment in other sectors. Spatially this has meant that people leave the place where agricultural production is carried out to look for work where industrial production occurs.[10]

The point, then, is that resource-adjustment has a more severe impact precisely on the small, inefficient family farms and society the Common Agricultural Policy was designed to preserve. Structural adjustments caused depopulation of rural areas and jeopardized the financial health of small family farms; they led to the establishment of large, mechanized farms with absent owners and local managers. The "rural problem" (Kearney 1991:126) refers to these threats to the mutual dependence between small family farming and rural society brought about by structural adjustments in the agricultural sector.

Mechanisms for Preserving Rural Localities

PRICE SUPPORT SCHEMES.

In order to achieve the aim of social equity and in effect to preserve the localities where farming and rural society could flourish, the Common Agricultural Policy adopted market intervention schemes to support the prices individual farmers received for their products. For example, farmers of cereals, sugar, milk, and beef received a guaranteed minimum price for their products either by selling them to an agency (like the wheat board) or by levies pushing the price of imported goods above the minimum. Another price support mechanism was to pay a subsidy to producers of wheat, cotton, tobacco, and sheep to make up for any deficiency between the market price and a target price that would ensure an adequate income without unduly increasing the cost of food to consumers.

The most important of these schemes for Teviothead hill sheep farmers was the Sheep Meat Regime introduced in 1980,[11] which exemplifies the way in which the design of price support mechanisms was based upon the mutually constitutive relation between agriculture and rural society. The Regime was based upon an analysis of sheep farming, particularly in marginal agricultural areas, such as the uplands of the Borders region. The analysis runs as follows: because of the poor quality, the land there results in inherent low productivity and poor financial returns; in turn, these characteristics of hill sheep farming mean fewer employment opportunities and less incentive to take it up as an occupation; further, while consumer demand for lamb is relatively constant, hill sheep farming is seasonal so that farmers sell their lambs when supply is high; this depressed demand, the prices farmers received and the level of income they could expect. Together, these were the ways hill sheep farms manifested the "farm problem", and threatened the viability of rural society by causing depopulation in locations like Teviothead (Scotland Agricultural College 1993a).

The solution adopted in the Sheep Meat Regime was a "variable premium" paid to farmers on their "finished" or fat lambs. Fat lambs are ready for slaughter at the time of sale. To be eligible for the variable premium, fat lambs must confirm to a Community "certification standard" that sets out the maximum dead weight, the maximum fat cover, and the confirmation class of the carcass for finished lambs.[12] The variable premium supplemented the market price a farmer received up to the "guide price," which in the U.K. was set at 85 percent of the "basic price." The basic price is a CAP-determined, seasonally adjusted, weekly market price that represented what farmers should receive for their lambs to realize a fair income level. The basic price in the September to November period is low because there is an increased supply of finished lambs, and is high in the February to April period when the supply of finished lambs is low.[13] During 1991, the variable premium was between £12 and £16. In addition, the Regime included a "ewe premium" paid to farmers for every breeding ewe maintained on their farms. It was meant to fill the 15 percent gap between the U.K. guide price and the Community-wide basic price. In Less Favoured Areas, the rate for ewes on severely disadvantaged hill land was £9.88, twice the rate for ewes on better quality low lying-fields. Farmers in Teviothead were unanimous in saying that without these two price supports, which represented at least 25 percent of their turnover, hill sheep farming would not be viable.

The general effect of these price support schemes on the agricultural sector was to (over)stimulate farm production: the more products sold on the market, the more a farmer received in price subsidies, and the greater the income. They represented nearly 90 percent of the CAP budget. This reflects the importance to the Community of rural space and the link between material production in agriculture and moral reproduction in social life.

STRUCTURAL MEASURES: IMPROVEMENT AND DEVELOPMENT GRANTS. In order to achieve economic efficiency in agriculture, the CAP adopted structural measures or resource-adjustments. These were aimed at controlling the productive capacity of the agricultural sector so that the supply of agricultural products would match the demand for food in the Community.

Structural measures involve decreasing the amount of land in agricultural production, increasing the size and technology input of farms in order to take advantage of economies of scale, and transferring labor and capital from farming to other sectors of the economy. The two structural adjustment schemes that were used by almost every Teviothead hill sheep farmer during the 1980s were the Agricultural Development Scheme (EC) and the Agricultural Improvement Scheme (U.K.). These grant schemes provided financial support for modifying the natural qualities of agricultural land, particularly the marginal land in Less Favoured Areas, as a means of increasing the efficiency of labor. This is explicitly conveyed in an explanatory leaflet:

> The aim of an improvement plan is to bring about a lasting and substantial improvement in the economic situation of your farms. The plan must therefore show that, within a period of not more than 6 years, the investments you propose to make will increase the earned income of each labour unit needed to run the business. (Department of Agriculture and Fisheries for Scotland, Leaflet AIS(EC)1 1986:1)

Grants, which in the Less Favoured Areas can cover up to 60 percent of the costs, are given to assist in a wide variety of expensive and technologically based improvements to hill pasture: planting of shelter belts; building and repairing stone dykes and fencing for controlled grazing and lambing; spraying bracken to improve the hill pasturage; building of roads for improved access to hill grazing areas for delivery of supplementary feeding; building of sheds to house ewes during lambing; and, most important of all for hill sheep farmers, installing land drainage, and reseeding and regeneration of grassland for permanent high-quality pasturage. These schemes were designed to improve the economic viability of farms by increasing labor productivity and maximizing profit.

Diversification of Rural Space

These mechanisms for increasing the efficiency of farming transformed rural space in the Community. Because of the strategic way some farmers were able to use the price support schemes, two contradictory effects were brought about. First, subsidizing market prices stimulated greater surplus because

farmers could increase their incomes by increasing production largely through technological innovation. This worsened
the "farm problem" because still more and more money had
to be used to subsidize noncompetitive agricultural commodity prices on the world market. Second, large technologically advanced, highly efficient and corporate-managed
farms were more able than small family farms to take advantage of price supports. These large farms produced a great
deal more than their proportion of the sector, and thus they
received a disproportionate share of the subsidies whose
principal target was the small, less efficient family farm. The
result was an increasing disparity in farm incomes and a concomitant increasing divergence in farm size between large,
wealthy agribusiness farms and small struggling family farms
that were the essence of rural society.

While the Common Agricultural Policy defined a common space for the agricultural sector by de-emphasizing
internal national partitioning, its programs created a different kind of internal partitioning. The Community was
divided into 166 regions (CEC 1987) as a way of conceptual-
izing and ameliorating the uneven effects of price support
mechanisms and structural transformations on rural society.
This regional spatialization was based not upon the political
differentiation of nations but upon diversity in topography,
resources, and potential for development in rural areas. This
marked an era of regional policymaking (Bowler 1985:57).
For the Borders of Scotland, the most important of these
regionalizing policies was Directive 75/268 establishing Less
Favoured Areas within the Community. The stated objective
of the Directive was, again, social rather than economic: to
ensure the continuation of farming in areas characterized by
poor natural resources for agricultural production and to
maintain the density of the rural population in these areas.
Less Favoured Areas were mountainous and hilly regions
with marginal agricultural potential because of the topography and soil quality, low and declining population, and/or
poor infrastructure. They were also the localities where family farms were concentrated.

As a result of this Directive, Teviothead and a large area
of the Borders took on a specific spatial quality. As a Less
Favoured Area, it was productively marginal but still a rural

space for moral reproduction within the Community that needed special assistance. It was necessary to differentiate this type of rural space because the price support mechanisms and structural measures were insufficient "to sustain the traditional pattern of small-scale family farming in the Community and to encourage the continued population of some remote rural areas" (Marsh 1991:16). Thus, farms in Less Favoured Areas were eligible for direct payments to compensate for the impediments to production imposed by the environment or caused by Common Agricultural Policy instruments that were beyond the control of farmers. These payments, known as Hill Livestock Compensatory Allowance (HLCA), were targeted to directly increase farmers' incomes by being based on input (livestock numbers grazing on hill land) rather than on output as were the price support mechanisms. In 1993, hill sheep farmers received £6.50 for each hill ewe and £63.30 for each hill cow (Scottish Agricultural College 1993b: 65).[14]

If, at a general level, the price support schemes and structural measures of the Common Agricultural Policy led to a diversification in agriculture and rural regions, the way Teviothead farmers used these programs led to an analogous diversification within and between their hill sheep farms. Those farms with a high proportion of rugged hill land that could not be converted into improved pasture were unable to switch production from purebred hill lambs to crossbred field lambs. Since hill lambs are often too small to meet fat lamb certification standards, they were sold on the store market where they were not eligible for the variable premium. While these farms used grants to convert as much land as possible to increase lamb production on improved pasture and used supplementary feeding to fatten more of their hill lambs, they largely remained "breeding" farms in the sense that the majority of their production was purebred hill lambs sold on the store market. Those farms that had a greater proportion of low-lying hill land and flat fields converted the former to improved pasture where they could raise less hardy but more prolific field sheep and where the larger lambs could be fattened to the certification standards of the Sheep Meat Regime. These farms sought to increase the production of crossbred fat lambs that were eligible for the variable premium. They were labeled "commercial" farms because there was less emphasis on breeding programs for purebred hill sheep and more emphasis on feeding programs for crossbred field sheep.

Phase 3: Rural as Social Representation in the Revision of the Common Agricultural Policy: The Future of Rural Society

In the third phase, discussion of the Common Agricultural Policy was again built upon a social representation of rurality, but now one based upon the changes the policies had wrought upon rural locations. The 1988 European Community Commission report, *The Future of Rural Society*, is a reflective portrayal of rural space describing the effects of the Common Agricultural Policy on farming and the then current state of rural society. Unlike the earlier image, rural space is now heterogeneous including areas for industry, leisure activities, and environmental preservation as well as agriculture.

The report begins with the following definition of the rural, which I quote at length not only because it highlights the different types of spaces that are now deemed to exist within it but also because it still recognizes the mutually constitutive relation between human activities in rural space and forms of social life.

> The concepts of the countryside or of rural society are by no means merely geographic in scope, since economic and social life outside our towns and cities is of great complexity, embracing a wide range of activities.
> But our rural areas are not only places where people live and work, for at the same time they have vital functions for society as a whole. As a buffer area and refuge for recreation, the countryside is vital to the general ecological equilibrium, and it is assuming an increasingly important role as the most popular location for relaxation and leisure. (CEC 1988:5)
> Rural society [as locality], as it is generally understood in Europe, extends over regions and areas presenting a variety of activities and landscapes comprising natural countryside, farmland, villages, small towns, regional centers and industrialized rural areas. It accounts for about half of the population and a little over 80 percent of the territory of the Community.

But the concept of rural society [as representation] implies more than geographical limits. It refers to a complex economic and social fabric made up of a wide range of activities: farming, small trades and businesses, small and medium-sized industries, commerce and services. Furthermore, it acts as a buffer and provides a regenerative environment which is essential for ecological balance.
[After the expansions of the Community in 1973 and 1987] ... the Community has acquired a distinctly higher proportion of areas the structures of which militate against proper economic—and social—development. Most of these areas are *rural in the extreme*, sometimes with 20–30 percent of the population still employed in *farming*. (CEC1988:15, brackets and italics added)

Unlike the original image, rural space is now heterogeneous. It was not just for agriculture, even a diversified agriculture, but also for leisure activities and environmental preservation in those areas where farming was driven out by structural measures. However, these two latter activities continued the moral reproductive function that the Common Agricultural Policy envisioned for farming in rural society. In one case, there is rural space for relaxation and leisure necessary for regenerating the human spirit for people throughout the entire Community; in the other case, there is rural space for regenerating the environment essential to the ecological balance of the entire Community. Again, to quote from *The Future of Rural Society*: "The countryside accounts for nearly 80 percent of the Community, and those living and/or working there form more than half of the entire population of the Community. These facts, and the sheer importance to civilized life of nature in its own right, demand of the Community that it take the proper action to ensure the development of rural society" (CEC 1988:14).
The last paragraph of the first quotation is also significant because it transforms the Common Agricultural Policy's original image of the rural. It constructs an ambiguous articulation of spaces (Creed and Ching 1997:12; Gupta and Ferguson 1997b:35) by placing agriculture and rural society within this new heterogeneous rural space. On the one hand, in relation to the large, technologically advanced agribusiness farms, leisure areas, and environmental buffer zones, the spaces where small family farming continues are "rural in

the extreme," remote, depopulated, and economically marginal because of their heavy dependence on agriculture. On
the other hand, the word "extreme" is important in the paragraph because it is a narrative form of distancing as well as
authenticity. Its use makes poorer agricultural regions, the
Less Favoured Areas like Teviothead, into a kind of distanced
landscape portraying the most authentic form of rural space
in which family farming and an idealized form of society continue to exist. Such spaces need to be preserved for the good
of the Community, and without doubt, this also makes good
political sense.[15]

Conclusion

This chapter brings to an end my account of what might be
called "a history of Borders space in three strata." It began in
1286 with the accidental death of King Alexander III that
changed the Borders into an international frontier where
lawlessness prevailed. In this politically undisciplined space,
feudal relations of loyalty, dependence, and service between
a laird and his agnatic kin were used to form large reiving
"families" living in and identified with territories covering
whole or part of river valleys they protected from raiding parties and English armies. With the union of the Scottish and
English crowns in 1603, the Borders was no longer politically
peripheral. They became the peaceful Middle Shires where
landlords commercially developed their large estates by
defining farm boundaries, encouraging tenants to improve
their farms and giving tenants security of tenure. In this disciplined capitalist space, individual tenant (nuclear) families
became associated with specific farms over several generations. By the middle of the twentieth century, the Borders was
again put on the periphery—this time more in economic
than locational terms—but now by and in the European
Community. It was classified as a Less Favoured Area and
"rural in the extreme," ironically because of its continuing
dependence on agriculture. In this agriculturally-marginal
space, farming families live and work on small, economically
inefficient farms that are maintained by Common Agricultural Policy programs because they function both as an image

of and a locality where the ideals of wider society are reproduced. Borders space thus is historically stratified, providing
a rich source of meanings for Teviothead hill sheep people to
cultivate in the process of creating a sense of place on what to
outsiders appears to be a bleak landscape.

Notes

1. I am writing this in Edinburgh during the 1997 United Kingdom election cam-
    paign in which "Euro-scepticism" is a central issue.
2. These structural problems and resulting small economic size of upland and hill
    sheep farming businesses has been recognized in Britain since the 1930s. From
    the 1940s, the United Kingdom government introduced improvement grants
    and headage payments to ameliorate the structural deficits inherent in hill
    sheep farming (see Grigg 1989:238-240).
3. For stylistic purposes, my use of the phrase Common Agricultural Policy
    includes the Less Favoured Area policy as well as other policy statements con-
    cerning agriculture and rural society produced by the Community.
4. The process of constructing a common agricultural policy became one of the
    ways of achieving the integration that the policy was itself meant to achieve. In
    addition, the policymakers privileged a conception of the form of economic
    relations that would characterize the envisioned European Community.
5. This was to be realized through the establishment of the European Agricultural
    Guidance and Guarantee Fund.
6. Murdoch and Pratt suggest that this conflation of agriculture and rural space
    was also pervasive in academic studies of agriculture in the 1970s (1993:418).
7. These are only two of the five objectives of agricultural policy identified in the
    Treaty of Rome. The other three stated in Article 39 are: to stabilize markets
    for agricultural products, to guarantee regular supplies of food throughout the
    Community, and to ensure that supplies reach consumers at reasonable prices
    (Folmer et al. 1995:11–12).
8. There is some support for Bowler's assertion of the pervasiveness of this image
    in Europe at the time when the Common Agricultural Policy was being devel-
    oped. His description of rural fundamentalism is reminiscent of Williams's
    (1975) historical analysis of the changing representation of the "country" in
    English literature and of Newby's notion of rural Romanticism (1979:14,18) as
    British society's living "museum" of its cherished values. In addition, Creed and
    Ching point to the notion of the "romantic trope of the countryside as idyllic
    retreat" (1997:19) in America. However, unlike Bowler, these analysts also iden-
    tify the negative images and realities of living in rural society.
9. As we will see below, there was an explicit social policy to preserve rural society
    by ensuring that farmers as the pivots of rural society were maintained.
10. The regions demarcated in the *Third Periodic Report* portrayed some of the
    uneven effects of structural measures.

11. In the early 1990s, the Beef Special Premium, a headage payment of beef cattle, was introduced. Since most hill sheep farms also carry some cattle, this was another important source of income. I do no more than mention this scheme because sheep are the most financially and socially important livestock for a hill sheep farm.

12. By the mid 1980s, the Regime's certification standards for fat lambs were changed, reducing the maximum weight upon which the premium is paid. The results were that the leaner and lighter lambs became eligible for the premium and that upland and hill farms could potentially produce lambs that would be certified for sale on the fat market.

13. The seasonal variations in the basic price were meant to act as incentives for sheep farmers to shift breeding and feeding practices so that lambs are ready for market at times when they would "naturally" receive higher prices because of lower supply.

14. By 1997, the respective Hill Livestock Compensatory Allowance subsidies were £5.75 for hill ewes and £97.50 for cattle (Scottish Agricultural College 1997:2). One result of the MacSharry reforms introduced in 1993 was to put a quota on the number of hill sheep and cows each farmer was able to claim for the Hill Livestock Compensatory Allowance and to vary these headage payments in line with market prices for lamb and beef. Also, in the mid-1990s, the HLCA was extended to ewes grazing on low-lying fields on hill sheep farms in Less Favoured Areas, but like the ewe premium, it was only half the amount as the payment on hill ewes.

15. It would be possible to take this analysis further into the 1990s based upon the report on the state of agriculture and rural society by Commissioner MacSharry and the reforms to the Common Agricultural Policy that he recommends. They continue the process of redefining the concept and nature of rural space. In MacSharry's report, the Community again observes and studies rural regions so as to find the geographical locations where these three types of rural spaces are objectified; then problems are identified in these locations (i.e., the "three standard problems," one for each type of space); and finally mechanisms are devised to address each of the problems in each of the spaces. These are the MacSharry reforms, and they will probably regenerate a further image of rurality in the late 1990s (see Gray 2000).

FORMS OF TENURE

Establishing Relations between Farm and Family

I now shift genres from a history of space to an ethnography of place, from those actions of governments, bureaucracies, and people that marked out a Borders territory and partitioned it in accordance with some political, economic, and/or social framework to the practices I shared with hill sheep farming people that create a sense of place in Teviothead.[1] Such emplacement involves people identifying a set of areas or sites in a given space, investing them with cultural, historical, and/or personal significance, and forming an attachment to them that is constitutive of both person and place. Heidegger's concept of "dwelling" (1975:143ff) entails some of the same processes. It refers to the embodied actions of humans using and doing things in everyday life; in such "praxical"[2] action, they create "locations" (1975:154) that together form a coherent surrounding world (see Tilley 1994:11ff). Through dwelling, humans build a world of locations that is experienced as an inherent part of their being; it produces a sense of place where humans feel they can carry out their lives in an understandable way. What Heidegger also emphasizes is that this world-building is intrinsic to social existence and that it has a spatial dimension: "Dwelling involves a lack of distance between people and things ... an engagement which is neither conceptualized nor articulated, and which arises through *using* the world rather than through scrutiny" (Thomas 1993:28).

Notes for this section begin on page 103.

Over the next several chapters I will be describing the farming practices through which hill sheep people of Teviothead constitute and become attached to the places that form their world. For them, building this sense of place in the Borders begins with establishing a relation with a farm through one of four types of land tenure. These are formal and contractual relations between legal entities that allow a farmer to use the farm. However, in the process their everyday concepts of farm and family are constituted and some features of a family's attachment to a farm are initiated.

Teviothead

Upper Teviotdale straddles an eighteen-kilometer stretch of the River Teviot that runs in a northeasterly direction from its source in the hills forming the watershed boundary with Ewesdale to the mill town of Hawick. In a formal sense, Teviothead refers to a parish and electoral district situated in the southwest of Upper Teviotdale. It is located in Roxburghshire, one of the central counties geographically and historically in the Scottish Borders. However, in this ethnography I use the place-name Teviothead in the same self-referential and constitutive way as local people to refer to the locality that incorporates those who tend to consider themselves a community. I use the term "community" with some reservations not only because of the debate in anthropology about its referent (see Bell and Newby 1971; Cohen 1985; Newby 1982), but also because people in Teviothead explicitly recognized that defining the existence, nature, and boundaries of their community was problematic. Indeed, throughout the 1980s there was ongoing debate among the residents of Upper Teviotdale about whether the formerly separate Parishes of Teviothead and neighboring Newmill should be considered one community. Discussions of this issue among people in both locales crystallized around the diminished membership of the Newmill and Teviothead chapters of the Women's Rural Institute and the Church Guild, the decreased patronage at the three local hotels, and the need for greater cross-participation in the activities sponsored by the Newmill and Teviothead Community Hall Committees. When I asked residents about the limits of their community, most prefaced their answer by clarifying that they were doing so in terms of the density of their social relations rather than in terms of formal Parish boundaries. In these terms, Teviothead included residents in both Parishes and most of the farms and cottages between the watershed and Hawick. Throughout the rest of the ethnography, I retain this fluid and emergent sense of the place referred to by the name "Teviothead."

Teviothead consists of between 150 and 200 residents of fifteen hill sheep farms and nearly thirty cottages spread over the valley in a form that Neville calls a "scattered open-country neighbourhood" (1994:91). There is no cluster of residences and shops that identifies Teviothead. Instead, there is merely a sign and a reduced speed limit zone on the A7 near a line of former workers' cottages and the primary school. The community hall, church and cemetery are situated off the main road and are not easily visible from it. The fifteen farms that are generally included in the community of Teviothead spread for several miles in all directions from this marked location (see Map 5).

Forms Of Tenure

Hill sheep farms in Teviothead are under four different forms of tenure. Tenure has an economic and spatial dimension. It refers to a contractual process of establishing rights of access to and enjoyment of the profits from a specific area of land and set of buildings; in turn, the land and buildings described in the contract precisely mark out the legal space of a hill sheep farm. As we saw in Chapter 2, most of the Teviothead farms described in tenure contracts were settled by the Buccleuch Estate during the seventeenth and eighteenth century.

Owner-Occupation

In this form of tenure, an individual or legal partnership purchases freehold possession of a farm's land and buildings. In the 1980s, the factors determining the value of land in Teviothead had more to do with its potential for forestry than for sheep farming. During that period, when farms or part of

Map 5   Teviotdale

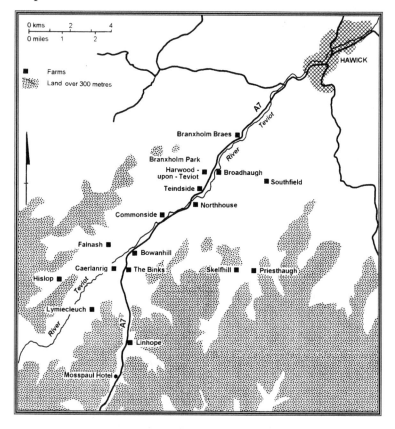

farms were up for sale, the demand for land came from investors from the South (i.e., England). Prices of £250–£300 per acre for agriculturally marginal hill grazing land were offered by companies acting on behalf of individuals who were taking advantage of government tax concessions for investment in forestry. Thus, to purchase a hill sheep farm, a potential owner-occupying farmer would have had to offer at least that amount. However, in the early 1990s, the government ended these tax concessions, and as a result the value of hill land in the Borders decreased by at least half. One farmer who looked into the possibility of selling some land found that its value had dropped to approximately £90–£100 per acre. In addition to purchasing the land and buildings, a new owner buys the existing livestock. The reason given is that the livestock already on the farm have become adapted genetically to the particularities of the land, grass, and parasites. If new livestock were brought in, it would take a number of generations for them to become adapted, and during this period they would be less healthy and productive. In the early 1990s, ewes were valued at approximately £50. Assuming an average stocking density of one ewe for every two acres of hill land and one ewe per acre on park land, the assets of an owner-occupied hill sheep farm in Teviothead with a majority of hill land and some fields can be roughly figured as (1) £100 per acre of hill land and £600 per acre of field or park land,[3] (2) machinery and equipment normally costing between £35,000 and £60,000, and (3) farmhouse, buildings, and other improvements of variable value. Based upon these figures, it is possible to estimate the value of the assets of a large owner-occupied farm (2500 acres) between £800,000 and £1,000,000. Owner-occupation is usually encumbered by borrowings that include bank loans, overdraft, and other liabilities that represent approximately 15 percent of these total assets (Scottish Agricultural College 1993a:50).

In the early 1980s, there were four owner-occupied farms in Teviothead. Skelfhill, covering over 4000 acres, the majority of which is hill grazing land, with 2000 hill ewes and nearly 100 cows, was purchased by the current owner-occupier's father in 1961. His son succeeded to it in the early 1990s. Priesthaugh consists of 2750 acres of which 2360 acres are hill land and 300 acres are fenced fields; it carries 1280 hill ewes, 360 park ewes, and 100 cattle.[4] It was purchased by the current owner-occupier's paternal grandfather just after World War II;[5] he passed it onto his son, and when the latter retired recently it was passed onto his daughter and her husband.[6] Hislop, covering 2200 acres of mostly hill land with a flock of 1100 purebred hill ewes and over 50 cattle, was purchased 30 years ago. Falnash, covering 720 acres of hill grazing and fields with a mixture of crossbred park ewes (480), purebred hill ewes (360), and a dozen cattle, was purchased in the 1970s from the Buccleuch Estate. In the mid-1980s when his son was reaching marriageable age, the owner of Hislop purchased Falnash. In the process, one-third of Hislop's land was sold for forestry planting so that the combined farms totaled 1650 acres with 900 hill ewes, 450 park ewes, and over 70 cattle.[7] Hislop-Falnash has now been passed onto the son.

Tenancy

In this form of tenure, an individual farmer or legal partnership contracts to pay an agreed annual rent to a landlord in return for the right to live on the farm and to use the land for agricultural production. The principal landlord in Teviothead is the Buccleuch Estate. The terms of its leases vary in length. For example, a lease signed in 1905 with the Buccleuch Estate had a term of four years; another lease signed in 1975 was on a year-to-year basis; leases for long-standing Buccleuch Estate tenants generally were up to nine years with more frequent rent reviews at three- to five-year intervals. As I described in Chapter 2, in the past the Buccleuch Estate has had a preference for families retaining tenancies over generations. This preference is underwritten by Scottish tenancy laws, which ensure that when a tenant dies, his or her successors have the right to continue the tenancy. Recently, the Buccleuch Estate has found these provisions of the tenancy laws unfavorable, so a new form of lease (to be described next) was developed that bypasses the rights of the successor enshrined in them.

Historically, the Buccleuch Estate has set rents by the number of sheep and/or by competition among prospective tenants. The contemporary method is the latter, although the Estate is well informed about the productive capacity of the farm and the European Community subsidies it will attract. When a farm comes up for rent, it is advertised in the local press. Retaining the disciplinary practices of the Middle Shires, the Buccleuch Estate supplies a detailed map of the farm's hill grazing areas and fields, a full description of the property and its improvements, and the terms of the lease. Prospective tenants must fill out an application specifying the amount of annual rent to be paid, personal and family circumstances, education, training and farming experience, current farm holdings and financial status, and proposed policies and budget for the farm. Prior to Britain joining the European Community, the method prospective tenants used to calculate the rent they would be able to pay was based on the number of ewes the farm could carry and thus the income that could be produced from selling lambs. With the introduction of "headage" payments, i.e., the ewe premium paid under the Sheep Meat Regime, the Beef Special Premium, and the Hill Livestock Compensatory Allowance (HLCA) paid under the Less Favoured Area policy, prospective tenants currently calculate their rent offer on the amount of these payments the livestock would attract. As several tenant farmers said, the premiums (ewe and beef) and HLCA "pay the rent," and the tenant in effect lives off the sale price of livestock.[8] In 1990, headage payments per hill ewe totaled £19.28 and for cattle it was about £62.

One effect of this competitive system of setting rents on newly tenanted farms in the context of European Community headage payments is an implicit two-tier rental structure. In the early 1990s, tenant farmers in Teviothead believed that the European Community payments accelerated the already escalating level of rents that was due to the shortage of farms in relation to the number of competing prospective tenants. As an example, in 1969 a tenant farmer of the Buccleuch Estate paid £750 annual rent for a small, relatively low-lying farm in Teviothead of just under 500 acres with 500 ewes. A decade later, his son was paying £3500, and when he left the farm in the early 1980s the new tenant was thought to have made an offer of £10,000 in his application. Rents for long-standing tenants, who are not in a competitive situation at their three- or five-yearly rent reviews, are generally lower than rents for new tenants on equivalent farms. Long-standing tenants negotiate with the Buccleuch Estate management on the basis of the farm's productive capacity, the state of the livestock market, the income from European Community headage payments, and the cost of living increases to set rents that allow a fair standard of living for the tenants and provide sufficient income to the Buccleuch Estate as return on its capital. Thus, at the same time that the rent escalated to £10,000 for the small 500-acre farm mentioned above, which went through two new competitive leases, another farm over double the size, which only had to renew the existing lease, negotiated a rent of just £6500.[9]

As with owner-occupation, the tenant has the responsibility to stock the farm and provide machinery. In normal leases, an incoming tenant is required to purchase the sheep already on the farm. Thus, there is a significant capital investment required of the tenant in terms of livestock and machinery. In early 1990s values, on the smallest farms, this amounted to just under £50,000 (£23,000 for sheep at £50 per ewe, £25,000 for machinery, plus any cattle purchased), rising to over £100,000 (£72,000 for sheep, £35,000 for machinery, plus cattle) on the largest farms. Tenants, therefore, also have significant borrowings averaging about 20 percent of total assets (Scottish Agricultural College 1993a:50).

Of the fifteen farms in the Upper Teviotdale, six remain under these "traditional" tenancy leases (see Newby et al. 1978). All the tenants are long-standing and together represent one tier of the rental structure. Linhope Farm owned by the Buccleuch Estate extends to 2720 acres, 2600 of which are hill grazing land (the highest proportion among farms in Upper Teviotdale) carrying between 1600 and 1700 hill ewes. The current tenant is the third generation of the family on Linhope. The Binks Farm is one of the smaller farms in Upper Teviotdale covering 460 acres, predominantly hill land, with 400 ewes, most of which are hill ewes, and over 20 cattle. The current tenant told me that The Binks has been owned by a family in Edinburgh "for a long time." He took up the tenancy in 1978 after coming out of his father's farm in the Yarrow Valley. Bowan Hill Farm is one of the longest running tenancies in the Buccleuch Estate. It has been in the current tenant's family since 1870 when his great-grandfather secured the lease. It covers 1284 acres—1170 acres of hill land and 100 acres of fields—with 800 hill ewes and 50 cattle. Commonside Farm is owned by the Buccleuch Estate, and the current tenant is the second generation of the family on the farm. It includes 2740 acres of which approximately 80 percent is hill grazing land. It carries 1100 purebred hill ewes, 550 crossbred park ewes, and 130 cattle. Branxholm Braes is one of the smaller farms with just over 500 acres carrying 400 park ewes. It is owned by the Buccleuch Estate, and the current tenant succeeded his father in the lease. Finally, one tenant has a lease on two neighboring Buccleuch Estate farms, Harwood-on-Teviot (600 acres) and Branxholm Park (600 acres), that are run as a single business. Unlike the other farms in Upper Teviotdale, sheep rearing is only a minor part of the farm operation with just 200 crossbred park ewes compared with the major investment in 1200 cattle, pigs, and a large egg producing operation. The current tenant is the second generation of the family on the combined farms.

Partnership[10]

Since the early 1980s, the Buccleuch Estate has modified its form of leasing so that instead of establishing a landlord-tenant relation, tenure on a farm was offered in the form of a Partnership Agreement between the Estate and the farmer. All the farms that have come up for lease in Teviothead over the past fifteen years have been on Partnership terms. These tenant-partners form the second tier of the rental structure. The process of selecting a partner is similar to the one used in the past for selecting tenants. The Buccleuch Estate advertises the property and provides details of the land and other fixed assets as well as the general terms of the two types of Partnership Agreements. Prospective Partners fill out an application form describing personal and financial circumstances, specifying the type of Partnership (Limited or Participating), and making an offer of the rent to be paid. Other terms of the Partnership Agreement are finalized between the selected Partner and the Estate. It is in relation to the rent offered for Partnerships that the accelerating effects of the European Community headage payments are most significant since the level of payment largely determines the rent offered. Partners on Buccleuch Estate farms in Teviothead told me that in calculating the rent they offered, they estimated the maximum number of ewes the farm could carry and multiplied that by the current total headage payments each ewe would attract. Thus differences in offers made by prospective Partners reflected their estimates of the farm's carrying capacity and the level of technological input they could use to increase it.

From the point of view of the Estate, there are four advantages of Partnerships over traditional tenancy. First, a Partnership is a different legal relation than tenancy. As a result, by entering into Partnerships the Estate is no longer bound by the tenancy laws and their provisions for security of tenure. Second, in Partnerships, payments other than, but in addition to, rent can be written into the Agreement increasing the income to the Estate. Third, because a Partnership involves the Buccleuch Estate contributing capital to the farm business, the income it earns in rent and other payments from the farmer Partner is no longer considered by the tax department as purely "unearned", and this decreases its tax liabilities. Fourth, as a Partner, the Buccleuch Estate retains greater control over farm policy, operations and improvements.

In a Partnership relation, the Estate becomes either a Limited Partner by contributing a small fixed amount of capital, usually £500, or a Participating Partner by contributing a significance percentage of the initial capital for the farm business, usually 25 percent. In a Limited Partnership Agreement, the farmer becomes the General Partner who contributes the remaining capital, including livestock, representing his or her interest in the partnership; in addition, the General Partner pays an annual rent and a further amount representing return on the capital contributed by the Estate. As a Limited Partner, the Buccleuch Estate cedes control of farm policy and operation to the General Partner to almost the same extent as in a tenancy lease.

In the case of Participating Partnerships, the farmer Partner contributes an equal amount of capital but is also obliged to put up additional capital to stock and equip the farm. As a Participating Partner, the Buccleuch Estate retains significant control of farm policy and operations. One example of a Participating Partnership Agreement offered by the Buccleuch Estate for a medium-size farm had the following six basic provisions. First, the Buccleuch Estate would become a Participating Partner by contributing £15,000 toward the farm costs. Second, the Buccleuch Estate was guaranteed a return of 2 percent above the normal rate of return on capital to be paid to them by the farmer partner. Third, the farmer partner would contribute £15,000. Fourth, the farmer partner also had to put in an additional minimum £40,000 for stocking the farm. If the partner had to borrow the money, it must be solely as an individual without legally involving the Buccleuch Estate. Thus the Buccleuch Estate would have no financial responsibility in case the partner defaulted on the loan. Fifth, the farmer Partner must also pay an annual rent of £7000 to £8000 per year. Finally, the initial duration of the terms of the Partnership Agreement was two years, after which it was renewable on an annual basis. In another proposed Participating Partnership Agreement, the Buccleuch Estate would contribute capital for a percentage of the farm's livestock; the Partner would pay the Buccleuch Estate 10 percent of the farm's gross income and allow the Estate access to the farm's books; the Partner would be limited to £500 for improvements to the farm without approval of the Buccleuch Estate; the Partner would pay annual rent; the Agreement would be renewable on an annual basis. Several farmers in Teviothead were critical of the unfavorable terms of a Participating Partnership Agreement. They said that the farmer Partner is "a glorified manager who has to pay rent." Another indication of the unfavorable character of this form of tenure is the example of a farmer in Teviothead who was in a Participating Partnership Agreement with the Buccleuch Estate. He saved and borrowed enough money as quickly as possible in order to pay back to the Buccleuch Estate the capital it had originally contributed so that the Agreement could be converted to a Limited Partnership.

During my most recent period of fieldwork, there were five farms in Teviothead that were leased by the Buccleuch Estate as Partnerships. All were or had become Limited Partnerships under terms similar to those described above including contributing the capital for the livestock and machinery. Teindside was the most recent farm to be let out as a Partnership by the Buccleuch Estate. It covers 443 acres of relatively gentle hill land and thus is able to carry over 500 crossbred park ewes and 50 cattle. The current Partner came into the Teindside in 1992 after he left his father's farm. The former tenant of Teindside had also been in a Partnership Agreement with the Buccleuch Estate. He had come into the farm in 1981 after the previous tenant, whose family had been traditional tenants for three generations, had to give up the farm because of financial difficulties brought on by death duties. Broadhaugh Farm has a total area of 746 acres of which about half is hill land. The farm carries 800 crossbred ewes. The current General Partner has held the lease for more than ten years. The last "traditional" tenant of Broadhaugh had to give up the farm ("come out") in the mid-1970s because of the financial strain brought about by death duties on his father's estate. When Northhouse Farm came up for let in 1987, the Buccleuch Estate reserved about 1000 acres of its former area for planting, leaving just over 1600 acres, two-thirds of which is classified as hill grazing land. The farm now carries 700 hill ewes, 900 park ewes and 50 cattle. The former tenant of Northhouse Farm moved to Southfield Farm. Southfield consists of 200 acres of hill grazing land and 428 acres of park land and carries a flock of 1075 crossbred ewes and 55 cattle. The current tenant of Caerlanrig Farm secured the lease as the General Partner with the Buccleuch Estate in 1988. Caerlanrig consists of 1200 acres of hill land carrying 770 purebred ewes and 100 acres of park land carrying 280 crossbred ewes.

Managerial

Lymiecleuch is the only farm in Teviothead run by a resident manager. It is the largest and topographically one of the wildest farms in the valley, covering 4500 acres most of which is hill grazing land carrying 1900 ewes and 70 cattle. It is one of the farms owned by the Strang-Steele family's Philliphaugh Estate and is "paired" with another farm, Philliphaugh, located near the town of Selkirk. These two farms are run as complementary operations. Philliphaugh has a more gentle topography of lowland arable fields. Cattle from the Philliphaugh are summered on the hills of Lymiecleuch, and draft hill ewes[11] from Lymiecleuch are sent to the Selkirk farm for crossbreeding to produce an additional crop of lambs.

Philliphaugh Estate hires a manager to engage in two types of labor: first, to do the farm work, and second to oversee the daily operation of the farm. The Estate provides all the capital for the farm—land, livestock, and machinery—and the manager is an employee with no capital investment in the farm who carries out the directions of the Estate. Since the principals of the Estate or its factor (administrator) are not experienced hill sheep farmers, the manager makes most of the decisions about the day-to-day running of the farm, i.e., buying and selling stock, ordering supplies, hiring other workers, and keeping accounts. The person who was manager of Lymiecleuch until the early 1990s said that he was obliged to consult with the Estate factor only on decisions that required a large capital outlay. Otherwise, as long as the farm was run profitably, there was a minimum of supervision by and reporting to the factor. In return, the manager was paid an annual salary, and provided with a house, telephone, coal, and potatoes.[12]

If we are discussing tenure as a relation between a person/family and a farm that includes possession with rights of access, use, and enjoyment of the property, then the managerial position is not strictly a form of tenure in the same sense as owner-occupation, tenancy, and Partnerships. The managerial relation is an employer-employee relation that does not entail the manager gaining possession of the property or livestock and thus rights to all or an agreed portion of the income from it. However, there is one aspect of the way Philliphaugh Estate practiced the managerial relation on Lymiecleuch that resembles a crucial aspect of the three forms of tenure. Since the 1930s, the Estate has given the son of a retiring manager the opportunity to take over the position in much the same way as sons historically succeeded to their fathers' tenancies on Buccleuch Estate farms.

In 1903 the Strang-Steele family took possession of Lymiecleuch and hired four shepherds. In the early 1930s, the Strang-Steele family decided to install a manager for the farm, and one of these shepherds was hired for the position. When this manager retired in 1938, his son was offered the position. This son had been born on Lymiecleuch in 1902, grew up and worked as a shepherd for sixteen years on the farm. He had moved to Linhope after he married in 1935 and returned to Lymiecleuch when he became manager. When he retired in 1973, his son, who like his father had grown up and worked as a shepherd on the farm, was offered the position; but he declined it. The Estate then hired another man. When he retired in the early 1990s, his son, who like the son of the previous manager had been a shepherd during his father's tenure as manager, was offered the position by the Estate, which he accepted.

The extension by the Philliphaugh Estate of the tendency in other forms of tenure to privilege a son's succession to the managerial position is the first indication in this ethnography of a general point about the nature of the relation between people and farms in Teviothead: living and working on the farm, in addition to owning some of its assets, created a sense of personal attachment between a farmer (often extending to his agnatic descendants) and a farm.

Interdependence Between Family and Farm

As we have seen, tenure is the first step in the process of a farmer acquiring a farm. More than just a legal relation, tenure establishes interdependence between a family and a hill sheep farm. Families are materially supported by the income from their farms so that they continue over time as a distinct group of kin (see de Haan 1994:289), and farms are viable as productive enterprises producing income, profit, and capital growth when their resources are leased and/or owned, managed, and worked by families. These material relations between particular families and farms in Teviothead express a more fundamental predilection toward building a constitutive relation between everyday concepts of family and farm that is both a precondition and a consequence of a family's sense of place on a farm.

Dependence of Family on a Farm

The most overt form of dependence of a family on a farm is economic. A family depends on the income from sheep farming production to maintain an acceptable standard of living. A hill sheep farm's gross income is made up of two components: sales of sheep, wool, cattle, and crops; and subsidies received on sheep and cattle from the U.K. and European Community agricultural programs. In the early 1990s, gross income ranged from approximately £50,000 to over £100,000, averaging about £75,000 (Scottish Agricultural College 1993a:27). After deducting variable and fixed costs, net farm profits allowed farming families to take as "personal drawings" from the business between £8,000 and £25,000, averaging nearly £13,000 (Scottish Agricultural College 1993a:27), for living expenses.[13]

Such economic reliance, however, is only one dimension of the mutual dependence between farms and families. In discussing the economic viability of farms, farmers relate them to the number of "families" that could be financially and socially accommodated rather than to other economic criteria such as net profit or management and investment income.[14] In doing so, they define their concept of family in terms of its relation to a farm. One farmer told me: "Burnthill Farm is not big enough for two families."[15] This statement was made in the context of describing a common situation faced by farms in Teviothead. Burnthill is a small Buccleuch Estate hill sheep farm of approximately 450 acres running 500 ewes in a neighboring valley. At the time, the farm tenants and personnel consisted of the farmer, Andrew Oliver, his wife and his son, Walter. They were actively looking for another farm to rent because Walter was about to get married and start another "family." Implicit in both the statement by the farmer and the act of the Olivers looking to rent another farm when Walter was about to get married is that a married couple (and their future children) forms a distinct family unit with separate interests. In strictly economic terms, the income from Burnthill Farm probably could have absorbed one additional person. However, culturally the newly married couple would have been a separate family needing their own residence (including automobile, furniture, etc.) and their own income to support it. The farm was too small in terms of the number of sheep that could be grazed to produce enough income for two such separate families to make personal drawings sufficient to satisfy their daily living requirements. Since Walter wanted to remain in farming and since his father was not ready to retire, the solution was for one family to rent (or buy if they had the capital) another farm to support itself in order to be a separate family. In seeking such a singular relation between a family and a farm through some form of tenure, hill sheep farming people define the specific membership, boundaries, and identity of their everyday concept of "family" as an intersection of marriage, common economic interests and access to a separate farm. Thus, when the farmer used the term "family" in telling me about Burnthill Farm and when the Olivers began looking for another farm for Walter and his prospective family, they were all defining the family to be what we analysts label a "nuclear family," consisting of husband, wife, and unmarried children.[16]

This is a clear case of what Bourdieu describes as the difference between a practical and theoretical relation to an object (1990a:96) and as the "intentionality without intention" of practice (1990a:12). The Olivers were not consciously attempting to theorize their everyday concepts of family and farm or the constitutive relation between family and farm that

I am suggesting are central to their sense of place and of family farming. Rather, the way their family came to be defined through its singular relation to a farm is both an unconscious disposition and an unintentioned byproduct of the Olivers' strategy for dealing practically with a very important issue in which all family members had a stake—finding a separate farm for Walter, who wanted to be a farmer, and his impending family in the conditions of the small size of Burnthill Farm and the scarcity of other hill sheep farms.

While it may appear that this practical definition of family as nuclear depends upon the physical size of a farm and its resulting economic capacity, similar statements and activities were engaged in by people with farms large enough to materially support more than one family. There are two types of situations in which this happens. The first is similar to that faced by the Olivers except that the farm has enough land and sheep to produce sufficient income to materially support two families. Even in this situation, however, the explicit goal is to find another farm to rent or purchase for the son. During the past decade, several farms faced this situation and only one secured another farm for the son. The others adopted transitional arrangements of establishing separate residences for the two families each drawing separate incomes while continuing to jointly work the farm until the parents retired from the partnership. The second situation is when a family has more than one son who wants to be a farmer. Almost everyone who discussed this situation said that it would be necessary to rent and/or purchase a separate farm for each son because partnerships between brothers on the same farm do not work, especially after "they marry and have their own families." Farmers were able to relate case after case in the Borders region of brothers eventually having to dissolve their partnership because of disagreements over farm policy and/or the distribution of income. There was only one farm known where brothers were able to continue a farming partnership for an extended period. This was achieved because the farm's size and mix of land types were capable of supporting two separate farming operations—one rearing cattle and growing arable crops, the other breeding sheep—with separate residences and financial arrangements which each brother could manage.

In these two types of situations, farms are not too small economically in terms of acreage, number of sheep and quantity of income, but socially in terms of insufficient space for the exercise of authority by two farmers with separate familial interests and in terms of the incapacity of one farm to represent the distinct identity of more than one family. As one farmer expressed it: "Partnerships incorporating a farmer, his wife and sons are an ideal situation to build up a strong family. But once sons get married, they want to build their own *empire* ... it's natural for everyone to want to farm on their own ... to be your own boss." Embedded in the metaphor of farm as empire are several important insights into the nature of the association between family and farm. First, it conveys that a farm is just as important for the social existence of a family as it is for its material existence. Second, it highlights the issue of authority and the distribution of control over all aspects of farming as a crucial factor in the social size of farms. To have one's own empire means that an individual farmer determines a hill sheep farm's policy (e.g., the mix of hill and park sheep raised, the number of cattle, and the use of fields for fodder or cash crops); the deployment of labor, land and livestock; and the disbursement of finances. Third, it assumes that such control originates in the farmer's ownership of the livestock and his or her ownership or tenancy over the landed estate of a farm. Fourth, it makes explicit that building an empire through a farmer having a singular relation to a farm is predicated upon marriage: by marrying, a farmer creates his or her own family whose separate existence is materially supported by a farm and whose separate social identity is represented by the farm. Moreover, through the children produced by marriage, the empire— the association of the family with the particular farm—has the potential to continue over time if the farmer passes control and ownership to the next generation. Fifth, the empire and its intergenerational continuity usually have a patrilineal bias. In fact, over the past ten years all but one inter-generational transfers of farms in Teviothead were from parents to son.[17] Given that the relation between farm and family is seen to be singular, one farm is not socially big enough for more than one family because a family needs to be associated with a distinct place for it to have a separate existence and identity.

Dependence of a Farm on a Family

While a family's material and social existence are dependent upon its ownership and/or tenure over a separate farm, conversely farms are dependent upon families for their existence and viability as productive enterprises. The following are two cases of the farms in Teviothead that failed in recent times largely because in some way they "lacked a family" residing and working on the farm (see Gasson and Errington 1993:18).

CASE 1: LONGKNOWE FARM. Will Elliot leased Blackrigg Farm from the Buccleuch Estate. Blackrigg covers approximately 1090 acres carrying nearly 1000 sheep. Will and his wife provided most of the labor supplemented by hiring part-time lambing shepherds. In the mid-1970s, Will rented Longknowe Farm, another Buccleuch Estate property of approximately 750 acres and over 700 sheep. Since none of his children expressed interest in becoming a hill sheep farmer, the motivation for Will renting a second farm was more to build an entrepreneurial than a familial empire. A condition of his Longknowe tenancy was that the farmhouse be occupied so that it could be maintained on a daily basis by the residents. The Estate agreed to a family of Will's relatives residing in Longknowe Farmhouse.

To minimize labor costs, Will worked on both farms, his wife on Blackrigg, a full-time hired shepherd on Longknowe, and part-time shepherds on Blackrigg during lambing. After eight years, Will decided to terminate his lease on Longknowe because it was making a loss. Will explained the failure to me as due to the financial strain caused by a downturn in the lamb market and a doubling of interest rates just after he had borrowed money to make capital improvements to Longknowe. For him, the core and symbol of his financial problems was having to pay the full-time shepherd's wages since this "money is not going back into the farm" in capital improvement that would increase production and income. What Will did not explicitly say was that the necessity to hire and pay the wages of a full-time shepherd was the result of insufficient family labor. Other farmers in the valley made this explicit. They told me that Will had "spread himself too thin," that there was not enough family labor for two farms and that Longknowe was too small in size and lamb production to partially support a family and pay a full-time shepherd's wages.

There are two points to highlight about this case. The first is that the requirement of the Estate that a family live in the farmhouse accords with the way farmers themselves see the close association of family residence and a farm. The second is that family labor, as opposed to hired labor, is an important component of a sheep farm's economic viability.

CASE 2: SHANKEND FARM. Shankend Farm had been in the Armstong family for over two hundred years. It was the longest continuous family tenancy in the Buccleuch Estates. The farm covers 630 acres of low, protected land and carries over 1000 ewes. In the early 1980s the current tenant was Robert Armstong. Before marrying Robert, his first wife had lived in town. She became discontented with rural country life, and the marriage ended in divorce. Robert eventually remarried, but the farm went downhill through his absences and neglect. He rarely did any farm work but rather paid wages to a shepherd and a tractorman. By 1986, Robert had gone bankrupt and was giving up the tenancy on Shankend.

For people of the Teviothead, the state of Shankend Farmhouse epitomized what happens when a family is not committed to a farm. Robert did not spend much time on the farm and his second wife cared little for farming. Several times during the last months of his tenancy, he "had gone missing." No one knew where he was, and he was not residing in the farmhouse. When the Estate came to inspect the farm, they found the consequences of his fifteen dogs living in the farmhouse with a side of beef hanging in the kitchen for food. The farmhouse was fouled and in shambles, as was the farm financially.

Ostensibly, the problems leading to the failure of Shankend Farm were different from those faced by Will Elliot. Will's problems, despite his sound business intentions to expand his family farming enterprise, stemmed from international and European Community economic processes beyond his control: the downturn in the sheep market and the upturn in interest rates. It was unlucky that these changes took place when he was financially most vulnerable. Robert's problems were of his own making, the result of poor business sense and lack of commitment to the farm. He chose to drink and gamble away profits, and he decided not to work and reside continuously on the farm at the same time as incurring the high costs of hired labor. Yet, while the specific events and relations that led to the failures of Longknowe and Shankend were different, their detrimental effect on the viability of the farms operated through the same mechanism crucial to the success of hill sheep farms: family labor. Both Longknowe and Shankend "lacked" a family. Will's family was living and working at Blackrigg, and Robert's was deficient in commitment: he spent less and less time at Shankend, and his wife was only interested in the dogs. In both cases there was an insufficient level of family labor to make these two farms viable as businesses.

This bring me to a central issue in the ongoing debate in the rural sociology literature over the definition of the family farm. The most recent instance is the dialogue between Gasson and Errington (1993) and Djurfeldt (1995) over the necessity of family labor in defining the family farm (see also Hill 1993). Gasson and Errington argue that the existence of hired labor supplementing family labor is not of crucial importance because the amount of family labor varies over a family cycle without changing the self-perception of being family farmers (1993:14–15). For Djurfeldt, a strict operational definition requires the recognition that "when hired labor becomes necessary to the reproduction of a farm, it has important implications for its way of functioning," which makes it fundamentally different from a family farm whose labor is not a fixed cost (1995:5). Despite this difference, both accept the competitive advantages of family labor to the success of a farm business. It reduces fixed costs, obviates the structural requirement for surplus production (Friedmann 1978:562 and note), increases flexibility in personal consumption (563), and can adjust to changes in income or labor resulting from wider political and economic forces. In these economic terms at least, hill sheep farms in Less Favoured Areas like Teviothead depend upon a family for their existence and success as businesses that in turn are able to materially support the families living on them. However, focusing exclusively on the economic advantages of family labor for the viability of a farm misses its more fundamental effect. I take up this theme in Chapter 6 where I show how farm labor transforms the economic and social interdependence between family and farm into a sensual attachment between people and their farms, that is, a sense of place. Before doing so I need to describe the characteristics of the land and sheep upon which farm labor is expended.

Notes

1. In writing this and the following ethnographic chapters, I was caught between Fabian's (1983) critique of the objectifying, distancing and disempowering effects of the "ethnographic present" tense and Hastrup's reassessment of the "ethnographic present" tense reflecting the reality of fieldwork (1995:20). Other than my descriptions of time-specific events for which I use the past tense, I decided to use the ethnographic present in Hastrup's sense: "Fieldwork is outside history quite irrespective of the fact that all societies have histories of their own and are deeply involved in global history as well. The reality of fieldwork is a liminal phase for both subjects and objects, in which the distinction between them is dissolved … The reality of the encounter is outside ordinary history; it is its own history, if you wish. … The ethnographic present is a narrative construct that clearly does not represent a truth about the timelessness of the others … But the betweenness implied in fieldwork, and the fact of the ethnographer's sharing the time *of* the others, makes ethnography escape the ordinary historical categories" (21,25). Rabinow 1977 makes a similar point about the betweenness of cultural encounter we call fieldwork.

2. Heidegger (1962) uses the term "praxis" to refer to knowledge emerging from doing things with entities in the world. "Praxis necessarily precedes, and provides the motive for, any merely theoretical inquiry into the being of entities" (Macaan 1993:73). I am using the adjectival form "praxical" to indicate the derivation of the concept from Heidegger.

3. A rule of thumb used by local valuers is that arable land is worth approximately six times hill grazing land.

4. As will be described in the following chapters, hill sheep are usually pure bred and park sheep crossbred. In order to avoid repetition, when I refer to hill ewes in the text it also means that they are purebred and when I refer to park or field ewes, it also means that they are cross bred. The parallel dichotomies of hill land and park land or fields, pure bred and crossbred sheep infuses much of hill sheep farming practice and meaning.

5. Both Skelfhill and Priesthaugh farms were owned by the government and used as military training areas during World War II. After the war, both were sold.

6. Originally, his son had been the prime successor to the farm. But he decided that he did not wish to be a farmer.

7. The statistics presented by Tweddle, Smith, and Anderson on farm size in terms of ewe-equivalents (Scottish Agricultural College 1993a:60) suggest that owner-occupied farms are smaller than tenanted farms. This pattern is not

repeated in Teviothead where the four owner-occupied farms are among the largest six farms.

8. In 1997, one established tenant farmer told me that the two headage payments for sheep and cattle more than pays the rent by a long way. This may be another advantage to being a long-standing tenant of the Buccleuch Estate.

9. As we will see in the next section, all farms that have come up for rent since the early 1980s have been leased under different arrangements, called Partnership Agreements, that include an annual rent in addition to other financial transfers to the Buccleuch Estate. Even in these cases, the rent is higher than for equivalent long-standing tenants.

10. It is important to distinguish between these Partnership Agreements between private Estates and farmers and the partnerships formed among members of a farming family. When referring to the former, Partnership is capitalized and when referring to the latter, partnership is not capitalized.

11. Draft ewes are at the end of their breeding career. On hill sheep farms, a ewe becomes a draft ewe after five or six breeding seasons; it then may be sold for slaughter as mutton. However, because of the gentler conditions on lowland farms, draft hill ewes may be relocated to park land and retained for another breeding season. For the last breeding season, they are usually crossed with less hardy but bigger rams. As a result, their lambs can be sold directly on the fat market and be eligible for the variable premium of the Sheep Meat Regime discussed in the previous chapter.

12. These latter perquisites are typical of what a hired shepherd receives in addition to his wage.

13. My access to details of the financial records of farms was restricted. The figures I use here are derived from average data published by the Scottish Agricultural College in the *Profitability of Farming in Scotland* series and from my own data on a cross-section of farms—some owner-occupied, some tenanted, some with few cattle, some with cattle more important, and some with crops. One of the striking features of my figures is the large variations in gross income and personal drawings. However, since I have only limited access to financial details of Teviothead farms, it is difficult to do more than use the published averages and note these large variations.

14. Management and investment income (M&II) and net profit are seen by the Scottish College of Agriculture as two of the most important measures of a farm's financial performance (Scottish Agricultural College 1993a:17).

15. I am using pseudonyms here.

16. In a later chapter, I will describe how families in Teviothead privilege the nuclear family in the way they organize intergenerational succession to farms.

17. The exception was a case where the son—who had been identified as the heir, who had lived on the farm with his wife for several years, and for whom the legal arrangement had been made for the transfer—decided for personal reasons that he did not want to be a farmer. As a result, he received the cash equivalent of his share of the farm, and his sister and her husband succeeded to the farm.

Chapter 5

SHEEP AND LAND

A Political Economy of Space

In describing the size and capitalization of Teviothead hill sheep farms in the previous chapter, I foreshadowed two aspects of these farms that form the central foci of this chapter: sheep and land. No matter what type of tenure—owner-occupation, tenancy, or Partnership—a hill sheep farmer owns the sheep that graze the lands. Sheep are a significant asset in themselves. With a value of approximately £50, farmers on the smaller farms carrying around 500 ewes have an asset worth £25,000, and farmers on the larger farms carrying up to 2000 ewes have an asset worth £100,000. In addition to the capital value of sheep is their social value in defining a farmer. Ownership of sheep overshadows the difference that varying forms of tenure might have had on the social identity and status of farmers in Teviothead. Hill sheep farms consist of two categories of land differentiated in terms of weather conditions, topography, soils and vegetation—each suitable for grazing quite different kinds of sheep. *Outbye* is rough grazing or hill land and *inbye* is "park" land or fields. All farms in Teviothead have some park land, but the amount varies considerably. The farms closer to Hawick—Branxholm Braes, Harwood/Branxholm Park, Southfield, and Teindside—are at least 50 percent inbye. They tend to be smaller than the larger, more outbye farms of over 500 acres nearer the watershed with hill land covering more than 70 percent of the farms.

Figure 5.1 Priesthaugh Farm with Inbye Fields (foreground) and Outbye Hill Land (background)

I begin by describing the two types of land, the sheep that are raised on them, and the way sheep bond to specific areas of the farm. The latter process is particularly important because I will argue in later chapters that through such bonding sheep embody farming spaces and people, and mediate the way those people create and become attached to places in their farm work. I then analyze how the European Community and the Common Agricultural Policy differentially affect the use of inbye and outbye land, how, as a result, inbye and outbye land become different types of productive spaces, and finally how this effects the potential of inbye and outbye sheep to act as economic values as well as social values.

Outbye

Outbye land lies at altitudes above 1000 feet. It has a complex topography and a correspondingly rich descriptive nomenclature consisting of hills (*law* [conical hill], *pen* [pointed hill]), hilltops *(heid)*, steep hillsides *(brae)*, enclosed valleys *(hope)*, passes *(hass)*, ridges *(rig)*, flowing streams *(burn)*, dry river beds *(syke)*, knolls *(knowe)*, gullies *(gill)*, and ravines *(cleuch).* Outbye land is normally unfenced, but it still has definite spatial divisions that are constructed on the basis of patterns of sheep grazing and, as I will describe in the next chapter, practices of shepherding.

Analysis of Borders hills environment by the Hill Farming Research Organisation identifies several characteristics of outbye land that make in unsuitable for arable cultivation and for all but the hardiest sheep (Hill Farm Research Organisation 1979:9-19). Because the seasonal variation in temperatures is relatively small, variations in altitude have a great impact on the length of the growing season and the nutritional quality of the vegetation. As altitude increases, temperatures drop, wind exposure increases, and the amount and quality of vegetation decreases. High rainfall and poor drainage produce excessively boggy soil that inhibits the breakdown of organic matter into minerals. As a result, outbye ground lacks important nutrients for plant growth and sheep nourishment. These environmental factors limit agricultural production on Border hills to extensive livestock farming characterized by a low carrying capacity of approximately 1.4 to 2.5 acres of outbye land per breeding ewe. This predominance of relatively infertile outbye land in the Border hills is the basis for the region's classification as a Less Favoured Area in danger of depopulation. Hill sheep people distinguish various types of outbye "ground." "Deep" or "black" ground is an area of wet, "boggy" or "peaty" soil with mineral-poor grasses and a predominance of heather and moss (which are dark in color, hence the term "black"). If on gently sloping and accessible ground, these areas of hill land can be drained to improve pasturage. "White ground" is a area where bent grass predominates. It provides poor grazing from September to May when the grass turns light brown ("white"). The best type of outbye ground has a mixed topography with a variety of grasses and rushes providing areas for grazing and shelter.

These properties of outbye land not only limit its use to sheep rearing but also to particular breeds of sheep that can survive in its harsh conditions. In Teviothead, two breeds of sheep are grazed on hill land: Blackface and South Country Cheviot. They are purebred to maintain and enhance what farmers and shepherds identify as three attributes that make them particularly suited to rearing lambs on the hills. The first is their "hardiness." By this they mean that the Blackface and South Country Cheviot sheep can survive on the open hill throughout the winter months without large inputs of supplementary feed. Other breeds of lowland or park sheep would perish. Because hill pastures in winter do not provide enough nutrition to maintain both mother and the gestating lamb, ewes lose body weight over the breeding cycle, making them less productive. One aspect of the hardiness of outbye sheep in comparison with lowland breeds is a genetic capacity to convert more quickly reserves of body fat and protein into energy and nourishment for the fetus (Hill Farm Research Organisation 1979:55).[1] Another dimension of hardiness is the wool or "skin." Given that hill sheep winter on exposed terrain characterized by wet and windy conditions, their fleece, which is coarse, rough, and not suited to high-quality wool products, has insulating properties that provide greater protection against heat loss. As a result, Blackface and Cheviot ewes are able to withstand the undernourishment of hill pastures because there is a reduced need for their metabolism to maintain body heat. This in turn reduces the amount of supplementary feeding that farmers need to provide to pregnant ewes to minimize weight loss on the hill during winter.

Associated with the hardiness of the breeds are small size, relatively low productivity measured by a lambing rate of less than 100 percent[2] and a certain wildness that makes them well suited to grazing on the low quality pasture of the hills. Even with the mid-1980s changes to the European Community fat lamb certification standards towards smaller and leaner carcasses, hill lambs were often too small to meet the criteria of fat lambs and thus were ineligible for the Sheep Meat Regime's variable premium. Before the MacSharry reforms that phased out the variable premium, farmers had two options. One was to sell hill lambs on the store market in autumn to lowland farmers in Scotland and England who fattened them in their fields and then sold them several months later on the fat market where they attracted the variable premium. Another was to bring the lambs off the hill and fatten them on the farm's inbye land for several months. This usually required the extra expense of buying in feed. In these circumstances, farmers had to calculate the risk that the extra

Figure 5.2   Hill Sheep (South Country Cheviot)

expense would be more than offset by higher prices and additional variable premium that the fattened lambs would attract on the fat market.

Compared with inbye sheep, hill ewes have fewer multiple births making them less productive. Hill sheep farmers recount the following chain of causation to explain outbye sheep's low rate of multiple birth: multiple births depend upon the ewes' ovulation rate; the ovulation rate is affected by the overall condition of the ewes at the time of tupping (mating) in November; the condition of the ewes at tupping time is dependent upon the level of nourishment throughout the breeding cycle; and the level of nourishment throughout the breeding cycle depends upon the quality of the pasture grazed by the ewes. It is difficult in these harsh conditions for a flock of hill ewes to produce an equivalent number of lambs to that of park ewes. By the beginning of the 1990s with strategic supplementary feeding and bringing ewes carrying twin lambs into lower-lying improved pastures, lambing percentages on the hill hovered around 100 percent or slightly higher (due to more multiple births) when the weather remained favorable.

In a recent nostalgic retrospective on shepherds, the wildness of outbye sheep compared with park sheep is described as follows:

Normally, [park] sheep are of a very gentle and timid disposition, a virtue well recognized ... A flockmaster rearing mutton or lamb for the butcher will choose to breed an animal with an enlarged capacity of the digestive organs, and a reduced capacity in the head and chest or the mental and respiratory organs. Restlessness is despised; a breeder ... will prefer a dull or indolent sheep that fills its paunch with pasture, then seeks a shady nook to chew his cud with closed eyes and blissful satisfaction. The adaptability, hardiness and restless temperament of our wild native island and mountain breeds make them especially useful for converting the sparse grazing of the crags and moors, albeit at a slower rate while in search of food and shelter. (Combe 1983:15)

Wildness is an attribute that hill sheep people use to characterize all the components of outbye: land, weather and sheep. Thus remote farms of primarily hill land distant from roads are called wild. In a diary of one farmer, the windy, rainy, and snowy conditions that often prevail from autumn through spring are described as wild. And hill sheep farmers and shepherds use the term to characterize the nature of hill sheep. One particularly striking example occurred at a local agricultural show. One event of the show was sheep dog trials in which working dogs are judged on their ability to herd sheep into pens. Unlike other shows, the sheep used in these trials were hill ewes from an almost purely outbye farm where it was reputed that the shepherding was not done as frequently as it should be. There were comments by the people helping with the show that things could not be more difficult for the dogs since normally the sheep used for the trials are the more docile inbye sheep. They also said that these particular hill sheep would be even "more wild" since they probably had not seen a human or a sheep dog for several weeks. So, hill sheep are wild not just genetically but also because, like the ground on which they live, they are less subject to everyday human contact and productive discipline than park sheep. As will be discussed in detail later, the wildness and restless temperament of hill sheep are part of an adaptive territorial grazing pattern that bonds them to an area in the hills where their survival needs for food and shelter can be fulfilled.

Hill sheep people identify a second quality of Blackface and South Country Cheviot sheep that makes them suited to

outbye land: the ewes are "good mothers." Most hill sheep
farms in Teviothead lack sufficient low altitude inbye fields
with good pasturage and easy access to enable farmers to
bring all the ewes in from the hill for lambing. Thus, one
measure of "good mothering" is the ability of ewes to lamb on
the hill without the constant attendance of a shepherd.[3]
Lambing by hill ewes requires less human intervention for
two reasons. First, because lambs are relatively small, hill ewes
have fewer abortions (*kebbing*) and difficult births that could
result in the death of the lamb and/or the ewe. Second, after
birthing, hill ewes stay with their lambs and quickly "mother
up" should they become separated from their lamb(s). This
is particularly crucial in bad weather conditions when young
lambs could die quickly if they are not able to suckle.
Another dimension of the hill ewes' good mothering is having enough milk to feed lambs. During the first few weeks
after birth, lambs' survival and growth rate are entirely dependent on how much milk the mother can produce.[4]

A third characteristic of Blackface and South Country
breeds is that they are territorial grazers. This is another way
of describing the restlessness and wildness of outbye sheep.
Hill sheep tend to move from the lower to the higher ground
during the late afternoon and throughout the evening,
spending the night at or near the tops of hills; conversely,
they tend to move from the higher ground to the lower
ground in the early morning and throughout the day. As they
range over the land during this diurnal grazing pattern,
sheep learn about those topographical and pasturage areas
on the hill of adaptive significance for eating, mating, lambing, and sheltering. These areas become the known and
remembered places of a grazing domain where the ewes
return to fulfill their survival needs; in doing so they create
and bond to a region in which they remain throughout their
lives. One shepherd described the effects of this attachment
as an "invisible fence," which forms one level of the spatial
partitioning of unfenced outbye land. Throughout the Borders, the process of creating this spatial bond between a
group of hill sheep and a specific territory on the hills was
called "hefting on." The area of the farm's hill land and the
group of sheep that form an attachment to it is called a "heft"
or "cut". I wish to emphasize here how, in referring to both a

group of sheep and a territorial division of hill land, the concept of cut or heft unifies sheep and the space created by the
way they use the land in carrying out their lives; it expresses
the mutually constitutive relation between a specific group of
sheep and the distinct area of the hill to which they bond so
that they become refractions of each other.

This synthesis of sheep and space characteristic of cuts is
also manifest in the type and extent of the terrain and the
number of sheep. Thus cuts are unfenced areas of outbye
land that should include a variety of topographical features,
hilltops, small valleys, and areas of low-lying protected
ground, where ewes find grass for grazing and shelter for
lambing. The names of cuts mostly derive from topographical features identified on Ordinance Survey maps. Further,
the "size" of a cut is determined neither solely by the area of
the hills over which sheep range in their grazing nor by the
number of sheep. Instead both the area and number of
sheep included in a cut depend upon the amount and quality of the vegetation and shelter available. In Teviothead, cuts
vary from 50 to over 100 ewes. Two cuts that might contain
approximately the same number of sheep cover quite different areas because of the different topography, shelter, and
carrying capacity of the land.

The breeding program of hill sheep farms is organized by
cuts. Each year tups (rams) are restricted to mating with the
ewes of only one cut. Further, ewes remain in the same cut
over their breeding lives of five to six years. Every year, the
oldest cohort, known as draft ewes, is replaced by a cohort of
ewe lambs selected from those born of the ewes within the
cut. Thus a cut consists of four to five generations of breeding ewes attached to a particular territory. One farmer
described a cut as a "family" line consisting of "daughters of
daughters." Further, because ewes stay on the same cut
throughout their lives, they are understood to adapt to the
characteristics of the land where they live and breed. Farmers
and shepherds continually told me how their sheep had over
generations become genetically adapted to the grasses and
resistant to the parasites of their specific cuts. Other characteristics of a cut are also understood to be genetically embodied and transmitted: one shepherd commented that one cut
of ewes had more twins than others; another shepherd

bragged that ewes of one of his cuts were particularly good mothers. The general understanding of hill sheep people is that each cut has distinctive characteristics that are "bred into them" and thus are passed down the generations through the selective breeding program. This "breeding in" of the adaptive relation between a cut of sheep and a grazing space is the reason why, when a farmer "comes into" (i.e., purchase, lease, or become a Partner with the Buccleuch Estate) a farm, he buys the ewes already on the farm rather than bringing ewes from his previous farm.

Before moving to a discussion of inbye land and sheep, I note here that in describing to me the nature of a cut and the bonding of sheep and territory that the concept expresses, hill farming people employed a genetic discourse: in hefting on and living in the same cut over generations, a line of sheep comes to literally embody the nature of the land in their genetic constitution. In this process there is a permeability between acquired behavioral adaptation and genetic transmission. What in one generation of ewes is a specific behavioral adaptation to the land becomes, through the selection of replacement stock, a part of the genetic make-up of the ewes of the following generations. This is perhaps a more profound sense of the term "cut" and how it constitutes and unifies the seemingly separate phenomena of a particular group of sheep and the land upon which they dwell. Or to say this in a more heuristic way, the concept of "cut" expresses both the process of creating and the resultant attachment between a group of beings linked by descent and a place. This genetically mediated association of descent and territory in mutually defining a distinct group of beings and their place has appeared on three previous occasions in this book. Reiving clans were not just constructed from common kinship as embedded in agnatically transmitted clan names. Rather, distinct reiving clans were constituted by common kinship and common territory whose center was the tower house of the laird. Through administrative reforms instituted by the Buccleuch Estate in the seventeenth and eighteenth centuries, individual families secured tenancies on separate farms and passed them on from father to son over generations. And in contemporary Teviothead, a separate farming family, as well as the everyday concept of the family, emerged only when it was singularly associated with a farm through a form of tenure.[5]

Inbye

"Inbye" or "park" are areas of gently sloping or level land at altitudes under 1000 feet. Because of milder weather conditions and flatter terrain than that of outbye lands, inbye land is used for arable cultivation or more fertile pasturage. It is usually fenced to form a number of fields, allowing farmers to more easily organize cultivation and/or grazing. The topography of the smaller, mostly inbye farms in Teviothead means that they have a higher percentage of land divided into enclosed pasture and fields for a longer time than the larger, mostly outbye farms. On the latter type of farms, such as Linhope, Lymiecleuch, Hislop, Priesthaugh, Skelfhill, and Northhouse, less than 25 percent of the land is inbye. A significant portion of what are presently inbye fields was formerly outbye land. During the 1970s and 1980s, these farms used the European Community and United Kingdom agricultural grants (described in Chapter 3) to improve the gentler sloping hill land at lower altitude in order to convert it into inbye fields. The most crucial and expensive improvement was to install drainage systems by digging a series of small canals on the hillsides to allow water to flow into streams. Once drained, the land was plowed, fertilized, seeded for high quality grasses, and fenced off. It could then be used as improved pasturage for crossbred ewes, as a refuge for hill ewes with twins at lambing time, and/or as arable fields for growing winter fodder (hay and silage) or turnips.

The most common use of inbye land is for rearing inbye or park sheep crossbred to produce larger lambs that can be sold as fat lambs. One type of park sheep is a crossbred ewe produced by mating purebred hill ewes with a tup (ram) of a large, docile, and less hardy lowland breed. The two most common crossbred ewes used as park sheep in Teviothead are the Greyface (Blackface ewe crossed with a Blue Leicester tup) and the Cheviot mule (South Country Cheviot ewe crossed with a Blue Leicester tup).[6] These crossbred park ewes are then crossed each year with Suffolk tups—another

of the large, docile, but less hardy lowland breed—to produce cross lambs. The breeding life of these crossbred park
ewes is about six seasons. Each year most Teviothead farms
have to "buy in" a cohort of these Greyface or Cheviot mule
park ewes from lowland farms more suited to their less hardy
nature. The other type of park sheep are draft hill ewes. Each
year, the best draft ewes from all the outbye cuts are brought
onto inbye land, where conditions are milder, for one more
breeding season before being sold for slaughter. They are
crossed with Suffolk tups to produce cross lambs.

Park sheep have two principal advantages over hill sheep.
First, through crossbreeding they are larger, more docile, and
more quickly able to reach fat lamb certification standards
especially since they graze on the higher quality and more
nutritious pasturage of inbye land during spring, summer,
and autumn. Thus they are sold directly on the fat market
where they attract the variable premium. Second, they have a
much higher rate of multiple births. In Teviothead, lambing
percentages for park sheep reach 150 percent (1.5 lambs per
ewe) whereas hill sheep lambing percentages are normally
between 95 percent and 105 percent. However, park sheep
are less hardy and more expensive to keep. Because of higher
stocking rates on inbye land (approximately one ewe per
acre), park sheep are more prone to illnesses and their con-
tagion, and they rely heavily on supplementary feeding for
the majority of their nutrition throughout the winter.

Farmers use the fencing of inbye fields to actively organize
where park sheep graze and lamb. When a field becomes
sparse, the sheep are moved to another field. Because park
ewes have large lambs and often have difficulties lambing,
they need more supervision than hill sheep. Accordingly, at
lambing time, park ewes are lambed in fields close to the
farmhouse or a shepherd's cottage to allow easy access for
constant supervision. In the past decade, several farms converted barns or built large sheds for lambing park ewes. Not
only does this allow constant supervision, but it gets them
out of the bad weather that often occurs during lambing in
late March to early April. Thus, the relation between sheep
behavior and spatial divisions of inbye land is the reverse of
outbye land. On the hill, diurnal patterns of sheep grazing
and territorial bonding are the basis for the unfenced divi-

Figure 5.3   Crossbred Sheep in Inbye Fields

sions known as cuts, and in this respect sheep play a part in creating them. On inbye land, farmers build fences to demarcate fields and inbye sheep are moved between them to suit the purposes of the farmer.

Inbye sheep are not as specifically adapted to the topography, vegetation, soil, and parasites of any particular area of the farm as are hill sheep. This is the result of several aspects of the way they are bred and grazed: Greyface and Cheviot mule ewes are bred on other farms; draft hill ewes are raised in another territory of the farm; park ewes are given a high level of supplementary feeding, and over a year they are moved several times between fields to maximize grazing and cultivation. Thus, they do not heft on or develop a bond to a specific territory through grazing patterns and are not thought to be divided into cuts as are hill sheep. For these reasons, inbye sheep do not embody the inbye land of the farm as strongly as cuts of hill sheep embody the outbye land.

Tups (Rams)

Tups that mate with hill and park ewes are kept on each farm in a ratio of one tup to between forty to sixty ewes. Except for

the seventeen-day mating season, a farm's tups are kept separate from the ewes and generally graze in lower altitude
fields so that they are in peak fitness for running with the
ewes. Most hill tups are "home bred," meaning that each year
the best of the male lambs are kept for breeding. Four farms
in Teviothead—Falnash-Hislop, Skelfhill, Priesthaugh, and
more lately Northhouse—also breed Cheviot hill tups for sale
at auctions in the Borders. Most park tups, while purebred,
are purchased from other farms. This is because park tups
are of a different breed than the crossbred park ewes and
purebred draft hill ewes with whom they mate.[7] Depending
on the particular circumstances of a farm, tups are mated for
five or six years. Tups in their prime, two to four years old,
can mate with up to seventy ewes while younger and older
tups can mate with forty to fifty ewes.[8]

A Political Economy of Farm Space

While expressed by hill sheep people in terms of their physical attributes, inbye and outbye lands are not neutral geo-
metric spaces, simple surfaces for action (Tilley 1994:9) upon
which they practice hill sheep farming. Rather, through the
sale of lambs raised on them, inbye and outbye are distinct
social spaces constituted by their differential relations to the
market for agricultural commodities and the policies of the
European Community that regulate it. The point I wish to
argue now is that outbye land, sheep, and (as I will describe
in the following chapter) shepherding work are more significant for the distinctive attachment to and sense of place of a
hill sheep farm despite the increasing importance of park
sheep for the financial viability of the farm business.

Tilley suggests that the space created by capitalist-moti-
vated human action is above all useful and rational (Tilley
1994:21) and that the control of such space is associated with
the disciplinary aims of institutions. Similarly, Relph identifies
"the paradox of modern [capitalist] landscapes" (1981:104) as
dehumanized, and by implication monosemous, precisely
because humans have excessively shaped and planned them
monolithically in terms of economic efficiency. While inbye
and outbye lands are both integrated into the capitalist market

through Common Agricultural Policy programs and European markets, they are integrated to varying degrees and thus are different social spaces with differing potential for hill sheep people to build a meaningful relation to them. Again, the starting point for this discussion is the categorizing of the Borders region by the European Community as a Less Favoured Area because of the high proportion of outbye land. One consequence of this spatial classification is that Teviothead hill sheep farms are eligible for extra subsidies and increased grants over and above those available to farmers in more productive areas. The most important of these special support measures are the Hill Livestock Compensatory Allowance, a supplement to the ewe premium of the Sheep Meat Regime for sheep farms in Less Favoured Areas, and the Agricultural Development and Agricultural Improvement Schemes described in Chapter 3. But while hill sheep farms in Teviothead are eligible for these extra support measures because they were in a Less Favoured Area, the distinction between inbye and outbye lands within each farm and the different types of lambs produced on them attract differential treatment from these schemes. Because inbye land with its tendency toward flatter, open space is more docile, in Tilley's and Relph's sense, than outbye land, it is more open to rational and useful control and to being humanized in service of more efficient capitalist production. The Agricultural Development Scheme was aimed specifically at funding the expensive technological inputs needed to improve the natural characteristics of the land that allow more efficient production and lower labor costs. The most common improvements carried out in Teviothead (i.e., draining to control excessive soil moisture, fencing to control sheep grazing movements, creating shelter belts to control the effects of weather, planting and spraying to control the type of pasturage) were too expensive or less possible on rough outbye land. While both park sheep bred on inbye land and hill sheep bred on outbye land are eligible for subsidies of the Sheep Meat Regime (i.e., variable premium on lambs that reach certification standards and annual ewe premium), inbye sheep do not receive the Less Favoured Area Supplement and thus in total attract only half the total subsidy of outbye sheep; in addition, they are not eligible for the Hill Livestock Compensatory Allowance (HLCA).

There are two effects of these differential applications of agricultural programs. One is inscribed on the land itself. Compared with outbye, inbye land on all farms in Teviothead has been subjected to more human intervention funded by improvement grants. The flatness of the fields, the monoculture of the grasses and/or crops planted, and the straight lines of drains and fencing are the expressions of the high-level discipline exercised upon inbye land in the singular pursuit of exchange value. As a result, for hill sheep people inbye land has fewer topographical differences than outbye. Like colors, as Sahlins points out, topographic features are potential "signs in vast schemes of social relations: meaningful structures by which persons and groups, objects and occasions, are differentiated and combined in cultural orders" (1977:167). Thus, the socially constituted perception of the greater "natural" topographic complexity of outbye land can function better than inbye land as a "metalanguage" (Sahlins 1977:172) to organize hill sheep farmers' polysemous experience of their sense of place. Further, since inbye sheep do not bond to the land as outbye sheep do, their grazing likewise has less behavioral potential for constructing meaningful divisions upon the land. Instead of topography and sheep behavior marking out different inbye spaces, it is humanly-constructed fencing that distinguishes between fields.

The other effect of the differential applications of agricultural programs is on the sheep. Park lambs are bred on fenced, easily accessible inbye ground where they are subject to greater surveillance and control by farming people. Because of their crossbreeding and better grazing, they are sold on the fat market as finished lambs ready for immediate slaughter and sale as an agricultural commodity. In comparison with the price of hill lambs sold on the store market, the price of finished lambs from crossbred park ewes is less subsidized. Park ewes attract only half the annual ewe premium as that of hill ewes, and until recently they were not eligible for the HLCA. Thus their lambs are less protected from the effects of the European and world agricultural markets.[9] The protection of inbye sheep has decreased even further in the last several years. Since the late 1980s, the level of price support for fat lambs under the variable premium continued to fall and was phased out by the MacSharry reforms in 1993. In addition, the MacSharry reforms placed a limit on the number of ewes in Less Favoured Areas eligible for the ewe premium. At the same time as protection for inbye sheep has been decreasing, the HLCA for hill sheep has been increasing, from £6.25 per ewe in 1986 to £8.75 per ewe in 1991.[10] If we can think of protection as a form of economic distancing from the market, and that the "closer" to the market (i.e., the less protection through price support subsidies and headage payments) the more a phenomenon is subject to commoditization, that is, the more its value is determined by its exchange value on the market, then crossbred park lambs sold on the fat market are more commoditized than hill lambs sold on the store market. Finally, since inbye lambs are more commoditized, their significance for hill sheep farmers is largely their economic value derived from their sale.

The characteristics of outbye land that diminish its potential as a resource for capitalist production of commodities enhance its potential for the production of polysemy about hill sheep farms and the identity of the people who live and work on them. As I have describe above, in terms of agricultural production, outbye land is marginal. Its harsh weather, complex topography, poor soil, and vegetation render it unsuited to any form of arable cultivation and to significant improvement. Outbye land is used for purebred hill sheep that are genetically adapted to the harsh conditions but whose small lambs are less marketable. As a result, they are also eligible for the ewe premium but with the Less Favoured Area supplement, and in addition, the HLCA payment. Thus, in comparison with inbye lambs, hill lambs are more protected and at a greater economic distance from the effects of the agricultural market. One consequence of this distancing, suggested by Tilley and Relph, is that outbye land, as well as the hill ewes and lambs living on it, are less humanized through technological intervention. Indeed, the attribution of wildness to all components of outbye attests to this. Thus, the significance of outbye land and sheep to hill sheep people is not as limited to one form of meaning as are inbye land and park sheep, that is, rational use and efficiency in terms of producing objects for sale on the capitalist market. In this respect, hill lambs are less commoditized, providing semantic space for them to be more an embodiment of the multidimensional character of hill sheep people and their way of life.

In the next several chapters, I take up this difference between economic and social value of sheep in detail by analyzing the shepherding labor that produces hill and park lambs, and the different kinds of auctions in which they are sold.

Notes

1. The Hill Farm Research Organisation suggests that one of the major impediments to hill sheep productivity is "the 'hungry gap' period from January to April, when hill pastures provide only a minimum growth and when the majority of hill ewes, though pregnant, live on a sub-maintenance diet and decline in weight" (1979:42).
2. A 100 percent lambing rate occurs when there are as many lambs born as there are breeding ewes in the flock.
3. During lambing, shepherds have time to go around the hill and observe the sheep only twice each day.
4. There is a positive feedback relation between lambs' health and the milk yield of their mothers. Lambs that are vigorous and demand more milk stimulate increased milk production in their mothers (see also Hill Farming Research Organisation 1979:57).
5. In future chapters, I describe how this association of descent and territory is the basis of what I will argue is a consubstantial relation between a family and a farm.
6. More recently, some farms have experimented by crossing Blackface hill ewes with Continental breeds, such as Texel, to produce lambs whose carcasses more closely match the certification standards and consumer preferences in Europe.
7. One farmer in Teviothead recently started breeding Suffolk tups.
8. The brevity of my treatment of tups in this chapter belies their importance, which I take up in later chapters.
9. The recent extension of HLCA payments to park sheep on hill farms in Less Favoured Areas does not affect the point I am making here since lambs of hill sheep are still more protected than lambs of park sheep.
10. All forms of subsidies decreased as a result of the MacSharry reforms. Thus by 1997, the Hill Livestock Compensatory Allowance was down to £5.75 for hill ewes, but this was still nearly double the rate for park ewes. Hill ewes still received the Less Favoured Area supplement of £5.25 on top of the ewe premium of £11.50.

Chapter 6

HILL SHEEP AND TUPS
Emplacement through Farm Work

There is a variety of work on hill sheep farms differentiated and distributed mainly in terms of the type of livestock to which it is applied: hill shepherding, inbye shepherding, looking after the tups, and caring for the cattle. In addition, there is tractor work on the fields and general maintenance of farm equipment, buildings, sheep pens, and fencing. In the two previous chapters, I suggested respectively that work on hill sheep farms transforms the relation between a family and a farm into something more than economic and social interdependence and that outbye land is the predominant terrain not only in terms of physical space but also in terms of semantic space for the process of emplacement on a hill sheep farm. I now begin to bring these two themes together in describing how farming practices concerning sheep mediate the attachment of people and place on Border hill sheep farms. I focus the analysis on hill shepherding and on tups and the breeding program because they are the most important farming practices for hill sheep people in creating a sentimental sense of place on their farms.

Hill Hirsels and Shepherds

The distinctive division of labor on Borders hill sheep farms and the work of hill shepherding appropriate the tendency

Notes for this section begin on page 145.

of outbye sheep to heft onto particular areas of the hill to form cuts. Spatially contiguous cuts of hill ewes are combined to form a *hirsel*, a term that refers simultaneously to the sheep for which one shepherd is responsible and the area of the hill where they graze. Like the concept of heft or cut, a hirsel unifies hill sheep and space on outbye land. The difference between these concepts is that a cut unifies sheep and the space created by the ways *ewes* use the land while a hirsel unifies sheep and the space created by the way farmers organize shepherding labor. Further, unlike cuts which vary in area *and* number of sheep depending upon the carrying capacity of the terrain, hirsels are relatively equal in terms of the number of ewes but, because they are built up from cuts, they vary in the area of the hill they cover.

Hill sheep people usually talk about the size of a farm in terms of the number of hirsels rather than acres, and because the number of sheep in a hirsel remains fairly constant across farms, it is straightforward to estimate accurately the number of sheep in a farm's flock and the number of shepherds needed to herd them. In the early 1970s, a hill hirsel consisted of approximately 500 ewes. Eight farms in Teviothead—Linhope, Lymiecleuch, Falnash, Hislop, Commonside, Northhouse, Priesthaugh, and Skelfhill—had over three hirsels, or 1500 sheep, requiring at least three hired shepherds; and there were approximately eleven small, one-hirsel farms, many of which were sold for forestry or merged with other farms over the next decade. Three small one-hirsel farms—Rashiegrain, Merrylaw, and Commonbrae that had been bought by one owner and made into a single holding in the 1960—were sold for forestry. Before selling the four-hirsel Falnash Farm in the early 1970s, the Buccleuch Estate joined part of one hirsel—Blackcleuch—to Caerlanrig Farm, making the latter into a two-hirsel farm, and sold other two hirsels—Westerrig and Lairhope—to forestry. After the sale, another hirsel of Falnash was sold by the new owner to forestry leaving it a one-hirsel farm with a significant portion being inbye fields for park sheep. As I have described earlier, the owner of Hislop had on two separate occasions sold land: one hirsel to fund land reclamation improvements in the 1970s, and another hirsel to raise capital to purchase Falnash and to make the combined farms viable as a single unit. Likewise, the owner of Priesthaugh sold off two hirsels of the farm in the early 1970s to fund the reclamation of hill land into enclosed park land. The Buccleuch Estate "decommissioned" Coltserscleuch Farm by moving one of its hirsels onto Bowan Hill and joining the remainder to Northhouse. When Northhouse came up for let in the late 1980s, the Buccleuch Estate reduced the size by one hirsel of about 1000 acres.

On large, multihirsel farms, the labor required for shepherding exceeded that available in the family, and most hirsels were the responsibility of hired shepherds (also called "herds"). In this respect, the large farms could not have been "family farms" in the strict sense (see Djurfeldt 1995) of only members providing labor. Even on some small, one-hirsel farms, farmers hired a shepherd. By working on the basis of the number of hirsels on all the farms extant in Teviothead in the early 1970s, I estimate that there were 41 people that would have been in full-time shepherding. Based upon recollections of several farmers, of these 41 herds, 11 were farmers or farmers' sons and the remaining were hired. By the early 1990s, farms in Teviothead ranged from one to three hill hirsels, and hirsels had increased in size to between 800 to 1000 ewes. Farmers were able to nearly double the size of hirsels in a number of ways in order to make their farms more efficient by reducing labor costs. First, they used European Community and United Kingdom agricultural improvement grants to increase the amount of enclosed pasture where hill ewes with twin lambs could be brought for lambing and to build roads for easier access to the hill grazing areas. In addition, they purchased four-wheel motor bikes that could negotiate the rough terrain of the hills. These improvements meant that shepherds were able to herd more sheep, spread over a larger grazing area. Using the bike, they could go around the hill more often, especially at lambing time in April, they could deliver more easily supplementary feeding to outbye ewes during winter pregnancy, and they could take care of more hill sheep in the enclosed fields during lambing. This enabled farmers to decrease the labor requirements of their farms and shift the ratio of hired to family labor. After the sales and restructuring of farms in the 1970s and 1980s, the number of farms in Teviothead was reduced from nineteen to fifteen and concomitantly the number of outbye hirsels from forty-one to twenty-three. Twelve of these hirsels were herded by the farmer or a family member and eleven by hired shepherds. Four farms that had previously hired shepherds no longer did so, and all but two of the remaining farms had decreased the numbers of hired shepherds. Thus, although I estimate that 75 percent of all farm personnel spent a majority of their time in hill shepherding tasks, less than half the labor force was hired.[1] One consequence is that a greater percentage of the farm's labor was provided by the family members who were owners and managers of the business. In this sense, the policies of the European Community created the conditions for hill sheep farms to become domestic enterprises and to use family labor as a means of maintaining some degree of autonomy and resisting the potential for capitalism to determine the nature of the farm's labor relations (see Friedmann 1978:559ff).

In recognition of this shift in the ratio of hired to family labor doing the shepherding work, I use the term "shepherd" to refer to any person engaged in shepherding a hill hirsel whether owner-occupier, tenant, or hired. However, I do so only in this chapter because it does not accurately reflect contemporary usage in which the farmer-shepherd distinction retains its class meaning—a topic I take up in detail in Chapter 9. In this chapter, I use it to suggest that the meaning and consequences of hill shepherding for creating a sense of place are similar both for farmers and hired shepherds.

"Going Around the Hill"

Shepherding a hirsel entails a herd spending most of his time alone traversing the hill terrain where the sheep graze.[2] The overall brief is to watch over and intervene if necessary in the natural habits of sheep through the breeding cycle. There are several tasks—dipping, weaning, castrating, selecting lambs for sale or replacement stock—that are done with other farm personnel, but these represent only a small proportion of a shepherd's yearly routine. Walking, and more recently biking, around the hill is the most important activity for ensuring the welfare of sheep and the successful breeding of lambs for sale on the European agricultural market.[3] Yet, just as hill sheep are less commoditized than park sheep, hill shepherding is more than merely an economically motivated activity, and the hills are not just spaces of work.

For most of the year, those engaged in shepherding are in the hills every day for several hours on treks that cover ten to twelve miles. Unlike other farm tasks, going around the hill is done at "customary hours", meaning that shepherds are available seven days a week at any and all hours appropriate for the care of their hirsel. Their workday varies from several circuits of the hill from dawn to dusk during lambing, to less frequent tours combined with maintenance tasks during the shorter days of winter when sheep need less attention in the early stages of pregnancy. Shepherds organize and experience their daily and annual lives around the requirements of their hirsel of sheep. They and other hill sheep people judge their herding skills and knowledge of sheep by the quality of the ewes and lambs in their hirsel. It is recognized that over time under the care of a shepherd, a hirsel of sheep comes to embody his personhood, identity, and herding ability. This understanding—that the physical attributes of a hirsel of sheep objectifies the shepherd who cares for them—parallels the way hill sheep people use a genetic discourse to explain the characteristics of a cut of sheep and its embodiment of the territory to which it is bonded. Thus, through hill herding, outbye sheep come to embody and mediate the farm's land and its personnel, both comingling in the sheep's genetic constitution.

Shepherding also creates an attachment between people and the hills of their hirsels. As a way to begin describing this process of emplacement, I turn to the work of de Certeau and Heidegger. In exploring the difference between "place" and "space,"[4] de Certeau descends from the 110th floor of New York's World Trade Center into the streets where he follows the wandering footsteps of the people who use the city. "Neither author nor spectator" (de Certeau 1984:93), pedestrians appropriate it kinesthetically through practices that resist the normative meanings of the anonymous subjects presumed by cartographers and city planners. "Space is practiced place" (117) where historically and culturally situated people create a locality of familiar here's and there's in the same way that speakers act out the language system in the creation of vernacular meanings. It is de Certeau's image of this constitutive *walking* in the city that suggests a way of understanding hill sheep herding as a process of emplacement.

One shepherd expressed what I came to understand as the special, sensual, and intimate attachment of hill sheep people to the hills they spend so much time in—a sentimental feeling of being in their proper place that I try to capture with the phrase "being-at-home in the hills":

> You know, while walking around these hills shepherding, you could die of a heart attack and no one would be able to find you very easily ... it tells you of the isolation of the hills and shepherding ... it's scary for certain folk [people from towns] but not to me. But in the same way, I'm uncomfortable in Hawick with the traffic and people. If someone didn't look out for me, I could easily be hit by a car in the traffic. I wonder about city folk who decide to give up living in the city and move to the country because they are out of place.

I use Heidegger's notion of dwelling (1975) as a framework for analyzing the practices of this constitutive walking and biking around the hill and for describing the nature of the attachment that is produced by them. Recall that dwelling refers to actions of humans in creating meaningful places that together form a surrounding world. It entails a relationship between humans and the world motivated by *concern* and consequently by *involvement*, an involvement that privileges the practical and the spatial in the constitution of human knowledge and meaning. The formative act of dwelling—and of knowing—is doing things with entities: picking them up, manipulating them, discarding them, using them. Human acts of dwelling have implications for organizing space and defining places in at least four ways. First, in doing things with entities humans abolish the distance between themselves and the things used and thereby bring them into a spatial relationship. Second, dwelling as the utilization of things in everyday life has a *referential function*: the use of any thing implicates the use of other things so that together they form a coherent totality, a world in which each has a proper—and thus meaningful and nameable—place in the sense of its spatial and practical relation to other things. Third, and following on from the referential function, dwelling is a way of *seeing* the things used as mutually entailed spatially as well as meaningfully. Finally, in the act of using these entities, humans *gather* them together to form a place.

Concern and Bringing Close

Going around the hill is motivated by shepherds' primary concern for the welfare of their hirsel.[5] Because of the poor quality of outbye land and harsh weather conditions, hill sheep farming is relatively small in scale with flocks ranging from 400 to 4000 breeding ewes. This magnifies the financial significance of each ewe for the success of the farm and increases the intensity of labor expended upon them. One aspect of labor-intensive hill herding is that shepherds are responsible for the care of a relatively small number of sheep, between 600 and 1000 ewes,[6] and they are expected to walk or bike around the hills relatively frequently—two to three times a day during lambing, twice a day from lambing until clipping in June when ewes were likely to "cowp,"[7] again twice a day in tup time (November) to ensure the tups are working, and once each day during other periods. It is an act that brought shepherds in close contact with their sheep. Such closeness, however, does not just have a physical dimension but is measured in terms of the quality and intimacy of knowledge that results from working with them on the hill. When going around the hill, shepherds draw near enough to each ewe so that it is literally seen at least once almost everyday. Often shepherds stop and stand for several minutes just looking over a group of sheep as they graze. If there is a problem, it is dealt with quickly and the results of the treatment closely monitored.

Such frequent seeing and handling result in shepherds knowing some individual characteristic of many ewes in the hirsel: the shape of the nose, the way one carries her ears, a ewe off a prize tup, one that likes to rest in a special place in the morning after grazing, the one that was "yeild"[8] last year. This is one aspect of being-at-home in the hills that is experienced and expressed as detailed knowledge of sheep. In almost every discussion of shepherding I engaged in, shepherds and farmers emphasized that one of the characteristics of a good shepherd is the ability to "ken (know) the sheep" or be a good "kenner". By this, shepherds mean the ability to visually recognize individual sheep and their unique physical attributes as well as to remember their history, bloodline, and distinctive behavioral habits, such as where they like to lamb. One shepherd described a good kenner as follows:

> It's only when you're with sheep all the time that you develop your ability as a kenner … you can learn about the ability of people as kenners by watching them at Shows … if you have 150 sheep in a pen and a ewe from another pen jumps in among the 150 sheep, that's when you know who is a kenner, the one who can pick out the ewe that jumped into the pen.

Paths of Seeing and Gathering

Going around the hill consists of seeing and gathering the sheep, terrain, and people into a totality called a hirsel. It is significant that the round—and the practices of seeing and gathering places—begin and end at the place where the shepherd and his family live. For hired shepherds, the provision of a cottage is usually part of the conditions of employment, and in most cases the cottage is located in or near the hirsel herded by the shepherd.[9] At their cottages, shepherds don boots and clothing to protect themselves from the weather and wet ground, they collect the dogs used to maneuver the sheep, and they gather the other equipment—crook, medicines, hoof clippers—that might be needed to treat problems likely to be encountered. In carrying out these preparations, shepherds extend the bounds of their homes to include the sheep of their hirsel as well as the topographical and climatic conditions that affect their flock and their movements. For example, in preparing for the evening walk around his hirsel, I watched a shepherd collect two dogs from the kennel behind the cottage. He explained to me: "one is good at running wide around the sheep [to herd straying ewes back into their territory] and the other is good for close work with sheep nearby that need to be caught or herded into a pen … a good dog saves a lot of work." Such referential implication constitutes a shepherd's home as one of the places within his hirsel and vice versa.

From the cottage, shepherds follow an established path—in both an historical and practical sense—around their hirsel.[10] By following this path on foot or bike, shepherds not only gather the sheep, but also create places of meaning and collect them into a region they call a hirsel. Upon coming into a farm or being hired by a farmer, those taking on shepherding duties spend the first weeks and months learning both the topography of the land and the habits of the sheep of their hirsel. Usually, a new shepherd starts out by following the path used by the previous shepherd. Over time he modifies this path to suit the knowledge he acquires in traversing the hill terrain, in observing the behavior of the sheep, and in handling individual ewes during his own walks around the hirsel.

The farmer of Hislop who also "did a hirsel" described his introduction to his farm as follows:

> It was John Tullie who "introduced" me to the farm by offering to walk around the whole farm with me to show me what the ground was like. John's son James drove us to Bents Hill where we started the walk … from there we followed the shepherd's path that took us to Ewesdown Fell, Shorter Syke, Stock Hill, Lamblair Edge to the top of the Aiky Grain …from there we walked to the Bye Hass Fell to the top of Tod Hill. From the Tod Hill, we could see the rest of the farm so we didn't need to walk around the rest of the ground … so from Tod Hill we walked straight down the Tod Hill Rig to the farmhouse where James was waiting to meet us in the Landrover.

A hired shepherd said that once he learned the basic grazing pattern of sheep during his first three-year period of herding, it only took him a week of going around the hill to learn the specific topography and grazing habits of the sheep on his present hirsel. Another farmer said that it took him about six months of herding on his new farm "to become familiar with the ground and to get to know where to take the bike to see all the sheep." Another hired shepherd described his first introduction to his hirsel as follows: "When I came into the hirsel, the farmer [who had been herding the hirsel] took me around the hill for two days showing me the morning and evening routes. After this, I was left on my own and the first day out by myself it was very misty and I got lost. So it takes more than just a few days to learn a hirsel."

All shepherds stressed to me that there are two principles for constructing the paths around their hirsels. First, the paths should be adapted to the terrain in order to allow a shepherd to see all the ground of the hirsel so that if a sheep is in trouble anywhere on the hill, he would be able to observe it during his round and take remedial steps so that he would not end up with a dead sheep. Because the topography of the land is complex with intersecting hills, ridges, ravines, knowles, streams, tall grasses, bracken, moss, and heather, shepherds realize that they have to go around the hirsel many times to become familiar with all the areas where a sheep would be difficult to see. The paths they established meander and double back over the terrain to ensure that they can see every part of the land during their rounds. While walking around the hills with shepherds, each pointed out to me locations that were "not very sighty ground." These were places that were difficult to see from their paths—in dips and sykes, behind knowles, in bracken. They remembered them as places where sheep had died because they could not be seen from the paths and described how they had modified the path so that these places could be seen. In these practices, seeing is a form of shepherds constituting meaningful places with respect to sheep activities and events and their memories of them. Paths are created in order to see these places; and seeing these places as part of following a path is a gathering of them into a hirsel. Spatially then, a hirsel is a set of places related both by the activities of sheep carrying out their lives on the hill and by the activities of humans in going around the hill.

Seeing—and gathering—everything, however, does not mean that paths had to go everywhere in the hirsel. The hilly terrain allows shepherds to clearly see some parts of the hirsel from strategically located vantage points. As I walked around the hill with another shepherd, he purposely stopped at various points on the path to show me the places he had created where, he said, "it is good to have binoculars because I can see parts of my hirsel from a long distance away and I don't have to walk there if there's nothing wrong [with the sheep] … if something is wrong, I can go there and sort out the problem." As another shepherd put it: "My two most important pieces of equipment are the bike and the binoculars … I have found places on the farm that are good vantage points so that I don't have to ride the bike over every inch of land."

The second principle of constructing a path around a hill hirsel is to adapt the direction of movement to the shepherd's knowledge of the grazing habits of sheep in their cuts. As described in the previous chapter, sheep tend to move up the hills during the late afternoon and throughout the evening, spending the night at or near the tops of hills, and down the hills in the early morning and throughout the day. Based upon their detailed knowledge of how the cuts of sheep on their hirsels use the topographical features of the land, shepherds construct their paths in order to come up behind but be moving in the same direction as the sheep so that they push them in the direction they are naturally going. Because sheep move in different directions in the morning and evening, there are different paths for going around the hill depending upon the time of day. The stated pattern is for the path to "go around the tops [of the hills]" in the morning in order to drive the sheep down and "to go around the bottoms [of the hills]" in the evening in order to drive the sheep up. This practice, known as "maintaining the cuts," consists of a shepherd keeping a hirsel of sheep in their proper place by gathering them together as groups in their cuts every morning and evening. If a shepherd walked "against" the natural movement of sheep, he would scatter them.[11]

Cuts as products of sheep grazing behavior, their consequent bonding to a specific territory, and shepherds' herding practices form one level of meaningful place within a hirsel. When shepherds go around the hill, when they described their routes to me in the context of going around the hill with me, or when they talked to me about walking around the hill, they organized their journeys and punctuated their narratives in terms of the cuts within their hirsel, as the following extract from my fieldnotes illustrates:[12]

> Then I move onto the Dyke Back Cut and chase the sheep down, and from there cut back along the road heading for the top end of the farm. At a high spot just off the road I can see most of the cut ... but there's a blind spot ... so I have to send the dogs to rouse any sheep. Then I cross the road, double back behind the sheep so I can see them again but now moving down towards the river; then onto the road again which I follow down the cattle grid. Then I go past the handling pens, swing across to the Blackcleuch Rig. The cut of sheep on the Blackcleuch Rig I first come to is the Commonbrae Cut. Heading up the Commonbrae Cut I can see sheep on both sides ... but at the top I zigzag [because] ... this is rough ground ... long grass,

some bracken, rough grass, tussocks … sheep could be lying in the long grass and you can't see them unless you get close. I double back to go along the back of the fence with Hislop [Farm], then I cut down on the Cottage Cut, heading down towards the Blackcleuch Cottage [hence the name of the cut] … this is a long slope … I have to come almost all the way into the Cottage to see the ground. Then back up the slope to the top of the Blackcleuch Rig … the Blackcleuch Syke is too steep and rough [for the bike] so I have to go up and around the top of the syke and come back down the other side to see the sheep.

The paths established take a shepherd to and through each cut of his hirsel so that he can see all the ground, make sure there are no problems with any of the sheep, and move stray sheep back into their proper cuts. The particular order in which a shepherd goes from cut to cut was adapted to the topography of the land and the grazing habits of the sheep such that he always comes in behind their natural movement over the terrain. Shepherds recognize two topographically different types of hirsels that affect the lengths of the morning and evening circuits. One type is a "rig hirsel," like the one described in the narrative above, whose prominent topographical feature is a single ridge top with the cuts of sheep that form the hirsel spreading down the slopes on both sides. On this type of hirsel, the morning route "around the tops" generally follows the ridge, and the evening route along the bottom of the slopes makes a long circuit around the ridge. The other type is a "hope hirsel" formed by horseshoe-shaped hills forming its outside limits with cuts of sheep spreading inwards towards the central valley enclosed by the hills. The morning route around the tops is the longer circuit while the evening route is a shorter circuit into the valley.

There was one incident that conveyed to me the extent to which, in using these paths established to see the sheep, shepherds also gathered the cuts into a coherent region. It was during a round of a hirsel with a farmer, Jock Turnbull, who did the shepherding on one of the two hirsels on his farm. Both he and his hired shepherd normally used bikes for the rounds of the hill. Since Jock's hirsel was less hilly and steep, he could use a pick-up truck for the evening run if the weather was bad. On one of these rounds of the hill, Jock pointed out to me the visible parallel tracks that the pickup had made on the ground over the past year or so that he had been using it for his evening shepherding. He said that these tracks represented the knowledge he had gained of the terrain and behavior patterns of his hirsel (where the sheep liked to lie or graze, where they were likely to cowp, etc.). By following them, he knew he could see everywhere and every ewe in his hirsel.

Naming and Taming

Seeing and gathering places into cuts and cuts into hirsels are also referential acts. In going around the hill, shepherds follow paths that link spatially and temporally the places where they know sheep are likely to be or to get into trouble. As a result, any one place refers to other places connected by the paths so that together these places form a coherent whole—the cut—in relation to a specific set of sheep. Likewise, these same paths connect several cuts into a coherent whole—the hirsel—in relation to the shepherds who follow them and whose daily life and reputation are determined by the quality of the sheep in the hirsel. As a referential practice, going around the hill includes acts of naming places. The geographer Porteous aptly describes the significance of naming in the creation of places and the sentimental attachment to them that I am trying to convey with the phrase "being-at-home":

> One familiar method of directing or controlling the external environment is the act of naming. Mapless travelers are often disturbed by their inability to discover the "correct" names of the landscape features they encounter. Naming is a powerful act. By naming landscape features, butterflies, persons, we in part possess them and simultaneously exorcise their chthonic magical powers. Nature, disturbing or fearsome, can be humanized by applying familiar terms to it. (Porteous 1990:72)

With the inclusion of naming practices, going around the hill is not just a taming of wild hill sheep to stay in their cuts; in naming places, shepherds domesticate the wild, semantically open space of outbye hills. Here I recall a theme introduced in the previous chapter: the perceived complexity of outbye terrain functions as a sign system composed of topographical differences for naming localities in the hills of significance to sheep and to shepherds. The place names used by hill sheep people are in most cases the same ones found on the Ordinance Survey maps. The most prominent feature of these place names in outbye land is that they are binomials. The first part derives from, or its character is similar to, names given to a person (e.g., Allen, Gray, Carsey), place (e.g., Skelfhill), thing, or attribute (e.g., Doe, Cow, Millstone, Peat, Stobiecote [cottage made with nails], Staney [stoney], Wester [westerly direction], Crummie [cow with crooked horns], White, Grey). While these words may have had some substantive meanings for identifying the locations when first created, those "original" meanings, usually derivable from their etymologies, have decayed over time so that they become more purely nominal. This is particularly the case for the names of farms. For example, the name "Skelfhill" is Scandinavian and "describes the shape of the hill which has a small peak at the end of a long, shelf-like plateau" (J.S.M. Macdonald 1991:38); the name "Falnash" is Old English meaning "fallen ash tree" (37); "Bowanhill", also Old English, means "rounded or bow-shaped hill" (38); and Caerlanrig, combining Celt, Old English, and Scandinavian, etymologically means "the long rig with the fort" (37). People in Teviothead were largely not aware of these etymologies.[13] The first words of the binomial place names have a similar character to these farm names: they are meaningful as names in identifying locations even if they have become etymologically meaningless as words (see Nicolaisen 1976:4).

Another feature of the naming system is that the entire binomial name of a place is often used as the first part of the binomial name of another place. Thus, on Skelfhill Farm, the whole place name "Crummie Cleuch" (etymologically, "the gorge or ravine of the cow with crooked horns") becomes the first part of the name of another close-by place, e.g.,. "Crummiecleuch Rig" for the ridge of high ground running above the Crummie Cleuch. This usage reveals an important feature of the words that make up the first part of place names. They can be used in the names for a number of different locations and are thus by themselves incapable of uniquely designating a place.

The second part of place names is a word that is topographically descriptive but spatially undefined. That is, these words can be used wherever it is appropriate to the topography of the location being named: *brae* (hillside), *burn* (stream, brook), *cleuch* (gorge, ravine), *fell* (steep, rocky hill), *foot* (lower end of a piece of ground or stream), *grain* (branch of a valley or stream), *hass* (neck of land), *haugh* (level ground), *head* (summit of a hill), *height* (hilltop), *hope* (enclosed valley), *knowe* (knoll), *law* (conical hill that is conspicuous), *loch* (natural lake or pond), *moor* (uncultivated, heathery land), *moss* (boggy ground), *pen* (pointed hill), *rig* (ridge or long narrow hill), *shiel* (temporary hut or shed), and *syke* (small stream).

It is the combination of these two types of words that forms a place name able to uniquely identify a location, and this was how they are used on maps. But maps, as I quoted earlier from de Certeau, are made up of the empty spaces and "normative meanings of the anonymous subjects presumed by cartographers ..." (1984:93). Perhaps the barrenness that outsiders, like the English and Scottish governments of the sixteenth century, attributed to Border hills landscapes expresses their lack of emplacement. It takes the use of these spaces by people, like the reivers between the fourteenth and sixteenth centuries, in carrying out their everyday lives to transform them into places that have significance. This is what happens in hill herding. In going around the hill, shepherds imbue these named but anonymous spaces drawn on the Ordinance Survey maps with meanings; in doing so they transform outbye spaces into hirsels where they feel at home. The following examples are extracts from fieldnotes of my walks around the hills with shepherds. They illustrate how shepherds tame the wild and (semantically) barren hills by associating their personal experiences, memories of shepherding, and their historical knowledge of Border reiving with these named locations thereby making them into places of their own both as individuals and as people of the Scottish Borders.

Excerpt 1

During a walk around the hill with Jimmy, he stopped and pointed out a particular location and described an experience he had had there one day:

It was a dull day and I was on the Blackcleuch Rig (the name of a hill within his hirsel) … I had stopped to look at the sheep and to do so I had to look towards the hills of Lymiecleuch (the neighboring farm). Just as I was looking over those hills, the sun broke through the clouds in one place and a bright ray of sunlight fell upon the top of one of the hills. I thought to myself that by the sunlight falling on that patch of ground it was saying to me, "this is the best place in the world."

Excerpt 2

When Watt and I arrived at the Byehass Cut, he said: "When I first came into the hirsel, the boss told me that this cut had done well in previous years and I found this to be true since I did not have to touch the sheep for the first 15 days of lambing … I was thankful for that since I had a lot of trouble near the Long Burn and Roundtree Knowe with ewes hanging lambs."

On the same farm a few years later, the new shepherd described part of the same hirsel as follows: "Travelling along the Peat Rig, I look back into the lower parts of the Long Burn cut but from here I can't see that blind spot in the Todhill Rig so I go down to the Peatrig Stell and I can see into the blind spot from there."

Excerpt 3

On a morning walk around the hill with Alex, a tenant farmer who herds a hill hirsel himself, he explained that he was not just looking at the sheep but rather he had organized his walk so that he could gather a cut of sheep and drive them back to the farmstead for castration and tailing. He said, "It's better to drive them up the glen between the Millstone Edge and Wetherlaw hills … it gets them in a tight bunch which is easier to control with the dogs."

Excerpt 4

When Davey and I came away from the Haggis Side, we made our way up to the top of the Wrang Way Burn. He then told me the story behind the name "Wrang Way Burn," which associates the place with Border reiving of the sixteenth century and recalls how the reivers' intimate knowledge of the hills, where they also felt at home, allowed them to elude capture:

Some raiders—the Johnnie Armstrong kind[14]—were being chased by the English. The English were getting close … so the raiders were going up the burn, but instead of continuing up the burn they slipped over to Eweslees (the neighboring farm) through Eweslees Doors and lay down in the bracken. The English did not see them and continued up the Wrang Way Burn and missed them, they went the "wrang way"!

Excerpt 5

A similar type of historical and cultural place associated with a similar type of story was related to me by Will, the tenant of a one-hirsel farm, which he herds himself on a bike.

> On the run from Pike Fell to Bloody Cleuch you are turning sheep down. Bloody Cleuch was named for a historical event. Sometime in the fourteenth or fifteenth centuries, the Cars of Carlisle chased some reivers from Scotland out of Carlisle into the Debatable Land.[15] The reivers decided to ambush the English and they chose the Bloody Cleuch as the place to hide and spring the ambush. The ambush was bloody— blood running into the cleuch and that's how it got its name, Bloody Cleuch.

In addition to these personal and historical places, there are some common types of places on hirsels that are reflective of the shepherding practices that created them. Almost every shepherd pointed out to me places where they had found a ewe that had cowped and survived for an extraordinarily long period of time, where they knew a particular ewe liked to lamb, where a dog had made a mess of moving ewes, or where lightning had almost struck them. Thus every time a shepherd goes around his hill hirsels, he not only gathers sheep, which as we have seen embody the shepherd and the land to which they are bonded, he also gathers places that together formed a world linking his residence, his memories, the work of shepherding, and Borders history—and where he feels at home.

Retro-Spection and E-Scaping

The final issue I take up with respect to hill shepherding is the process by which this sentiment of being-at-home in the hills becomes a synecdoche for a way of life and Border identity. A synecdoche is a type of metaphor in which a part stands for the whole and the character of the part pervades the meaning of the whole (Daniel 1984:107). I suggest that this process itself occurs in the act of going around the hill. It is based upon a distinction between *scaping* as outlined in Chapter 1 and *dwelling* as described in this chapter. Unlike scaping, which imposes distance between the observer and the thing observed, dwelling entails involvement with and a closeness to the land and the sheep that graze upon it. It is the externality, distancing, disengagement with the scene that is the reason scapes have the quality of beauty or ugliness. It is also the condition for them being used by humans as tropes through which they can e-scape the dimensions of their world and relate it to the more distant horizons of other worlds of which they are also a part. In the case of the people of Teviothead, these distant horizons are hill sheep farming as a way of life and Border society.

Such e-scaping is enabled by another practice of hill shepherding. As I described earlier, shepherds establish places on the hill from which they can see other places in their hirsel *from a distance*. At these places they are constructing scapes as part of building the hirsel. Yet they do more than just construct scapes. Shepherds also make some paths that allow them to see a second time places where they have already walked or biked without retracing their steps. One shepherd explained why he did this: "After walking through the cut of sheep, [by taking this path] I can see a few minutes later that all the sheep have moved and that none are in trouble … a sheep in distress does not roam." Thus, shepherds construct their paths not only to see distant places where they do not have to go unless there are problems, but also to enable them to see a second time from a distance a place where they have already been—a visceral enactment of reflexivity. One illustration of this process of scaping, reflexivity, and e-scaping happened during a walk around the hirsel of a shepherd named Davey. He was explaining to me that a good shepherd knows the individual sheep and the places where each one likes to lamb. As we looked over an idyllic landscape of a cut of sheep placidly grazing with their young lambs, one ewe broke from the group and approached us. As she did, Davey used a metaphor likening the existence of natural differences among sheep to differences among humans:

Each ewe is different; after lambing some will stay by themselves for a day or two and others will return to the rest of the
cut after a couple of hours. The ewe approaching us is very
friendly ... she's looking for some food ... there's a ewe in [he
named another of his cuts] that was also friendly but her
daughter was not as friendly ... [at this point he e-scapes] ewes
are like humans, each individual [human] is different.

Metaphors as means of understanding have directional-
ity: people use their knowledge of one phenomenon to gain
knowledge of another unknown, less well understood, or
inchoate (see Fernandez 1974) phenomenon, which in turn
may enable the understanding of yet another phenomenon.
The direction is from the known to the unknown. This movement has a spatiality that is central to its effectiveness as a
mode of understanding. Fernandez expresses this spatiality
of tropes figuratively in his representation of how they work:
tropes build "a bridge across the abyss of [cognitively] separated, discriminated experience" (1986:178). However, the
use of such a spatial metaphor in describing how metaphors
work may be insufficient because spatial experience may be
literal to how metaphors work. Davey's metaphor illustrates
this very clearly. His knowledge of his hirsel and of the individual differences among his sheep was gained through
going around the hill, which, as I have described earlier,
entails being spatially close to sheep in order to achieve success in caring for them. In this context, the objects of knowledge were the sheep themselves, and such knowledge was
achieved through spatial proximity. When these same sheep
were viewed from a distance in a landscape, Davey was able to
reflect upon his knowledge of the sheep. That is, his knowledge of the differences among sheep itself became an object
of knowledge, and he used it as a means for understanding
another phenomenon, the differences among humans. My
point is that the spatial distance from sheep created by the
scaping practices of shepherding enabled Davey to reflect
upon his knowledge of his sheep, to use this reflexivity to e-
scape beyond the hirsel, and to infuse his knowledge of
sheep to enhance and express his understanding of inchoate
humanity of which he is a part.

This same tropic process of distancing, reflexivity, and
metaphorical understanding is evident in three of the previ-

ous fieldnotes extracts of other shepherds talking about places in their hirsels. For Ian, the ray of light falling on the distant hills where he felt at home enabled him to e-scape and to infuse the farm and the Borders regions with the same sentiment: they were felt to be the best places on earth. The vistas of the Wrang Way Burn and the Bloody Cleuch continually reminded Davey and Will of the reivers whose historical exploits were central to their identity as Borderers. They too e-scaped the lived dwelling places and transmuted their attachment to a hirsel to the Borders region.

Breeding and Hill Tups

The other main kind of farm work associated with hill sheep farming is the breeding program, which is designed to modify the genetically based characteristics of the flock. Its aim is to produce ewes whose lambs have the body confirmation (i.e., physical characteristics of body length, meat to fat ratio, and large haunches) that, with fattening, would meet consumer demand, satisfy European Community certification standards, and attract high prices on the market. The most important part of any breeding program is the tups. One farmer described the overriding significance of tups for the characteristics and quality of a flock of sheep.

> Tups can change the look of a whole flock…the confirmation and milkedness of the ewes of a whole flock can be affected by a tup. So if you have a good tup, he can put his influence through a flock for a good few years beyond the time he was tupping the ewes. Similarly, a bad tup will badly influence a flock for a long time and it is hard to get rid of this bad influence. That is why it is important not to let a bad tup go on tupping a flock longer than necessary and to get rid of it as soon as its bad influence is spotted.

A breeding program has two aspects: selecting tups and deciding with which cuts of ewes they would best mate. Replacement tups are selected each year from two sources. Most are chosen in spring when lambs are castrated. The farmer, with the help of the shepherd who herded them, selects those tup lambs born on each cut that exhibit the characteristics needed for selling lambs on the market and wintering ewes on the hill. One or two additional tups are purchased at auctions from other farms that specialized in tup breeding. Again, it is the farmer who has the final say, particularly on the amount to be spent, even if he depends heavily on the advice of a hired shepherd in choosing which tups to bid on. The overall effect of the selection practices is that while there is a gradual introduction of new genetic material into the flock through buying in tups, most of a farm's tups are homebred.

Once the tups are selected, mating is organized in terms of cuts, so it is necessary to decide which tups mate with which cuts of ewes. This is an important decision because, as I described in the previous chapter, each cut of ewes is considered to be a descent line with distinctive characteristics. Hill sheep people recognize that there is always a possibility that a tup and a cut of ewes might be incompatible and produce poor quality lambs. In the mating season (27 November to 1 January for hill sheep) a tup mates only with the ewes of one cut. Because a cut's replacement stock is drawn from the ewes born to it and because these ewe lambs are not mated until their second year, tups have to be rotated around the farms' cuts after two seasons to avoid inbreeding. It is this biennial rotation that distributes the tups' genetic characteristics widely throughout a farm's flock. In addition, because they are rotated around a number of cuts in various hirsels, tups are not linked to any particular shepherd but to the whole farm.

Both aspects of the breeding program are the responsibility of the farmer. Whether or not he does a hill hirsel, a farmer's specific contribution to the characteristics of his farm's hill sheep is made through the tups he selects from all the cuts, the tups he decides to purchase, and the ewes he mates with these tups. It is through the selection and circulation of tups over several generations that a farm's flock *as a whole* becomes a relatively closed breeding population with distinctive characteristics. The whole flock reflects a farmer's persona—his stockmanship, knowledge of hill sheep, and understanding of the agricultural market. In a manner analogous to the relation between shepherds and their hirsels, a farm's flock embodies the tups, the stockmanship skills and knowledge of the farmer who selects them, and the qualities of the farm's land upon which they graze. Moreover, just as ewes mediate a shepherd's sense of place on his hirsel, tups and the flock mediate a farmer's sense of place on his farm.

Inbye Shepherding

By the early 1990s, ten farms in Teviothead had flocks of inbye ewes that required a significant input of capital and labor. In this section, I am primarily concerned with the shepherding tasks used for inbye sheep. My aim is to highlight a number of differences in the way park sheep are raised in comparison with hill sheep and to demonstrate that, because of these differences, park sheep do not embody the land or the person responsible for them as do hill sheep, and park shepherding does not engender the sense of place that hill shepherding and breeding do.

First, as I described in the last chapter, park sheep are constantly moved around a farm's fields and are more dependent upon supplementary feeding. Therefore, they do not heft onto and embody a farm's inbye land as strongly as hill sheep embody the outbye land. In addition, all park lambs are sold each year so that replacement stock has to be bought in from other farms. This means that flocks of park ewes do not consist of "daughters of daughters" in a genealogical line through which the land is bred into them over generations. Thus, unlike hill sheep, there is little need for incoming tenants or owners to purchase the existing flock of park sheep.

Second, the terms "cut" and "hirsel," and the labor practices entailed by them, are not used to divide up the flock of inbye ewes. On most farms, one person is primarily responsible for all the park sheep that are spread around the farm's fields. Because fields are small and flat relative to hill hirsels, there is no need to construct paths through fields because a shepherd can easily see all the sheep from one or two vantage points. Instead of the treks that take a hill shepherd between one and one-half and three hours to see all his hirsel, a person shepherding park sheep can see in a few minutes all the sheep in each field. During spring and summer when the fields provide sufficient grazing to fatten the lambs, there is little to do on a daily basis. In winter, the main daily task is putting out fodder. This involves bringing hay or silage to one or two feeding stations within each field. Unlike hill shepherding, in which a shepherd moves the sheep around a cut that they had defined by hefting on, park sheep come to the feeding places defined by the shepherd.

Third, fields are named but there were no places within them imbued with meanings derived from personal experiences and memories of the shepherd or with historical referents to reiving. This lack of meaningful places within fields is exacerbated by the practice of bringing park ewes into barns or sheds for lambing. Lambing is one of the most intense and important periods for a hill shepherd since the number and quality of lambs produced by his hirsel reflect upon his stockmanship. Usually shepherds' most vivid memories concern events that occurred during lambing, and each of these events is associated with a place in the hirsel. For example, on my walks around the hills, shepherds pointed to places where a lamb had died, or they had helped a ewe in trouble giving birth, or to a depression in the ground where they had found a ewe and lamb during a snowstorm. Thus, shepherding practices for park sheep do not infuse inbye fields with a sense of place. Inbye fields remain more a space for the production of commodities than the construction of a world.

Notes

1. Anderson (1986) notes that between 1974 and 1984, the paid work force on farms in southeast Scotland—most of which are hill sheep farms—decreased by 11 percent, with an 8 percent decrease between 1983 and 1984. The exact proportion of domestic and hired labor on hill sheep farms in Teviothead is difficult to calculate because of the varying amount of labor provided by wives of farmers. The figure of less than 50 percent hired labor was derived as follows. There were as many full-time working farmers and sons as hired workers on Teviothead farms. In addition, on most farms, wives provided significant part-time farm labor as well as book work for the business. The specific amount was difficult to calculate. It could be argued that the wife's domestic labor (e.g., rearing children and farm housekeeping) should be considered full-time because she is as much involved in reproducing the farm as a whole as her husband. However, this would not affect the proportion of hired versus employed labor on farms since the same argument could be made for the hired workers' wives. Thus, only the wife's farming labor is included in the calculations.
2. At the time of my fieldwork, all those involved in hill shepherding work on Teviothead hill sheep farms were men, though there were a few instances in other localities of women herds. Accordingly, I use the pronoun "he" in the narrative.
3. The use of four-wheel motor bikes for hill shepherding became widespread in Teviothead around 1990. I have asked most of those doing hill herding what difference the bikes have made. Other than enabling them to cover more ground more quickly so that their hirsels are larger, the practices of hill herding that I describe in this chapter seem to have remained the same. In fact, one or two shepherds have told me that they were able to approach closer to hill sheep on a bike than they were able to on foot. Hill sheep run away from a herd on foot with his dog.
4. As will be discussed below, the terminology used by de Certeau to distinguish between "place, " i.e., localities as positions on maps and plans, and "space," i.e., meaningful localities constituted through practice, is the reverse of the terminology used by many phenomenological geographers (see for example Pickles 1985; Relph 1985). I use de Certeau's terminology at this point in the chapter because I am drawing upon his ideas in framing the analysis. Throughout the remainder of the chapter I revert to the terminology of the phenomenological geographers.
5. Given that the concept of "hirsel" unifies a group of sheep and the land they graze, hill sheep people can use the word to refer to the sheep of the hirsel or the area of the hill where they graze. In both usages the constitutive relation between sheep and place is assumed.
6. On other types of sheep farms located on more productive land, shepherds may be responsible for 2000 sheep. One shepherd, who had been a shepherd in New Zealand, said that he had been responsible for over 5000 sheep and hardly had any contact with them except occasionally from the cab of a jeep.
7. "Cowping" refers to the tendency of ewes in late spring when they are heavy with wool and weak from lambing to fall over on their backs. If they do not right themselves, gas builds up in their stomachs leaving too little space for their lungs to expand so that they eventually suffocate.
8. A "yeild" ewe is one that did not become pregnant.
9. In the past, hill shepherd's cottages were located in the hirsel itself, often very isolated but indicative of the intimacy and identification between a shepherd and his sheep. Contemporary shepherds' cottages are located near their hirsels but also on roads that allow access to the town.

10. I derive my concept of "path" from Relph, who describes them as "routes which reflect the direction and intensities of intentions and experiences and which serve as the structural axis of existential space. They radiate from and lead toward nodes or centres of special importance and meaning ..." (1976:20-21). See also Weiner 1991: 33f.

11. This practice also maintains the cuts in land management sense, since the movement of sheep over the land ensures even grazing and "clean ground" where there is not an excessive buildup of dung allowing fluke to become a problem.

12. This was narrative I solicited from the farmer of Caerlanrig Farm who did the hill shepherding. With a detailed map of the farm, I asked him to describe the routes he took for the morning and evening rounds of the hirsel. I had been around this hirsel on foot twice on previous field trips with a shepherd hired by the previous tenant. The route described by the farmer was very similar to the one the previous shepherd had used except for those places, like the Black-cleuch Syke, that were too steep for a bike.

13. If these farm names had any specific meaning, it was more likely to be derived from a historical event or personal memory. For example, the name "Caerlan-rig" is associated with a historical event from the reiving period. It was the place where one of the most notorious reivers, Johnnie Armstrong, was betrayed and hanged by James V.

14. The most famous of the Border reivers who was captured and hanged at Caerlanrig Farm in Teviothead.

15. The "Debatable Land" refers to territory between the Rivers Esk and Sark, whose center was the neighboring valley of Liddesdale, which was under dispute from the fifteenth century. It was called the Debatable Land because neither the English nor Scottish kingdoms could be held responsible for the activities of the people living there. It became the home of the most renowned raiders of the Borders including, Johnnie Armstrong, hanged at Caerlanrig in Teviothead, and Kinmont Willie Armstrong, rescued from Carlisle prison by Sir Walter Scott of Buccleuch.

LAMB AUCTIONS

Spectacles of Hill Sheep Farming

There are three types of auctions where hill sheep farmers sell sheep.[1] Store lamb auctions are for lambs that do not meet the Sheep Meat Regime's certification standards for fat lambs. Fat lamb auctions are only for lambs that meet the certification standards and are eligible for the variable premium. Finally, there are ram auctions where purebred hill tups raised on Borders farms are sold. In thinking about these auctions, I was struck by the title of Appadurai's book, *The Social Life of Things* (1986). He is alluding to the fact that types of objects in a society move in a patterned fashion through a series of contexts that change their nature and significance in much the same way people do in their social lives. Adopting this reading, Kopytoff (1986) suggests the concept of social biography that in turn Salazar (1996) uses in tracing the fate of cattle in Ireland from farm to auction. But there could be another sense of the title. In this reading, things make possible a form of social life. Both readings can be simultaneous, and that is the way I treat them in this chapter. I trace the social biography of sheep from hill farms to auctions (the first sense) in order to describe the social life that sheep made possible by being sold in auctions (the second sense). Store lamb auctions are particularly significant for both senses because they entail a physical assemblage in one place of hill sheep people who on most days are spatially separated and socially individualized on their farms. For them, the import of taking their lambs to the auction is not exhausted in the financial exchanges that take place, even though they are necessary to the viability of their farm businesses. To leave the matter there would be to ignore the way lambs come to embody the land, shepherd and farmer in shepherding and breeding practices.

Drawing upon this expressive quality of hill lambs, I develop two themes in the following analysis of store lamb auctions. The first is that they are spectacles in the sense described by MacAloon as public, visually engaging, deliberate, and dramatic exhibitions for an audience (1984:240ff), with the additional attribute I particularly highlight that they consist of several "reflexive moments."[2] The second theme is that by participating in store lamb auctions individuals experience hill sheep farming as a distinctive form of social life—a way of life, if you will—and the Borders as the rural space for it.

Sheep as Values

In the previous two chapters, I described the contexts and farming practices of the production of sheep. The point I made was that, compared to park sheep, hill sheep are cultural objects through being endowed with *specific* meanings that referred to and constituted the specific farmers and shepherds who cared for them and the specific farms and hirsels on which they were raised. The specificity of hill sheep encompasses all the major practices and personnel of a hill sheep farm. First, by the process of hefting on, groups of hill ewes and their lambs create a separate space on the land for themselves and embody the particular attributes of the land upon which they graze. Second, through the division of labor and going around the hill, the physical attributes of a hirsel of hill sheep incarnate the stockmanship of the shepherd responsible for their care; conversely, a shepherd's identity and reputation is objectified in the quality of the lambs of his hirsel. Third, and likewise, through the selection and rotation of tups around the flock, hill sheep manifest the stockmanship of the farmer and the farm as a whole; thus, the reputation of the farmer and his farm is based upon the quality of the lambs and tups produced. As cultural objects, hill sheep are a self-reflexive end in themselves. In this respect, their value lay in what they portrayed about hill sheep people to hill sheep people. To produce hill sheep is to produce hill sheep people, their farms, and their way of life.[3]

Absent from this discussion is the obvious point that these same farming practices are aimed at producing lambs to be sold on the agricultural market to realize income for the farm business. In this respect, sheep become instruments of profit by being endowed with a *general* significance that refers to the general labor skills and stockmanship of anonymous person(s) that went into their production and to the universal certification standards that apply to lambs produced on *any* farm by *any* individual and sold in *any* auction in the European Community. While all sheep are raised to be exchanged and in this sense all are commodities (see Appadurai 1986:6-16), I suggested earlier that such commodity value is more prominent in park sheep than in hill sheep because of the way they are raised. Park sheep are moved from field to field so that they do not heft on to and embody a specific territory. While one person is responsible for them for most of the year, during lambing other farm personnel often take care of them so that park sheep embody the farm's labor more generally rather than that of one specific person. This general and anonymous significance is manifest in the visible physical attributes of the lambs with little reference to the personhood of the specific people who raised them and the specific farm where they were produced. In this mode, sheep are teleological. Their potential value lay in what they can be exchanged for—money for food, clothing, farm machinery, and business profit. In Simmel's terms, sheep as commodities are "preliminary forms" (Weingartner 1959:47) whose value is expressed in the universal measure of money.

In general, hill lambs are sold at store auctions and park lambs at fat auctions. I begin with a comprehensive account of store lamb auctions because store lambs are the most important for hill sheep farmers in terms of both forms of value. As commodities, store lambs off the hill provide the bulk of the farm's income from sales and subsidies; as cultural objects, they embody the people, livestock and land that are quintessential to hill sheep farming. Fat lamb auctions are described more schematically. Park sheep are viewed by hill sheep people more as commodities, valued principally for the money for which they could be exchanged.[4] Tups are more aesthetic objects valued for what they express about hill sheep farming, but that will have to wait until the next chapter.

Store Lamb Auctions[5]

Store lamb sales are held at auction marts around the Borders from late August until November.[6] Teviothead farmers sell a majority of their hill lambs at store market auctions because they do not have enough fields to fatten them to European Community certification standards without expensive supplementary feeding. As I have indicated above, purebred hill lambs are cultural objects in expressing the stockmanship of the particular shepherd or farmer who raised them. This is not to say that hill sheep are not significant for the money they are exchanged for. Indeed, the fact that breeding programs are designed to produce lambs whose carcasses potentially meet consumer demands and the general standards set by the European Community is evidence that outbye sheep are also valued as commodities.

These two modes of significance are incorporated into the auction before the sales in the way hill lambs are chosen. Lambs are sold in lots of between 40 and 150. The lambs that make up a lot all come from the same cut, although on occasion they come from two cuts, but always from the same hirsel. Thus, each sale lot of lambs is associated with the shepherd of the hirsel. In selecting their best lambs for sale from their hirsels, shepherds try to compose the sale lot in such a way as to accentuate their good qualities and hide their bad qualities. To achieve this, they make what is called a "level draw" of lambs. On the day before an auction, they gather one or more cuts of ewes and their lambs from their hirsels and drive them to the "folds" where there are a series of pens and races with gates. There they "shed off" the sheep into separate pens of ewes, ewe lambs, and wedder (castrated) lambs.[7] Shepherds, often with the farmer's advice, then walk through the pen inspecting the lambs and lifting the best ones into another pen. Then, from the latter pen, some lambs that do not look as good as the rest are removed, and the remaining lambs make up the sale lot. The goal is to get a set of lambs that look the same: similar weight, height, body shape, head shape, leg length, wool color and quality. Paraphrasing one shepherd's explanation:

> If you have a draw of sheep that do not weigh and look the same, the smaller lambs look even smaller; this lowers the price buyers are willing to pay for the whole draw because the lambs will not fatten as much and [will] realize less profit as smaller finished lambs. Similarly, the bigger lambs look even bigger, and this too is a disadvantage since buyers reason that if the lambs are already large, they will fatten less and thus decrease the difference in store price and fat price that is the essence of their profit. If they all look the same, there is no reference point from within the lot which buyers can use for differential assessment. This makes it a bit more difficult to spot the bad points of the lambs.

In making a level draw, shepherds and farmers attend to the visible physical characteristics that they know buyers look for in store lambs. These are body shape (rib length and size of hindquarters, where most of the meat is), quality of wool, clear and sharp line separating neck wool and head hair, straight and strong legs. For buyers, these qualities are general objective signs of the lambs' potential to realize profit through fattening; for the shepherd who is responsible for them, the same qualities specifically reflect upon his stockmanship; and for the farmer upon whose farm the sheep are raised, they are also a manifestation of his breeding knowledge.

The Buyers

There are usually thirty or so buyers participating in store market auctions. For them, store lambs are significant as cultural objects and commodities, but in different ways and proportions. Buyers are usually farmers of lowland farms, most of which are located in northern England just across the Border, where the milder climate and better pasturage are suited to fattening lambs in autumn and winter. These lowland English farmers then sell the "finished" lambs to abattoirs at fat market auctions from January to March when supplies of lamb are low, when demand is high, and when prices and the variable premium reach their maximum levels. In this series of exchanges, the value of store lambs is their potential as commodities to produce profit when resold on the fat market. As an indication of the amount of profit that can be made, in autumn of 1993, good Cheviot store lambs sold for an average of £25; after fattening, these lambs sold for £42 (sale price plus variable premium) on the fat market in early 1994. With estimated costs of feeding and transport averaging £5 per head, buyers could realize a profit of £10 per lamb in just over four months. Buyers assess the commodity value of store lambs on the visible physical characteristics of the lambs. It is less important to know on which farm the lambs were raised and who the shepherd was as long as the lambs present the right physical attributes for fattening, reaching the certification standards and attracting high prices from abattoirs at fat auctions.

Yet buyers also realize that store lambs' potential for fattening and profit is not totally revealed by their visible physical qualities. Rather, it is to some extent latent in lambs' genetic make-up, and this is the contribution of the farm's breeding program nurtured by skilled shepherding during the first five months on the hill. Together, breeding and shepherding—the work of a farmer and a shepherd—produce the capacity for fattening on lowland farms in the second five months just prior to sale and slaughter. As a result, in assessing lambs' commodity value, buyers also take into account the farmer and shepherd who produced them. Since most buyers have been purchasing and fattening store lambs for a number of years, they have built up knowledge of how lambs raised on particular farms by particular shepherds fattened in the past. In this process of creating a farm's reputation, buyers transform the cultural value that lambs have for farmers and shepherds in embodying their stockmanship into an instrumental value for them in the lambs' ability to fatten and produce a profit. Most farmers in Teviothead told me of at least one buyer who would bid aggressively for their lambs on the basis of their reputations. Several farmers had private arrangements with one or two buyers to sell their top or second draw of lambs directly to them, thus avoiding the transportation and commission costs of auctions.

The Audience

In comparison with fat lamb auctions, the audience at store lamb auctions is large, especially at the auctions when the "top" draw of lambs from many farms are likely to be up for sale. It is comprised mainly of other local hill sheep people. Farmers, shepherds and some family members from farms throughout the Borders attend store lamb auctions even if they are not selling lambs. It is a special day out, and most "dressed up" for these occasions with men usually wearing fine wool trousers, tie, tweed jacket, cap, and dress stick and women wearing dressy clothes. Those selling arrive early in the morning to deliver their lambs, and, even though the sale would not begin for a couple of hours, they remain at the mart to look over the lambs of other farms in the holding pens, talk among themselves about sheep, and speculate about the state of the market.

People from Teviothead explained to me that the main reasons for so many people attending auctions and staying throughout is that they were occasions when it was possible to see sheep raised and herded by others, to assess the quality of other farms' lambs in comparison with their own, and to socialize with other hill sheep farming people. In this respect, store lamb auctions are arenas for public displays of self, farm, and Borders hill sheep farming. Selling lambs and attending auctions is one act of defining Teviothead and the Borders as a place where a set of people are involved in a common way of life. At the same time and place, they confront buyers who represent the economic forces of the agricultural market as it is shaped by the Common Agricultural Policy and whose actions are a reflection and cause of hill sheep farmers' economic marginality.

Spatial and Temporal Layout

The auction marts all have a similar spatial layout. They consist of a series of concentric circles within and around the sale ring that focus the action on the lambs. The sale rings are approximately twenty feet in diameter bounded by a three-foot wall. A bench lining most of the interior of this wall gives the best view of the lambs, and this is where most of the active buyers sat for the bidding.[8] The auctioneer's box is perched above the wall and affords a clear view of the buyers' benches and the audience. There are two gates in the wall for the entrance and exit of lambs. Around this wall is the next concentric structure: a walkway where members of the audience can move around to find the best place to stand and look directly into the ring. Surrounding this are tiers of benches where the majority of the audience view the proceedings.

Complementing this spatial structuring of the auction is the sale catalog that organizes the temporal ordering of the sales. Upon arrival at the auction mart, almost the first thing participants do is to purchase a catalog. The auction day and catalog are divided into separate sessions for Cheviot and Blackface lambs. Each sale lot of lambs is numbered serially, and the farm where they were raised identified by name. If a farm is offering lambs from more than one hirsel, the draw from each hirsel makes up a distinct sale lot, separately listed and named by the hirsel. Sale lots from one farm do not occur sequentially in the sale; they are treated separately in the draw that determines the sale order. Because the catalog is prepared for an audience of hill sheep people, it is a contemplative document in the sense of representing the quintessential organization and operation of a hill sheep farm to hill sheep farming people. Like the ensuing sale events it summarizes, the organization of the catalog uses the medium of temporal sequencing to portray farms as independent units, which the audience know to be associated with particular farmers and their families, and hirsels as separate divisions within farms where the lambs being sold were raised, which again the audience know to be the responsibility of an individual shepherd.

Presenting Lambs and Selves

At most store lamb auctions I attended, there were about two hundred sale events. Like cockfights in Bali (Geertz 1975), there is no ordering of sale events except the randomness of drawing lots. A sale event begins with the posting of some information about the lambs: the sale lot, number, and/or weight of lambs being sold.[9] Then the entrance gates to the sale ring are opened, and representatives of each living component of a hill sheep farm—its owner, tenant or manager, shepherd(s), and the sheep that embody them—enter the ring together as a social unit. There is an air of spectacle. The lambs are herded into the ring by their shepherd with the help of the farmer, both dressed in their best clothes. The auctioneer provides a "ring master" who stands stationary in the middle of the sale ring. Throughout the bidding, the

farmer and shepherd herd the lambs so that the animals circle in one direction around the ring master while they move
in the opposite direction around the lambs. Hill sheep people in the audience explained to me that controlling the
sheep circling the ring gives the buyers sitting on the ring
side benches an opportunity to examine all the lambs from
various angles as they pass in front of them during the bidding. The overall effect of the spatial layout of the mart, the
organization of the catalog, and the actions of the participants during the sale event is a deliberate visual presentation
of farm, farmer, shepherd, herding skills, and the lambs that
embody them to buyers seated around the ring.[10] It is also an
instance and simulation of the relation between hill sheep
farms and the European Community. Enclosed and united
inside the ring are the hill sheep farm, personified by its
products, personnel, and their social relations, and the CAP-
shaped agricultural market, personified by the buyers. In this
respect, store lamb auctions have the quality of "resonance"
that Greenblatt attributed to museum exhibitions: "the
power of the displayed object to reach out beyond its formal
boundaries to a larger world, to evoke in the viewer the complex, dynamic cultural forces from which it has emerged and
for which it may be taken by a viewer to stand" (1991:42).

Figure 7.1   Presenting Store Lambs, Hawick Auction Mart

However, the buyers are not the only group in relation to which the sheep are presented for evaluation. Auctions are one of the three contexts (local farm shows and tup sales are the others) in which hill sheep people gather and inspect each other's lambs. As such, they are punctuated by what I call "reflexive moments." The entrance of the farmer, shepherd, and lambs and the exhibition of their herding skills in the sale ring is the first of them in store market auctions. I described in the previous chapter how hill herding is mostly solitary work creating a singular attachment between a shepherd and his hirsel—as a group of sheep *and* a place. During most of the work day, there is only minimal contact with the farmer or other farm personnel who are carrying out their work on park sheep or cattle largely by themselves. In this respect, the way work is organized tended toward individualizing people's experience of hill sheep farming. The concentric structure of the mart and the performance of the sale events engages the attention of the audience on the portrayal of the farm in the ring. It is a moment when there was a spatio-temporal collectivization of audience members' individualized experiences of their way of life as they evaluate the particular hill sheep farm presented in the ring. Over the store lamb auction season, then, all the farms in Teviothead and the Borders present themselves to their peers. The specificity of the hill sheep farm that is emergent for individual hill sheep people in their work routines and embodied in their sheep become a shared experience of a common world that is reflected upon in the act of evaluating the lambs, farmer, and shepherd in the ring.

This presentation of hill sheep farming is juxtaposed to the buyers' bidding, a process that neutralizes its distinctiveness. Buyers interpret hill lambs in terms of the universal certification standards of the European Community and as commodities measured in terms of a universal standard, money. Further, once the lambs are sold on the fat market, they become even more anonymous commodities and less cultural objects. They are no longer specific breeds of hill sheep embodying the farm where they were raised but merely British or Scottish "lambs" sold in shops throughout the European Community. The auction is the boundary where the hill sheep farming world of cultural value of lambs confronts the European Community world of commodity value of lamb carcasses. As we shall see, the dickering that Weber (1978:635) said was the market's most distinctive feature takes place on this boundary.

Competitive Bidding Between Buyers over Price

As soon as the lambs enter the ring, the auctioneer explicitly identifies the farm—and, if needed, the hirsel—on which they were raised, thus emphasizing their embodiment of the farmer's and shepherd's stockmanship. He also makes a brief comment about the lambs and/or farm's reputation for producing quality (i.e., profit-making) lambs: "these lambs are just off the hill," "these are fine looking lambs," "the lambs from this farm are always good." Here the auctioneer sets the frame of the sale event: the lambs in the ring are commodities, and the bidding is a process for determining their value as instruments of profit. The auctioneer then kicks off the bidding by suggesting a starting price that is supposed to reflect the lambs' commodity value. In almost all cases, he has to lower this price before a buyer signals acceptance and starts the competitive bidding.[11]

While the bidding takes place between the buyers, all participants know that at the end farmers have to decide whether or not to accept the last bid. In this respect, dickering between buyers and seller is always immanent in the competitive bidding between buyers. As the bidding slows, dickering becomes explicit as the farmer has to determine if the bids are approaching an acceptable price in terms of income and his judgments of the lambs' value as an embodiment of his farm in relation to other lambs at the auction. Since no reserve price is established between the seller and auctioneer prior to the bidding, successive sellers continually revise their judgments of what is an acceptable bid (above the break-even point) in light of preceding sale events. If the buyers' evaluation of the lambs' commodity value for themselves is not sufficient for the farmer's economic and cultural requirements, the farmer shakes his head, rejecting the bid before the hammer falls. The auctioneer then renews his exhortations for higher bids from the buyers, which are usually forthcoming. The highest bid then extracted from the buyers is their collective final offer for the lambs; the farmer has just seconds to decide to accept it.

Dickering between Farmer and Buyers over Value

Throughout the immanent and explicit dickering between buyers and sellers, the issue is not so much the price as what form of value the price should reflect. In the few moments that the dickering takes, a number of aspects of the auction are brought into the calculations by the farmer selling the lambs as he assesses the last bid. He does not judge bids solely in terms of monetary income. The high bid as a price reflecting the commodity value of lambs may be economically profitable to both the buyer and the farmer. Yet it may not be sufficient to represent the farmer's estimation of the cultural value of lambs in embodying the shepherd's stockmanship, the farmer's breeding program, and hill sheep farming in general. In purely financial terms, if the lambs are "passed in" (the final bid rejected and the lambs not sold), the farmer incurs extra transportation costs that have to be recouped at the next auction to vindicate the farmer's interpretation of his lambs' value as more than mere income-producing objects. Whether he takes this financial risk of rejecting the buyers' low evaluation for the sake of his farm's reputation among other hill sheep men depends upon his immediate cash needs and the audience's interpretation of the bidding. I re-emphasize here that within the sale-ring the commodity value of lambs is dominant—by entering it a farmer subjects himself and his lambs to that evaluative framework. But that does not automatically render it decisive for the outcome of the dickering between buyers and seller because in the moments of judging the fairness of the final bid, sellers appropriate the audience and their interpretations of lambs as more than commodities. This in effect moves the boundaries of the sale ring outward to encompass the audience where the lambs are also cultural objects.

There are two ways in which the sale ring expands. First, the distinction between audience and seller is spatio-temporal rather than rigidly categorical. The audience is mostly farmers and shepherds who have been, were, and would be sellers at past, present and future auctions, and the seller in the ring at any one time was and would again be a member of the audience. In this sense, the seller is the personification of the audience in the ring and the audience is a collection of past and future sellers. Second, members of the audience engage in the practice of "marking the catalog." Almost everyone in the audience keeps a record in their sale catalogs of the prices bid for each lot of hill lambs. Shepherds in particular have quite accurate memories of the prices (and the consequent judgment of their skills) paid for their lambs in auctions in the present and preceding years. This detailed knowledge of the market enables the audience (including the farmer currently in the ring) to make a number of comparisons between the bid price of lambs in the ring and (1) the prices of their own lambs in auctions of the current sale season and previous seasons and (2) the general price of store lambs of other hill sheep farms in the current auction and in other auctions that season and previous seasons. In this respect, marking the catalog engenders a collective sense of the market for lambs of various quality among the audience and its personification in the ring, the farmer selling the lambs. Thus, in the moments of deciding whether or not to accept the high bid, the farmer in the ring does so not just as an individual assessing the bid in relation to the financial needs of his own farm but also as part of the audience watching the event and assessing the lambs as objectifications of hill sheep farming This is a second reflexive moment when hill sheep people in the ring and in the audience experience themselves to be part of a distinctive group through a common sense of the cultural value of hill lambs as opposed to their commodity value for buyers.[12]

The final act of the dickering is accepting or rejecting the last bid. Here, the issue for the seller is to interpret it in relation to the hill sheep farmers' collective knowledge of the market, and in particular to the price differential between the bids for his lambs and those of other farmers in this and other auctions. There are always price differences between lots of lambs of the same breed within an auction. Thus, deciding whether or not to accept a low bid hinges upon the meaning the seller attributes to the price difference as a reflection of the lambs' cultural value. Here again, the sale ring expands to include the audience because throughout the day, as they mark their catalogs and discuss the sale prices around the pens and in the pub, the audience collectively adopts one of two explanations for differences in the prices offered for lambs in the bidding. One is the "steady price" explanation. This occurs when, in the audience's view, hill lambs of comparable quality attract similar bids from the buyers. Thus in steady price bidding, price differences that reflect the buyers judgment of differences in the commodity value of lambs are accepted as accurate indicators of the differences in the quality of shepherds' stockmanship and farmers' breeding skill embodied by the lambs. This is the case even if the absolute level of prices is low since it is the price relative to other lambs from other hirsels and farms that express the differences in stockmanship. It was easy for me to identify shepherds who had received praise for their skills in the comparatively high prices their lambs had fetched. They were the ones most willing to buy drinks and discuss the sale with fellow shepherds in the pub. There is also the potential in a steady price auction to disconfirm judgments made by farmers of shepherds' stockmanship in nonauction contexts. In one case, a farmer, who himself herded a hirsel, had been quite critical of his hired shepherd's competence. His criticisms ceased after a steady price sale in which his lambs fetched a significantly lower price that those of his supposedly incompetent shepherd. The point here is that establishing a steady-price explanation is a third reflexive moment in which the audience of hill sheep people recognize their shared valuation of lambs as cultural objects.

The other explanation of price differences suggests that they are artificial evaluations of buyers who are outsiders and not hill sheep farmers. Most of them bid only on Cheviot or Blackface lambs, and of the thirty buyers at an auction, less than half purchase large numbers. As a result, there are relatively few major buyers for each breed of lambs at a given auction and because of this, the explanation goes, it was possible for any one of these buyers to have a disproportionate effect on the bidding. At several auctions when prices seemed to go up and down on what farmers thought were similar lambs, they told me that some buyers who wanted to purchase a particular breed of hill lamb had withheld bids on the first six or seven lots in order to get an idea of the going price. This depressed the price for the early lots of lambs. Then when the major buyers simultaneously entered the bidding on the eighth or so lot, the price rose sharply—and for farmers artificially—giving an inaccurate evaluation of the lambs in comparison to previous lots.[13] This understanding of price fluctuation emphasizes that buyers are not hill sheep farmers but crass profiteers and agents of the European Community agricultural market who are ignorant of the art of hill sheep farming and whose bids are not sensitive to the cultural value of the lambs. This is the fourth reflexive moment when, juxtaposed to the agricultural market in commodities personified by the buyers, hill sheep people recognize a common oppositional component of their way of life as they haggle with buyers over the value—commodity or cultural—of lambs, not their price.

In analyzing store market auctions, I have characterized them as reflexive and resonant spectacles referring to a larger world and evoking for individualized hill sheep people an experience of hill sheep farming as a way of life and the Borders as the place of hill sheep farming. I can now say something substantive about the nature of this way of life. First is the quintessential people and relations that define a hill sheep farm as a distinctive enterprise: farmer, shepherd, stockmanship, and the lambs that embody them. Second is the common understanding that lambs are cultural objects whose value derives from their specific relation to particular farms and shepherds. Third is the juxtaposition of hill sheep farming and its valuation of lambs to buyers who personify the European Community and the agricultural market where lambs are commodities whose value derives from meeting general criteria and is measured in a universal standard of money. Fourth is the Borders as the place of hill sheep farming.

Fat Market Auctions

Auctions for finished lambs, that is, lambs meeting European Community certification standards, are held at the same auction marts as store lambs. Almost all the park lambs, and a number of hill lambs, raised on Teviothead farms are sold on the fat market. Compared with store lamb auctions, the nature and procedures of fat lamb auctions render finished lambs as commodities whose value derives from the profit that can be realized both by farmers in selling them and by buyers on selling the carcasses to distributors and retail outlets.

As with store lambs, the evaluative process begins before the auction with the selection of the lambs to be offered for sale. The lambs are drawn from all the farm's park lambs so they are not linked to and do not embody the personhood of a specific individual. Again, the objective is to select a "level" draw of lambs—as one farmer said: "The aim is to get the biggest lambs that are not too fat"—but for different reasons. Unlike store lambs, fat lambs are graded by officials of the European Community. Any lambs that are overfat or overlean are rejected by the grader and can not be sold as lambs eligible for the variable premium.[14] It is in relation to the grading that a level draw was important. As one shepherd explained: "Graders tend to reject those lambs in a lot that are different from the majority ... the decision to reject [lambs] does not seem to be based on the amount of fat ... so if you bring a very level draw, they would probably be accepted ... I've never seen a grader reject all the lambs in a lot." Even in lots of lambs that graders accepted, I often saw the graders separate out ones that were larger or smaller than the average to make up other sale lots so that each lot had lambs of similar weight.

The Buyers

The buyers are employees of or agents for abattoir companies that transport the lambs directly to their slaughterhouses and then distribute the carcasses throughout the United Kingdom and the European Community. For them, lambs are teleological instruments and the bidding of their representatives reflects the goal of buying at the lowest possible price lambs whose carcasses they believe are preferred by consumers and would fetch the highest prices from retail outlets. Thus, it does not matter to them on which farm the lambs are raised and who does the shepherding because it is their inspection of the physical confirmation of the lambs and their estimation of the quality of the carcasses that determines their evaluation and bidding. It is for this reason that in most of the fat auctions, the only information posted about the lambs when they enter the ring is the average net dead weight.[15] This is the most important information about the lambs for the buyers. It is also important for the sellers because the variable premium is calculated on the difference between average price per kilogram for lambs at fat sales during the week in Britain and a target price per kilogram established each week by the European Community. As a result, the average price per kilogram is a target weight for lambs offered for sale because at that weight they are most cost effective. If lambs are well under the average weight, the total income is significantly less; if they are over the target weight, they are still less cost effective even though the total income is higher than for lambs at the target weight. This is because lambs much heavier than the target weight have been fattening too long, incurring extra production costs, which decrease net income.

The Audience

In comparison with store markets, the audience is small and transient. At any one time there are twenty or less people watching the bidding. They are mainly farmers whose lambs are to be sold within the next several lots or so.[16] Unlike store lamb auctions, fat sales are not all-day affairs but are treated as part of the workday. Farmers and shepherds come dressed in their everyday work clothes. After delivering the lambs and taking them through the grading process, if there is to be a long wait before their own lambs are to be sold, they often go back to the farm and return to the mart at the time they estimate the lambs are to be sold. It is these farmers who form the audience and judge the "trade" while waiting for their lot of lambs to come into the ring. Once the lambs are sold, they return to their farms. Some farmers leave after the grading process and do not return for the sale, thereby accepting in advance the last bid. This is part of an overall strategic cost- and time-efficient approach farmers take to fat lamb sales and is another dimension of their practice through which they render these sheep more as instruments of profit than as cultural objects of self-expression.

The Auction

Fat lamb sales have the air of a "production line," focusing attention on the lambs as instruments of profit rather than as expressions of the farmer, shepherd, or farm. The aim is selling the most lambs as quickly as possible, and the sale procedures highlight the physical qualities of the lambs that make them valuable as commodities rather than the personhood of the farming people that make them valuable as cultural objects.

As mentioned previously, one of the major differences between store and fat lamb auctions is that fat lambs are graded to make sure they comply with the certification standards that make them eligible for the subsidy. In the grading process, lambs are herded into small pens where the officials estimate the level of fat on the carcasses by feeling their backs and tails; lambs that are too fat or lean are rejected and marked; lambs that meet certification standards but are smaller or larger than the average are made into separate sale lots; the lots are then weighed to determine the average gross dead weight (one-half the live weight); the grader makes a deduction, usually between .5 and 2.5 kilos, from the gross dead weight to take into account dirt or water in the wool, producing an average net dead weight for each sale lot. Both average gross and net dead weights are recorded and are later displayed to buyers and audiences when the lambs are sold.

Graders do not take into account the reputation of the farm where the lambs were raised in the grading process. Instead, they base their judgments only on their visual and physical examination of the lambs. Further, in recent sales the name of the farm was not posted with the weights of the lambs so that the only way the buyers knew where the lambs were raised was in recognizing the farm personnel who herded them into the sale ring.

The spatial layout of the auction mart again emphasizes the dominant orientation to fat lambs as commodities. Before the Hawick auction mart closed in 1993, both store and fat lamb auctions were held there, but on different days. Much of my earlier description of store lamb auctions and the spatial layout of the mart is based upon those at Hawick. For the fat lamb auctions, a temporary sale ring of approximately ten-foot diameter is set up. In other marts, there are separate small rings used for fat lambs sales with a small area for standing and a few benches around them. Catalogs are less important or not provided because farmers can decide to sell fat lambs up to the morning of the sale, and it is not possible then for the auctioneer to print up an accurate catalog beforehand.

The lambs are herded into the ring by a mart employee and the farmer, if he has stayed for the sale. There are no introductory comments about the quality of the lambs or the farm as they enter the ring, and there is no formalized presentation of the lambs and farmer's self to the buyers and audience by herding them in a circle around the ring. Instead, the lambs are tightly bunched in the smaller ring making it easier for the buyers to move among the lambs and physically examine them in much the same way as graders. Because there are usually only four or five active bidders who are close and visible to the auctioneer, the bidding proceeds much faster. When the last bid is made, the auctioneer rarely consults the farmer, if he was present, to see if he accepts the bid. This is an indication that, unlike store mart auctions, there is little, if any, dickering between buyers and sellers in fat market auctions. In fact, during my observations of fat sales over a number of years, I did not record a farmer rejecting a bid.

The issue for farmers, then, is not so much whether or not to accept the final bid but whether or not to offer lambs for sale on a particular day at a particular mart. Like the buyers, they treat fat lambs as commodities and adopt a similar economically strategic orientation. They could consult the daily newspapers to find out the current level of the variable premium and the lamb prices in the previous day's fat sales. On this basis, farmers estimate the price his lambs would have to fetch in order to reach the average sale price for the week so that together with the variable premium he would be receiving the maximum income with minimum production costs; he also has to decide if by waiting to sell at another sale with a different average sale price and target price the total income would be better given additional production costs. The following is an extract from my fieldnotes taken during an outing with a farmer to a fat lamb auction. It illustrates, in the complex calculations made by farmers, that fat lambs are primarily treated as commodities. It also demonstrates that once a commodity framework is adopted toward their lambs, farmers are more willing to accept "what the market will bear" as reflected in the final bid from the buyers.

Selling Lambs on the Fat Market
Before the sales (but after the lambs had been graded):

Robert said that the fat market is a very strategic one: "… you always have to plan and scheme to get the best out of it in selling lambs. This is especially so in November and December when the lambs are getting quite big. You want them as big as possible without being overfat. So in November and December you have to watch the lambs carefully so that they don't get too fat before you sell them. There are plenty of fat markets near Teviothead, so you can find a place to sell lambs most every day of the week … you can bring the lambs to the fat market when they are at their best … this is why you have to watch the lambs carefully so you can sell them at their heaviest without them being fat."

Robert told me that at today's sales he would have to get a good price for his fat lambs for him to sell them. He wanted to get around £38 per lamb (including the variable premium). This meant getting a bid of about £30 in the ring. He based his figuring on the graded net dead weight of 18.5 kilos at which his lambs were assessed this morning. The European Community target price for the week is 206.6 pence per kilo (net dead weight) making his lambs worth £38.22 (18.5 x 206.6). The subsidy the European Community will pay is based upon the difference between the week's target price (206.6/kg) and the average sale price of fat lambs during the same week. Auction marts post the projected subsidy for the week to help farmers estimate an acceptable ring price for their lambs. This week's projected subsidy is 47.5 p per kilo. For Robert this means that if his lambs sell for about £30 in the ring, he will receive a subsidy of £8.79 per lamb (18.5 x 47.5p); in effect, his lambs could sell for slightly below £30 to achieve his £38 per lamb target. He said that if the lambs did not make £30 bid in the ring, he would likely pass them in and sell them at a store market where he thinks he could get £38 in the ring. He said that he would check the recent store lamb prices for Suffolk-cross fat lambs before his lambs are sold.

After the sales:

The final bid in the ring for his lambs was £29.60 despite other 18.5kg Suffolk-cross lambs getting higher prices. He accepted the bid saying that the buyers lowered their bid for his lambs because there were two Texel cross lambs in the lot, which diminished the level nature of the draw. Still the price was high enough to reach the £38 target, i.e., £29.60 + £8.79 (subsidy) = £38.39 per lamb.

Conclusion

By way of conclusion, there is one further point to make from this vignette beside its demonstration of the level of economic calculations that dominate farmer's practices in the sale. First, the commodity mode of fat lambs and the auctions at which they are sold, with their peripheral position and dominance by the European Community, confront farmers more starkly than store lamb auctions. Like most Teviothead hill sheep farmers, Robert accepted the ring bid even though it was below the target he had set—a target that was calculated principally on the value of lambs as economic instruments of profit. (There was no evidence that he included the cultural value of lambs in his calculations.) Robert's actions highlighted the greater dominance by and the impersonality of the European agricultural market experienced by farmers in fat lamb sales. This impersonality and dominance was also the theme of a genre of story about the grading process that I heard at almost every fat sale I attended. I quote one example of this story:

> A farmer took his fat lambs to the Wigtown mart for the weekly fat sale. There were three men grading the lambs because it was a big sale. Just before the farmer's lambs were due to be graded, the senior grader at the grading station went off for tea or something. The grader who took over that grading station rejected six of the farmer's lambs as overlean and they were taken away and put in a separate pen until the farmer was ready to take them back to his farm.
>
> Still the farmer was upset that the six lambs had been rejected. When the senior grader returned not ten minutes later, the farmer took him over to the pen where his rejected sheep were being held and asked this senior grader what was wrong with the lambs. After the usual physical examination, he said they were overfat.
>
> One farmer then made the moral of the story—the impersonal and capricious nature of the dominating European Community and agricultural market—explicit: "If graders can't agree on the quality of a lamb, how can anybody know what to bring to the fat market."

Notes

1. I am not including here the auctions where draft ewes are sold. At these auctions there are two types of buyers: farmers who buy draft hill ewes to be used as park ewes and to cross with a lowland tup for fat lambs, and abattoirs who slaughter the draft ewes for mutton carcasses.

2. Debord's (1994) conception of spectacle focuses more upon the pervasive commoditization of life in modern society and its use as a means of domination. While there are a number of attributes of his vision of spectacle that store lamb auctions display, my point is to highlight how in such auctions hill sheep farming people resist the total commoditization of lambs and their consequent detachment from their way of life.

3. It is for this reason that hill sheep have an aesthetic quality that acts as a medium through which the moral dimensions of hill sheep significance is expressed. This aesthetic quality is particularly strong in tup sales because the audience is composed of other hill sheep people who are more appreciative of the hill sheep farming way of life—it is a context for aficionados of hill sheep.

4. During the early 1990s when the variable premium was still being paid, most hill sheep farms increased the number of lambs they sold on the fat market. This was done by fattening hill lambs with supplementary feeding. At that time, the amount of the variable premium was large enough to offset the extra expense of fattening hill lambs. However, after the MacSharry reforms phased out the variable premium, the difference between the price of fat lambs and store lambs was lessened to the point where the cost benefit of fattening hill lambs with supplementary feeding was minimal. Thus, in 1996 to 1997, Teviothead farmers increased the number of lambs they sold on the store market.

5. In this section of the chapter, I draw upon the description of store lamb auctions in my previously published article (Gray 1984), updated by material collected on auctions in 1986 and 1991 and with a different analytic emphasis. I continue to use the "ethnographic present" for the reasons identified by Hastrup (1995).

6. These were located at Hawick, Annan, and Longtown. Teviothead farmers sold their store lambs mostly at Hawick and Annan. In 1993, the Hawick mart closed; since then most store lambs are sold at Annan. The present account is based upon my observations at Hawick and Annan up to 1991.

7. Since replacement stock is selected from the ewe lambs, most store lambs sold are wedder lambs.

8. Some buyers prefer the anonymity of sitting among the audience in the bleachers.

9. In some marts, only the number of lambs in the lot was posted. In this situation, it was the audience of hill sheep farmers who could best know where the lambs were raised, since they recognized by sight most of the farmers in the Borders. This is an indication that Border hill sheep farmers form at least a community of recognition. Experienced buyers had a similar advantage.

10. If more than one of the farm's shepherds are present in the sale ring, the farmer may not actively participate in the herding. Instead he stands near the auctioneer's box with a view of the lambs, the shepherds and the bidders similar to that of the auctioneer's. In taking this position in the ring and the actions linked to it, the farmer assumes a social location in the sale event analogous to the one he has on the farm. From this position he can keep an eye on his interests as the bidding proceeds without necessarily engaging in herding activities.

11. The tactic of suggesting a very high opening price appeared to me to be directed more at farmers than buyers. It was perhaps a means of acknowledging the cultural value of lambs to the farm people in the ring.

12. This is perhaps an even more dynamic form of spectacle than even MacAloon imagined when he stated that they demanded "movement, action, change, and exchange on the part of the human actors who are center stage, and the spectators must be excited in turn" (1984:244).
13. Farmers claimed that the same artificial bidding also occurred when one of the buyers went to lunch.
14. Lambs that are graded as too fat are often still sold at the auction, but the farmer does not receive any subsidy in addition to the bid price. Lambs that are graded as too lean are taken back to the farm for further fattening.
15. When the Hawick mart held fat lamb auctions, they did include the name of the farm on the information postings about the lambs. Other marts, such as Longtown, did not.
16. When Teviothead farmers first started selling fat lambs in the mid 1980s, they often watched the trade for an hour or so before their lambs came into the ring. By the early 1990s, these same farmers no longer did this.

Chapter 8

RAM AUCTIONS
Tups of Value, Men of Renown

In September, hill sheep people from around the Borders gather at the Lockerbie Auction Mart for the annual sale of Cheviot rams. Nearly five hundred tups raised by approximately fifty breeders are sold. Each breeder offers between two and twenty tups, with the "big" breeders having the larger number for sale. While there are other ram auctions in Scotland, the one at Lockerbie relates more closely to hill sheep farming in the Borders region. South Country Cheviot sheep were developed as a breed in the Borders, and they are still the sheep raised on most Border hill farms. Their name spatially links them to the Cheviot Hills, which is one of the defining features of Border landscapes. Thus the place-meaning of South Country Cheviot sheep, as icons of hill farming and its way of life, is sharply focused on the Borders. A number of farms in Teviothead raise Blackface sheep. However, this breed is farmed throughout Scotland. One of the major ram sales is held in the town of Lanark. Sheep farmers and shepherds from a wider area of Scotland than just the Borders region attend this auction. The origins of Blackface sheep are more in the highlands. Thus, the place where Blackface sheep both originated and are farmed makes them less exclusively a symbol of hill sheep farming in the Borders. For this reason, I base my account on the Lockerbie Auction.

Over several field trips since 1981, I attended the Cheviot ram sales at Lockerbie and the Blackface ram sales at Lanark.

Notes for this section begin on page 186.

They were similar in most respects, though the sales at Lanark were much larger with over 2300 rams sold and the prices were much higher. By way of capturing the spirit and ambience of ram auctions, I can do no better than Appadurai's paradigm of "tournaments of value" and Baudrillard's description of art auctions, both of which I quote at length.

> Tournaments of value are complex periodic events that are removed in some culturally well-defined way from the routines of economic life. Participation in them is likely to be both a privilege of those in power and an instrument of status contests between them. The currency of such tournaments is also likely to be set apart through well understood cultural diacritics. Finally, what is at issue in such tournaments is not just status, rank, fame or reputation of actors, but the disposition of the central tokens of value in the society in question. Finally, though such tournaments of value occur in special times and places, their forms and outcomes are always consequential for the more mundane realities of power and value in ordinary life. (Appadurai 1986:21)

> Contrary to commercial operations, which institute a relation of economic rivalry between individuals on the footing of formal equality with each one guiding his own calculation of individual appropriation, the [art] auction, like the fete or game, institutes a concrete community of exchange among peers. Whoever the vanquisher in the challenge, the essential function of the auction is the institution of a community of the privileged who define themselves as such by agonistic speculation upon a restricted corpus of signs. Competition of the aristocratic sort seals their parity (which has nothing to do with the formal equality of economic competition), and thus their collective caste privilege with respect to all others, from whom they are no longer separated merely by their purchasing power, but by the sumptuary and collective act of the production and exchange of sign values. (Baudrillard 1981:117, quoted in Appadurai 1986:21)

Like art auctions, the sign value of tups is presented in an aesthetic mode that highlights their function as cultural objects expressing breeders' personal value as hill sheep stockmen rather than as teleological instruments exchanged for profit; like tournaments of value, tup sales are vehicles of the privileged for status differentiation among Border hill sheep farmers. Tup sales have a *kula*-like pattern of exchange in which, to closely paraphrase Munn's description of the kula on Gawa (1983:283), tup breeders appear to be the agents in defining the value of tups. In fact, without tups, breeders could not define their *own* value; in this respect, tups and breeders are reciprocally agents of each other's value definition. However, despite themes of status differentiation and distance from economic realities, tup sales are also a mechanism for constituting a community of hill sheep people of the Borders through a redistribution of hill sheep farming skills and knowledge in the form of tups and their genetic make-up. Here again, in the social biography of tups we see the theme of sheep as synecdoches embodying, suffusing, and enabling a form of social life and a place (the Borders) where it is lived.

Of Tups and Hill Sheep Men

One evening after a walk around his hirsel and a meal with Charlie Nixon, a hill shepherd on one of the larger farms, I accompanied him on his final chore of the day—feeding the sale tups. When we arrived at the pens where the tups were kept, Charlie just stood in silence, doing nothing but gazing at them blissfully for nearly ten minutes. I was reminded of Geertz's graphic account of "cock crazy" Balinese men whose self is expressed in their cocks; like Balinese men, tup breeders "spend an enormous amount of time with their favourites, grooming them, feeding them, discussing them, trying them out against one another, or just gazing at them with a mixture of rapt admiration and dreamy self-absorption" (1975:418-419). Certainly one of the most respected breeders of South Country Cheviot tups in the Borders made the expressive link between self and tup explicit when he said: "The Lockerbie tup sales is an event when you present your farm and your self to your peers. Your peers view your tups as indicative of you as a farmer and pass judgment on you and your farm in the way they bid on your tups." As we will see, the more expensive the tups, the more important is their expressive function and the less important their commodity function of producing profit.

Again, like cockfighting in Bali, tup breeding is done by hill sheep men—but not just any hill sheep men. Breeding tups—and being accepted as a serious breeder—is both a privilege and mechanism of eminence (esteem, respect, prestige) though which an elite of hill sheep farmers defined the parity amongst themselves and represented their self-defined high standing in relation to "commercial" farmers and shepherds. Recall from Chapter 3 that commercial farmers are those who, with respect to raising lambs, were shifting production away from pure-bred hill lambs sold on the store market to cross-bred park lambs sold on the fat market. Now, with respect to tups, the term "commercial" referred to another dimension of these farmers: they raised and purchased less expensive sale tups (also referred to as "commercial" tups) or they were the non-tup-breeding farmers who bought them. As one farmer of the latter category ironically put it: "with tup breeding you are approaching the heights of the gods." He added, in comments I was to find typical of commercial farmers' critical views of the pomp and prices surrounding the tups of the "big" (elite) breeders:

> "I don't think that using an expensive tup necessarily improves the sheep on a farm. I know a farmer who bought a tup for a lot of money, £1000, and another from the same breeder and sire for £10. It ended up that the £10 tup produced better lambs than the expensive one. I don't think the elaborate ritual over tups is worth it. It gives farmers a bad name. When town folk look in the newspaper and see on page one that a farmer paid £5000-£6000 for a tup and on the next page that farmers are claiming to be in very bad financial striats, it looks funny and people don't believe the farmers' economic situation."

In Teviothead there were four tup breeding farms.[1] The farmer of one of them was respected throughout the Borders as one of the best tup breeders not just by the quality of his tups and the prices they fetched but also by the amount he was willing to spend purchasing tups from other "big" breeders. Like most of these breeders, he offered at least ten tups for sale each year, recognising that only two or three of these were the really good ones that other top breeders would buy. The rest were commercial grade tups that the "commercial men" would buy. Much of my knowledge of tup breeding and selling came from the time I spent with him, his son and hired shepherd. Another farm had just started a tup breeding program in the early 1990s. At first the breeder had not had the years to develop tups that the elite breeders were willing to acknowledge as top class by bidding high prices; but by the 1997 auction one of his tups attracted bids. The term "tup breeder" was applied to a farmer even if it was the farm's hired shepherds, like Charlie, who were "tup crazy" and whose knowledge and skills were applied to raising, selecting and preparing them for the sales. Two of the tup breeding farms in Teviothead fit into this category, one of them with the aim of entering the group of big breeders. Whether by design or default, these farms produced "commercial tups", that is, less expensive tups with good breeding that most farmers who were not among the top breeders would be willing to buy.

In addition to these breeders, there were three shepherds in Teviothead—and several others on farms throughout the Borders—who bred tups for the Lockerbie Sales. Most shepherds kept a "pack" of ewes whose lambs they sold for extra income.[2] The pack ewes were mated with the farm's tups and, if a shepherd was keen on breeding sale tups, he carefully selected tup lambs. Since a shepherd had access to the farm's tups, shepherds working on the farms of the big breeders had access to better tups and thus had the potential to produce higher quality sale tups. The majority of shepherds who did sell rams at the Lockerbie Sales were from farms of the big breeders.

Grooming[3]

The value of tups ultimately lies in the genetic make-up that they will contribute to a farm's flock. Since this is determined at conception, in grooming them for the Lockerbie Sales, breeders attempted to manipulate their external appearance to emphasize the desired physical attributes and to hide the faults. Their aim was to enhance the tups' value as signs of their stockmanship in detecting the quality of the tups' genetic make-up and thus as instruments of their status and renown. In explaining these practices of appearance, they used a discourse of aesthetics to emphasize the value of tups as cultural objects rather than a discourse of pragmatics that emphasized their value as commodities. Breeders expended a lot of time and effort preparing their tups for the Sales for, as the quotation above suggests, they recognized that they presented themselves, their stockmanship, and their farms for evaluation through their tups. Like store lambs, tups embodied the farm and its personnel, but unlike store lambs, it was more the farmer-breeder's self, even if it was a hired shepherd's stockmanship that was principally responsible for their quality. The exception, of course, was with shepherds' pack tups for they were understood to be unambiguous expressions of the shepherds' stockmanship and were a basis for a separate status differentiation among shepherd-breeders. However, while shepherds did not have an input into the status implications of breeders' sale tups because they did not bid at the Sales, breeders had control over status differentiation among shepherds since it was they who did the bidding and thus the evaluation of tups and shepherds.

The process of tup breeding began with the selection of tup lambs in May, over two years before they would be sold at Lockerbie. At that time breeders had to decide which male lambs to castrate for store sales and which to leave uncastrated as potential sale tups. Over the next year, the breeder further culled the tup lambs that were not developing the desired physical characteristics. As I described in a previous chapter, tups, whether raised for home breeding or for sale, were the province of farmers. This was particularly the case with tup breeders, the best of whom were renowned for their ability to see in young and undeveloped lambs the genetic potential to grow into a mature tups with the physical characteristic of hardiness that other tup breeders valued and that would produce lambs with the bodily configuration valued by the agricultural market.[4] Of great interest to and given extra scrutiny by breeders were the tup lambs from tups bought at the previous years' sales. It was only in these lambs that it was possible to tell if a good looking tup "bred well" with the ewes on the buyer's farm—even top quality tups may be incompatible with a flock on another farm and produce poor quality lambs—and it was often from these lambs that future sale tups were selected.[5]

To foreshadow a theme I develop later, there is in these practices of genetic reproduction an ingredient of status self-fulfilment and social involution among the group of top breeders that was explicitly referred to as "the clique." Those tups bred by top breeders that fetch high prices produced tup lambs that the purchasing breeders tended to select for return to the sales where they received high prices as products of top breeders because they were bred from high price tups of top breeders. The sale catalog provided some evidence of this circulation of tups, genes, skills and status among the clique of breeders. Every tup sold is listed individually in the sale catalog and its sire identified. Tups are individually named by breeders and the name of the farm was included in it. For example, some tups bred on Glenochar farm were named "Glenochar Big Yin", "Glenochar Sam", and "Glenochar Stamper", and some tups from Hislop Farm in Teviothead were named "Hislop Supersoft", "Hislop Topstar", "Hislop Supermac", and "Hislop Baron." Thus sire names identify the farm where they were raised so it was always possible to know the recent genealogy of the tup. In analysing the entries in the sale catalog, over ninety percent of the sires of tups sold by breeders whose tups generally received both the highest individual prices (over £1500) and highest average price (over £450) were raised on farms of these same breeders.[6] That is, over time the most expensive tups that epitomized Border hill sheep farming and embodied farmers' expertise were bought and sold among a distinct group of breeders. This was both an expression and instrument of being a top breeder that also defined the clique of big breeders.

Preparations occurred in stages beginning several months prior to the Sales with clipping the tups in June. Some breeders clipped the tups in March so that there was less new wool on the tups at sale time and it would be easier to dress the wool as part of manipulating their appearance. Others waited until the normal clipping time in June so that the tups' condition would not be jeopardized by exposure to the poor weather conditions of Spring. On the big tup breeding farms, the major grooming was a co-operative task done by the farmers and shepherds in early September, three weeks before the auction.[7] First, the horns are shaped and oiled. Electric sanding machines and hand files were used to smooth down the natural growth ripples in the horns and give them a "a nice curve away from the face", to allow the ears "to sit at a pleasing angle in relation to the head", and to produce a fine point at the ends.[8] If the horns are especially fat at the base, they are thinned because "you want to display as much of the tup's crown as possible"—a big crown being a sign of hardiness that buyers want to perpetuate in their hill flocks. Second, the wool was fluffed up with a wire brush to add lift and body so that it fills the hand and feels fine and heavy rather than coarse. Then the neck wool was trimmed with hand shears so that there was a distinct line where the wool meets the hair on the neck. If a tup had a particularly noticeable fault in this respect with wool growing too far up the neck, it was plucked out by hand because it is harder for a buyer to see the trimming that signals the fault. Third, the tups were then specially washed in the dipper to generally clean the wool. However, instead of just dropping them in and dunking as was done with the ewes, each tup was gently lowered into the water and the back end and face hand-washed with special soap.

A day or so later after they have dried, the wool was dressed. This entailed clipping to give an overall shape to the appearance of the body: straight back, wide and square back end. Instead of using the normal electric clippers, hand shears were used because they gave greater control. Then the top of the wool was colored a light brown with a sprayer to give it an "attractive bloom"; the hair on the head, neck and legs was left its natural white. One breeder told me how he had looked around for a number of years to find a sprayer that would allow him to finely adjust the depth and evenness of the color. He explained: "A white undercoat of wool showing through a light brown coloring on the outside makes a pleasing color … the tups really look grand." Finally, on the day before the sale, the tups' faces are whitened to make the hair look a consistent texture and color by hiding "blue" areas of dark hair on the face and pink areas of sparse hair on the ears and to enlarge the appearance of the head by increasing the contrast to the colored wool.

Under my questioning, they admitted that grooming the tups would not fool other breeders, who might buy them, into thinking the animals were better than they actually were. For a couple of hours before the sale, the tups were in holding pens and buyers were able to closely examine them visually and physically. Instead, they said that they wanted to make the tups "look good for the crowd." Most of the audience did not go to the pens for a close examination of the tups. They remained in the stands throughout the auction and would see the tups only from a distance when the first impression of their appearance was paramount as they entered the sale ring. Unverbalized during the preparations that I observed was an air of self-fulfilment in making the tups look good. Farmers and shepherds continually stood back to discuss critically the good points and faults of each tup and to gaze at the appearance they were developing as a result of the grooming. It was almost as if the tups actually improved in quality as a result and in this respect the breeders' selves and stockmanship moved from tups' internal genetics to their external visual impact through these practices of appearance.

A Circle of Visiting

In understanding the reproduction of hierarchy in South Asia, Marriott (1959, 1968, 1976) developed the concept of interactional practices. These were the transactions in food, water, and wives through which castes marked and maintained their social separation and ranking. Castes that symmetrically exchanged were equal because they shared a common substance as a result of the exchange, while those between which there was asymmetrical exchange were considered unequal in status. A caste that was attempting to raise its status might adopt the attributes of higher status, but if members of higher caste refused to exchange food, water and wives reciprocally, their claim to higher status was practically denied. Similar transactional strategies existed among the clique of tup breeders for similar social purposes.

One of these was the reciprocal visiting among the big breeders prior to the Lockerbie Sales that was a privilege and mechanism of creating a relatively closed clique. During this two-week visiting season, breeders brought their sale tups into pens near the farmhouse and most of the evenings were spent gazing at and discussing the tups individually over liberal amounts of whisky. In most cases, if a hired shepherd was respected for his knowledge and skill in breeding tups, he was invited along, but they were mostly occasions for farmers. The ostensive purpose of the visiting was to preview others breeders' tups. However, those invited to visit were known to be the breeders who in the past had paid high prices for tups from the farms they visited; and the farms they visited were those in the past that had produced tups fetching the highest prices. Over the two weeks, each breeder in the circle was both visited by and visited most of the other breeders in the clique.

To become a member of the clique, a breeder needed to be invited to other breeders' farms *and* be successful in other breeders coming to view his tups. I watched the efforts of one farmer who wanted to enter the clique. One of his difficulties was that he had not been brought up as a hill sheep farmer but bought a farm in mid-career. As a result, he did not have the stockmanship necessary to be a big breeder. However, he did hire a shepherd who other breeders acknowledged was a expert stockman. After a couple of years of buying expensive tups from breeders in the clique, he began inviting some of them to his farm during the visiting season. He did so quite strategically by inviting one of the top breeders with whom he was friendly and thus who found it difficult to refuse even though his visiting book was full. By doing this every year, he became a regular, if brief, stop on a visiting night of that breeder. Even after several years he was not a regular invitee to other breeders, and his tups continued to attract lower bids so that he was unable to effect the transactional symmetry necessary for membership.

There were just over a dozen farms included in the visiting circle and together they formed the annually self-perpetuating and socially-differentiating clique. The following is an outline of one year's round of visiting from the point of view of one breeder. What is also important to note is how the visiting, and the resulting clique, was spatially organized, taking in farms located in the valleys—Ettrick, Yarrow, Eskdalemuir, Teviothead, Ewesdale, Annandale—that defined the place of Border hill sheep farming.

A Visiting Circle[9]

Day 1: Meet up with the "Langholm Group" consisting of four breeders whose farms are situated near the that town; together they visit six breeders whose farms were located in Lanark, Eskdalemuir and Moffat.

Day 2:   Visited by a breeder from Lockerbie
Day 3:   Return visit by the four farms of the Langholm
         Group, as well as by a farm of the neighbouring
         Ewesdale Valley.
Day 4:   Visited by two breeders from Yarrow Valley; then
         return visit to the breeder from Lockerbie (Day 3)
Day 5:   Meet up with a breeder from Ettrick Valley and
         return visit to two Yarrow Valley farms (Day 4) plus
         four other Yarrow Valley breeders
Day 6:   Visited by one breeders from Yarrow and three
         from Lockerbie and Eskdalemuir; after the visit,
         join with three from Lockerbie/Eskdalemuir to
         visit the Langholm Group and three others nearby;
         stop off on the way at a farm in Ewesdale.
Day 7:   Return visit by one of the Langholm farms

The Sales: A Circle of Differential Value[10]

Tup Sales had self-presentation practices, similar to those
described in my earlier account of store lamb auctions, that
continued the process of linking the personhood of the
breeder to his sale tups. Breeders, commercial farmers and
shepherds from farms around the Borders attended the
show. Everyone wore their best clothes, brought their show
sticks, and members of the breeders' and shepherds' families
attended and formed a large part of the audience. There was
a catalog setting out the temporal order of sale by farm. It
identified the farmer, the farm and its location in the Borders; then the tups being offered for sale were listed in order
of the breeder's judgement of their quality—best first—and
numbered individually as the consecutive sale lots; the sire of
each tup was named; and if a hired shepherd from the farm
was offering his pack tup for sale, it was listed separately and
specifically identified as "Shepherd's ram." If one of the sires
had a particularly illustrious reputation or had been bought
for an especially high price, it was noted at the end of the
farm's section of the catalog.

   Like all auction marts, the spatial layout of the Lockerbie
mart was concentrically structured and focused on the sale
ring that was bounded by a three-foot wall, around which was
a walkway, itself surrounded by several tiers of stands for the
audience. The spatial organization of the audience segmented

them into groups that reflected their knowledge, personal stake in the quality of the tups, and participation in the bidding. In the top tiers of the stands that were furthest from the ring sat the wives, daughters and young children of the breeders. It was the expectation that these women would "mark the catalog", noting down the price and buyer name of every ram sold, not just those from their farm. They came prepared with food and drinks so that they could remain in their places throughout the auction. At the fall of the hammer for each tup sold, I could see all the heads of these women drop down simultaneously to mark the catalog. In the lower tiers of the stand and spilling onto the walkway surrounding the ring were the commercial farmers, mostly men, who were there to bid for commercial tups that would sell for £400 or less. Most of the farmers and shepherds from Teviothead who attended the Sales were in this section of the audience. There was movement up and down within this section. When a tup that a farmer wanted to bid for was in the ring, he would move down closer to the ring to get a better look at the tup and to be more visible to the auctioneer. He would drift back up into the stands when he was not bidding where he marked his catalog and discussed the sale with those nearby. The breeders who were socially closest to the tups were also physically closest to the ring. They took up the best and closest vantage points just around the central stage of the auction: they leaned over the wall of the ring, they sat on the benches lining the inside of the wall, and they congregated just outside the exit gates where they could see the tups in the holding pens just prior to their entry into the ring, could peer over and through the exit gates during the bidding, and could be seen by the auctioneer.

For the bidding, each tup was herded into the ring individually by its breeder/s (including the son if there was one involved in the breeding). The auctioneer provided two men to help control the tup. This was a presentation of an exclusive link between breeder and tup because, unless there was no one else, the farm's shepherd was not in the ring, even if he had helped with the preparations. In some cases, if it was widely known that an expert shepherd was responsible for breeding the tup, he joined the farmer in the ring as an acknowledgement of his skills. Other of the farm personnel and their friends stayed outside to help push each successive tup into the ring in the correct order. Like store lamb auctions, there was no official reserve price set for each tup. Instead, prior to the sale of their tups breeders had to get a feel for the bidding to determine whether or not to accept the highest bid. The few tups that were passed in were the ones that received bids of less than £40. This seemed to be the level at which criticism became insult; it was equivalent to what the animal would get at cast tup sales where poor quality rams are sold for slaughter.

Figure 8.1   Ram Auction, Lockerbie Auction Mart

At the end of the bidding, the auctioneer announced the final purchase price and identified the buyer by name. Prices for tups ranged from £40 to £3000 with occasional tups attracting bids as high as £6000; the average prices of tups from individual breeders ranged from £50 to £900. From my discussions with breeders, commercial farmers and shepherds, there was general agreement on two points: first, individual tups fetching prices less than £800 were "commercial" tups and those in excess of £1200 were definitely top class tups; and second, those breeders whose tups averaged more than £450 were usually among the clique of top breeders.

These certainly seem to be accurate assessments of the bidding patterns. In the Lockerbie Sales I attended, the ten to twelve breeders with the highest averages and highest priced tups were from the visiting circle that formed the limits of the clique; and the buyers of the ten to twelve most expensive tups were also from the clique. But, then, as I described earlier, I was not the only one at the auction carefully taking notes. When all the tups from each breeder had been sold, the average price was immediately calculated by those marking catalogs and a list was kept of the tups that received the highest bids. Thus throughout the auction a sort of "community of knowledge" about how each breeder was faring in relation to others spread among all the participants, and by the end of the auction everyone knew whose tups received the best prices and which breeders had the highest averages.

At the Lockerbie Sales I attended in the 1980s and early 1990s, about twenty tups fetched prices in excess of £1500 and all were from breeders in the visiting circle and all were purchased by breeders from the clique or those wishing to enter it; and about ten breeders attained averages in excess of £450 and again all were in the clique. The members of the clique lived up to the "I'll buy yours and you buy mine" strategy, as one onlooker put it to me. However, despite the seeming inevitability of this *general outcome*, there was a genuine air of excitement and suspense to the auction. One important feature of this excitement was the *particular outcome* that individual breeders in the clique would experience. The fortunes of individual breeders varied from year to year: in one year achieving among the highest averages and individual price and in the following year a low average and relatively low price for the "best" tup. And given the practice of marking the catalogs, the results for each breeder were known and communicated around the audience so that as the auction continued there was constant and building suspense about how the next breeder would fare in relation to the previous ones. The joy of victory was palpably evident in the bar as the breeder with the highest average and/or individual tup bought drinks expansively. Another feature of the excitement and suspense was seeing which individual breeders bid against each other for the best tups and how much they were willing to pay. Again, there was delight on the part of the breeder who bought the highest price tup and disappointment for those who were unsuccessful in purchasing a top quality tup. But then, there was always next year.

Circulation and Redistribution of Tups, Status and Identity

There are several analytic comments to make about patterns of bidding that relate to the transactional strategies of status differentiation and closure adopted by members of the clique. Some of these strategies were remarkably similar to marriage strategies that in the anthropological literature are called direct exchange and circulating connubium and they had similar consequences for inclusion and exclusion. I have already hinted at the essence of the strategies which breeders and commercial farmers alike recognized and understood. Breeders in the clique symmetrically offer very high prices for each others' tups. It was also said that members of the clique bid artificially high prices for each others' tup "so that *everyone* in the clique gets the respect, esteem and reputation as a top breeder."

There were four consequences of their bidding strategies. First, by *reciprocally* buying each others' best tups, members of the clique did not have to actually expend money for the tups because over several years they would spend on tups of other breeders what they received from other breeders who bought their tups. Some members even organized before hand a direct exchange: two breeders would agree to buy a specific tup from the other for the same price. Although there were not identified trading partners, the overall effect was a kula-like ring with money and tups moving around the clique both within one auction and over several years of auctions. As tups and money circulate, at any one auction the status fortunes of individual breeders fluctuate in relation to the others with some breeder or breeders in the clique getting a very low average and their best tup receiving lower than expected bids. But as long as they continued purchasing expensive tups, their status fortunes and the prices of their tups improved in later years. Over time, then, nothing happened to the financial and social status of members in relation to each other. To put this another way, the result of this circulation was a general pool of money and genes that constituted, reproduced, and socially differentiated the clique and that represented their common identity.[11]

Second, breeders in the clique made money from the sale of their lesser quality tups to commercial farmers outside the clique. In this pattern of exchange, there was in effect a redistributive system. Money from commercial farmers flowed into the clique and the knowledge and stockmanship of the breeders embodied in the genetic pool, that even their lesser quality tups benefited from, flowed back into the flocks of the commercial farmers. In this sense, then, the genetic pool of top breeders' tups that embodies their consummate stockmanship infuses flocks of hill sheep farms generally in the Borders. This is why the annual Lockerbie Sales was so important: it was on the one hand a celebration and mechanism for creating a shared sentiment of Border hill sheep farming inclusive of both breeders and commercial farmers and on the other hand it reproduced the status differentiation between them.

Third, because of the financial neutrality of the "I'll buy yours if you buy mine" strategy, clique members could bid quite high prices for the tups. These inflated prices excluded most non-clique breeders of only commercial tups from buying their tups, entering the clique and being accorded the status as a top breeder. This was an exclusion that shepherds particularly felt because in several cases they were the better stockmen. In the sales that I attended, shepherds' rams rarely fetched the same prices as those of the breeders for whom they worked. One shepherd who had an acknowledged very good tup received bids of less than £1000. He told me bitterly . that if this same tup had been the breeders, his mates would have bid it up to nearly £2000. He was even more embittered several years later when a shepherd's ram that he felt was no better than his fetched over £3000. Just as tups and breeder were reciprocal reflections of each other, so were pack tups and shepherds; and just as there was a dimension of competition among the top breeders each year to see whose tups— and whose stockmanship—were best, so there was a separate competition among the shepherds of these top breeders to see whose tups fetched the highest bids. These two realms of competition were kept separate by the high price of the breeders tups which shepherds could not afford to buy. The difference between them was that the top breeders controlled the relative status among shepherds because they gave their evaluations of the shepherds through their bidding.

Fourth, the strategy was used to drop members from the clique on the principle that "the tup breeders will not buy expensive tups off you if you do not buy expensive tups off them." One of the breeders suffered this fate when for two successive years he stopped bidding high prices at the sales. In the third year, the average price of this tups dropped dramatically because, as one onlooker remarked to me, "he's no longer in the clique."

What I have been trying to demonstrate in this discussion is that, like the art auctions described by Baudrillard, through reciprocally bidding high prices that other farmers and shepherds cannot afford to pay, the clique of top breeders "seals their parity…and thus their collective caste privilege with respect to all others, from whom they are no longer separated merely by their purchasing power, but by the sumptuary and collective act of the production and exchange of sign values" (1981:117). Yet, Baudrillard's account does not recognize the way tups were not just sign values of the clique of top breeders but also, through the redistribution of commercial tups, they were sign values for a hill sheep farming community in the Borders.

Notes

1. In the 1997 Lockerbie Auction, a fifth farmer from Teviothead offered his first tups for sale.
2. They were considered by the farmer and by the tax department to own the pack.
3. Unless otherwise specified, the following account refers to the farmer breeders rather than shepherd breeders.
4. Even on tup breeding farms where the hired shepherd is the expert, farmers attended the selections of sale tup lambs because *their* tups—I purposely emphasize the possessive here—presented for sale at Lockerbie expressed their personhood and farms, though it was known that the tups embodied the skills of the expert shepherds. There is a tendency for shepherds who are interested in tup breeding to apply for jobs at farms specialising in tup breeding. Just as the Australian economy is said to ride on the back of its sheep so the status of a tup breeder rides on the back of his sale tups.
5. This notion of "breeding well" with a specific flock of ewes was the defence breeders put up to the kind of critical story I presented above where the less expensive tup produced the better lambs.

6. The prices quoted throughout this chapter are representative of the late 1980s and early 1990s sales. By 1996, there had been significant inflation in these prices so that highest price tups were over £2000 up to £10,000 and the highest averages were about £1000.

7. On the two farms in Teviothead where the shepherds stockmanship was primary, they did the grooming with little help from the farmer.

8. On some tups, a portion of a horn may be cut off to repair damage done in a fight or to prevent it from growing back into the head.

9. In addition to the top breeders who visited this farm, there were several farmers and shepherds from Teviothead farms, interested in breeding but not part of the clique, who were invited to visit on the quieter nights.

10. A couple of hours before the auction begins, there is a judged competition to select the best individual tup and the best group of three tups. Entry into the competition is voluntary, but most of the top breeders entered because, if their tups win any prizes, it enhances their chances of attracting high bids.

11. From the mid-1990s, responding to the criticisms and to the necessity of expanding the market for high priced tups, the clique began to become self-consciously less exclusive and the tups of breeders who wished to enter it began to attract high bids, some of them from members of the clique from whom they had for several years been purchasing expensive tups.

THE BIG HOUSE

Farmers and Shepherds

I turn to the notion of "class" to draw together and elaborate upon ethnographic material about the relations between farmers and shepherds scattered throughout the preceding chapters. The concept of class has everyday and academic contexts of use for describing rural localities in the United Kingdom. People in Teviothead used it as freely in their discussions of their own social relations as scholars like Littlejohn (1963) did in analyzing social relations in the neighboring valley of Eskdalemuir.[1] In this respect, Bourdieu (1990a:59ff) reminds us not to conflate the understanding that arises from an ethnologist adopting a disinterested and external theoretical posture to a social phenomenon with the understanding that arises from people adopting a committed and interested practical relation to it in their everyday lives. His caution is particularly important for the analysis of "class" on Border hill sheep farms because there is an apparent similarity in the meaning of the word as used by farming people and by academic anthropologists and sociologists. For both, farmers and shepherds are members of different classes because of their differing relations to the means of production, i.e., capital, that are the result of large-scale historical, economic, and/or political processes. However, the particular ways farmers and shepherds experience class membership and practice class interactions with each other—the ways of making sense of their place in social space (Bourdieu

1990a:128)—are not reducible to these relations of production nor can they be treated as simply sequiturs to forces of a
materialist history, policies of the European Community, or
impacts of agricultural markets.

This perspective on the analysis of class is consonant with
that adopted by a number of scholars (see Sahlins 1981, 1985;
de Certeau 1984; Bourdieu 1984, 1987, 1990a; Ortner 1989;
and Jackson 1996) to deal with the issue of how to relate global
and local processes. In one form or another, they resist simply
according decisiveness to global institutions and processes in
the shaping of local social life. Privileging the fields or context
of everyday action, some argue that local social worlds have an
endogenous particularity and inertia that "refracts external
forces according to its internal structure" (Wacquant 1992:17)
or "mediates the impact of external events by shaping the ways
in which actors experience and respond to those events" (Ortner 1989:200). Privileging the agent, others argue that "no
matter what constituting power we assign to the impersonal
forces of history, language, and upbringing, the subject always
figures ... as the [local] site where these forces find expression
and are played out" (Jackson 1996:22), or in consuming the
representations "imposed by a dominant economic order,"
people in everyday life "use them with respect to ends and references foreign to the system they had no choice but to
accept" (de Certeau 1984:xiii). In another ethnographic context I adopted a similar stance phrased as a critique of an "outside-in" approach in anthropology (see Gray 1995; Gray and
Mearns 1989). I was referring to the common theoretical
stance and narrative strategy in which smaller-scale social phenomena, like households or family farms, are best understood
by locating them in national or global social, historical, and
cultural processes and that these latter determine the character and function of the former. It is like the determinist
assumptions of Newtonian physics in which universal laws of
motion are used to predict (i.e., explain) the action of any
body of mass no matter what its particular form; or it is like the
structuralist assumptions of Dumont's (1980) portrayal of
Indian society in which a society-wide principle (the opposition between the pure and the impure) is manifest in (i.e.,
explains) a variety of social phenomena (marriage rules, food
exchanges, *jajmani* relations, and political organization within

villages) with little attention given to their distinctiveness. One consequence of this approach is that smaller-scale realms of social life, and the people living in them, become epiphenomena because their attributes and actions are analytically exhausted in manifesting these wider forces. In this approach, small-scale social domains have no particularity in their own right and the people living in them are denied the creative and constitutive effects of their actions that are motivated by their pragmatic concerns of daily life.

While not denying the insights afforded by an outside-in approach, I adopt an ethnographic strategy that identifies what might be thought of as an existentially primary social domain whose structure "refracts" and "mediates" external forces and in which these forces are "played out" by agents living their daily lives. Such domains, where people spend qualitatively and quantitatively most of their lives, are usually small in social scale. They are characterized by a high density of face-to-face social relations and an intimacy of mutual knowledge. In Nepal I suggested that the *pariwar* (household) is this type of small-scale social domain and that it mediates and refracts hierarchical caste relations in Nepal. It is the principal domain where villagers engage in and directly experience caste relations on a daily basis; and the household imparts a particular spin upon the practice of these relations and villagers' understanding of them (Gray 1995). In Teviothead, it is the hill sheep farm that is the principal small-scale, socially dense and intimate domain where people practice and understand class relations.[2] My analysis of class, then, follows how it is consumed or played out on hill sheep farms and how hill sheep farms inflect the way farmers and shepherds experience class. In this respect, a subtext of the previous chapters has been to describe some dimensions of a hill sheep farm's social relations that give it a particularity and social inertia in refracting external forces so that each class has its own "place" spatially and socially on hill sheep farms.

Farmers and Shepherds

In the neighboring hill sheep farming valley of Eskdalemuir, Littlejohn describes a three-tiered class structure consisting of "gentleman farmers," "working farmer," and "working folk" (1963:80). He conducted his research between 1949 and 1951. By the time I arrived in the Borders thirty years later, there were hardly any farms left in Eskdalemuir and no "gentleman farmers" in Teviothead.[3] The words "farmer" and "shepherd" were used to name class categories and to designate the class membership of people living and working on hill sheep farms. In Chapter 5, I suggested that ownership of sheep overshadows the status implications of different forms of tenure relations to a farm. Thus in materialist terms, "farmers" are those who had some form of legal access to the means of production: as owner-occupiers, tenants or Partners of a farm but most importantly as private owners of livestock. The designation is also used, with the kin terms of reference, for members of the farmer's family (i.e., farmer's wife, farmer's son, farmer's daughter) to indicate their inclusion in the class labelled "farmer." In this respect, in the early 1990s, there were approximately seventy "farmers" in Teviothead. The term "shepherd" refers to those who own neither land nor livestock and who are hired by farmers to take care of a hirsel of sheep. In these terms, in the early 1990s there were eleven shepherds working on eight farms. Because of the cultural and financial importance of sheep, the term "shepherd" is sometimes extended to include other "farm workers" that are hired to do cattle rearing and/or tractor work on the four farms where there is significant arable cultivation. As with the term "farmer", "shepherd" or "farm worker" is used for members of employees' families to indicate their inclusion in that class. The population of shepherds and farm workers was approximately fifty persons.[4]

The global or national conditions that led to this situation are inadequate to understand how farmers and shepherds interact with each other except in the most general terms of control and resistance or dominance and subordination. These themes are present in class relations, but the specific way they are understood and practiced by farmers and shepherds is inflected by the nature of hill sheep farms. I address them indirectly at first through analyzing three facets of the way people relate themselves and others to class that I found remarkable in Teviothead: an ambivalence about the existence or importance of classes, a presumed gender difference in sensitivity to class, and a pattern of mutual mis-representation of each other's financial situation as a way of explaining class position and lack of mobility.[5]

Do Classes Exist?

One of the most striking attributes of class in Teviothead was the differing views of farmers and shepherds about the existence and significance of classes in understanding their relations.

FARMERS. A few farmers denied the existence of class differences, but most suggested that they were much less important in the social relations between farmers and shepherds now than in the past. In making these assessments they were using the presence or absence of "gentleman farmers"—the highest class in Littlejohn's (1963) three-tier model—as the point of comparison. Several made this explicit in a manner similar to this farmer and his wife:

> *Husband*: Class used to be an important part of life in the community but very little is left of it now. There used to be gentleman farmers who did no farm work on the farm but had hired laborers to do it all. Now most farms are "working farms" where the farmer does farm work along side his workers.

> *Wife*: When Bill's [her husband's] father was farming, he was that kind of gentleman farmer. They lived in the "big house," but he did get out and help his workers at the busy times, like clipping. Everyone had to work at the busy times. In this area [Teviothead] when most farmers were gentlemen farmers ... every farm had a tennis court but now very few still have them.

The argument embedded in these comments is that in the past there had been gentleman farmers in Teviothead—the last ones leaving or retiring in the early 1980s—but now that there are no longer any in Teviothead, class does not exist or is much less a dimension of social relations between farmers and shepherds. What practical concerns motivates this stance, which as we shall see is contradicted by shepherds?

The image of gentleman farmers is a taken-for-granted historical background that continues to provide the archetype of a person to whom class is important. Gentlemen farmers are attributed with four characteristics. First, they did not do any farm work and hired workers to do the shepherding and other tasks. From the perspective of contemporary farmers and shepherds, this is indicative of the wealth of gentleman farmers. They could afford to pay at least one extra worker so that the gentleman farmer and family members did not have to engage in any farm work but were at leisure all day—hence the reference to tennis courts. Second and consequently, gentleman farmers were not skilled stockmen and had little practical knowledge of farming. Third, they lived in "the big house," a phrase that one farmer explained as follows: "When people use the phrase 'the big house' they are saying that the person who lives in it owned or tenanted the place [farm]." Gentleman farmers displayed their class status in the form of an imposing farmhouse that was expensively furnished relative to workers' cottages. Fourth, gentleman farmers were "snobs," translating their economic difference into moral superiority through acts of social distancing. Snobbery is a way of talking about people as if class difference is indicative of a fundamental moral inequality between people. As snobs, gentleman farmers "did not mix" with people of lower classes: they did not talk with those working on the farm in both farm and nonfarm contexts; they did not invite them into the big house; they generally avoided interacting with them; they did not go to the pub where shepherds spent their leisure; and they acted as if they were better than those working on the farms. The use of the term "snob" or "snobbery" in discussions with me was often accompanied by the gesture of pushing the nose up with a finger that people said meant gentleman farmers "had their noses in the air" and "looked down their nose" at those in lower classes. It is this portrayal of social distancing, accompanied by vertical images of up and down for the stance of moral superiority, and a denial of a fundamental equality between humans taken by gentleman farmers that Teviothead farmers (and shepherds) find most distasteful.

Embedded in this representation of gentleman farmers is a model of class relations. Farmers are in a separate class because they own the livestock. One farmer was quite explicit about this saying: "The Buccleuch Estate would want a prospective tenant to have enough capital to stock the farm properly ... the biggest obstacle [to becoming a farmer] is a shepherd's lack of capital to start a farm." However, it is not this economic difference per se that farmers are attempting to deny by their de-emphasizing the importance of class in contemporary social relations. The fact of differences between farmers and shepherds is freely admitted but what is not accepted is that difference is indicative of moral inequality. One farmer told me: "The communist ideal [i.e., classless society with everyone equal] is fine in theory but it will not work in practice. People will always make classes … they will always make differences between themselves. Even if the people are poor, they will still make classes." Another said:

> In an agricultural community, there are two kinds or classes of people—farmers and shepherds. But all are involved with sheep—it is a common interest which binds everyone together in the farming community. Within this community and its type of people, you find a level and accept an individual at that level. But no matter at what level an individual may be, he is still a respected member of the community.

The other dimension of the gentleman farmer model of class relations is that farmers act morally superior to shepherds and other farm workers. It is this association of class with gentleman farmers and the infamous snobbery of gentleman farmers—and its denial of equality—that contemporary farmers in Teviothead are attempting to disavow in disputing the existence or strength of class in social relations in local social life. If they accept the existence or continuing importance of class, they have to accept that as farmers they are in the superordinate position; and if they are in the superordinate position, it implies that they are snobs. One of the farmers who had most explicitly and fervently rejected the existence of class relations in Teviothead said: "It's like we should feel wrong to be in a farmer's class." Here he recognized the existence of a farmer class but was denying the snobbery historically associated with it. After hearing the outlines of this interpretation from me one evening, a shepherd's wife said to me: "You've really sussed them out … you really ken the farmers."

Farmers distance themselves from the snobbery implications of the gentleman farmer class model by referring to themselves as "practical" or "working" farmers. In effect, they adopt a two-tier class structure of farmer and shepherd. The characteristics of working farmers are precisely the converse of those of gentleman farmers that are objectionable because of the denial of individual moral equality. Again, farmers use the same code of social distance/closeness for expressing their rejection of moral superiority and the acceptance of equality. Working farmers, as the term is meant to indicate, actually do farm work so that for them their mode of life more closely resembled that of shepherds than that of gentleman farmers. Second, working farmers are good stockmen and have farming knowledge and skills so that they can do most of the jobs on the farm that hired shepherds do. Third, in cooperative tasks where they work with and beside hired shepherds, working farmers mix with their workers, speaking with them freely and comfortably. Fourth, working farmers do not have the excessive wealth of gentleman farmers so that they are not economically different from shepherds. As I will describe later, farmers elaborate on this theme by saying that shepherds are financially better off than farmers.

SHEPHERDS. Whereas farmers deny or distance themselves from class, shepherds accept that class exists, that they are in a distinct class subordinate to farmers, and that farmers avoid mixing with them, and they feel they are treated as inferior by farmers. In addition, they also are aware that some farmers say that class does not exist. As one shepherd said: "Those farmers who deny class the most are the worst … that's a general rule." The following three excerpts from my fieldnotes typify shepherds' views on the existence of classes in Teviothead and the nature of their relations with farmers.

Excerpt 1

One evening, I was talking with a farmer and his wife about whether or not class differences existed or were still important in Teviothead. The farmer said: "it depends who you talk to." He then named three shepherds of other farms who definitely acted on the basis of class differences. They were known to "do a farmer" at the pub, that is, to spend an evening exchanging stories and comments that were highly critical of one farmer for his class characteristics: not being a good stockman, not mixing, and being snobbish. The farmer then mentioned that the shepherd working on his farm was not like this. Yet this same shepherd told me: "There's a lot of class distinction in Teviothead compared to Liddesdale … In Liddesdale, workers, farmers and ordinary people mixed better … here farmers don't seem to want to mix."

Excerpt 2

I mentioned to a shepherd that some farmers said there was no class in the valley. He responded: "I don't know which farmers you've been talking to!… I don't know how a farmer could say that." Then he went on to say, in a way that recalled some attributes of gentleman farmers:

> Farmers think they are a wee bit better than the working man … a working man has to watch what he's saying now because jobs are scarce … farmers don't think they need the working man as much … farms are becoming more family farms [farms where family members of the owner/tenant do most of the farm work] … farmers think they can do without the farm workers if it came to the crunch … but in the end farmers couldn't do the work and couldn't do without the working man.

Excerpt 3

Mary responded to my question about the existence of classes with some vehemence:

> They do exist! I know, I am the daughter of a worker. As a young girl and teenager, I would bring eggs and bread to the house of a farmer. For all the years I brought eggs and bread to their house, I was never invited in. My mother was never invited in either. Then, the farmer got very sick. One day I was asked to come in and help nurse him. That day the farmer died. I was comforting the wife and children—some were crying on my shoulder. People who wouldn't speak to me or my family were crying on my shoulder. I'm cheeky. I said to them, "You know this is the first time I've ever been in your house in all these years."

I mentioned to her one of the farmers who had denied the existence of class relations. Mary's immediate response was: "That's because he's one of the worst. I went to school at the same time as he did and he never really spoke with children of workers. It's sheer snobbery … and one of the worst snobs in the valley was his mother."

There is a remarkable converse similarity between these views and those expressed by farmers. We saw above that farmers differentiate themselves from the characteristics of gentleman farmers and liken themselves to hired shepherds as a mode of denying the implications of class for social distancing, moral superiority, and snobbery. Implicitly shepherds use the same class archetype of the gentleman farmer, but their discourse moves in the opposite direction, pushing the actions and attitudes of farmers closer to gentlemen farmers and further from their own characteristics and style of life. Like farmers, they use it as a strategy for accepting the existence of class differences; but unlike farmers they also use it to criticize contemporary farmers, even if they are working farmers, for the superiority that they display toward them. They draw upon the same attributes of gentleman farmers—not being as good stockman as shepherds, not mixing with and acting superior to shepherds. As discussed in an earlier chapter on hill herding, an attribute of stockmanship is the ability to "ken your sheep." As one shepherd explained:

> It's the ability to recognize individual sheep and to remember them. If you're a kenner, you get to know individual sheep after the first year of herding them, even after they have been clipped when it's not so easy to ken the sheep without their wool … people are born kenners of sheep. It's only when you're with sheep all the time that you develop your ability as a kenner.

I then asked him to name the good kenners in Teviothead. He named nine, including himself. When I pointed out that all of the good kenners he named were hired shepherds, he thought for a moment and said, "that's about right", adding: "It's more than just being able to look at a sheep and judge its qualities … most folk, including farmers, would be able to do that." Another shepherd, who had "flit" from a farm to herding on another farm, explained: "William [the farmer] was a bit too bossy, always looking over my shoulder [scrutinizing how I was doing my job and telling me how to do my job], and *really not knowing that much about sheep.*"

Shepherds talked critically about farmers among themselves in pubs and with me in their homes or while we were walking around their hirsels. A constant theme of their discussions was that farmers "do not mix": they don't drink often at the pub like shepherds and when they do, they form their own "companies"; they do not join in the winter indoor bowls at the community hall, but rather go curling at commercial ice rinks, which shepherds said made the sport too expensive for them; and they do not invite workers into their houses socially. In the words of a shepherd: "when was a shepherd ever invited to a farmer's dinner party?" One person pointed out that farmers and shepherds did mix at dances and Whist Drives at the Community Hall. But then after a moment's reflection, he added: "People in Teviothead are supporting the Hall rather than going out and mixing with farmers and shepherds." Here he was implying that farmers and shepherds do not go to these functions for the purpose of mixing with each other; rather farmers and shepherds go "to support the Hall" (more precisely to support their community that the Hall symbolizes) and because of that they are in a situation where they meet each other.

Shepherds even use the same nasal and directional metaphor for class position and the moral inequality implied by acts of snobbery. When farmers talk about snobbery [though they did not consider themselves as snobs], they push their noses up in the air with a finger. One shepherd described a farmer he thought was a "snobby" as follows: "John Elliott [farmer] is stuck up, I wouldn't want to work for him, he thinks he is above everyone ... His nose is always in the air." Two other farmers were said to "look down their noses at shepherds and farm workers."

Gender and Class

There is a perceived difference between men and women in the sensitivity to and importance of class. This difference was remarked upon widely by men and women of both classes. Women are said to be more conscious of class differences: farmers' wives are more likely to act "classy" in the company of shepherds' wives, and shepherds' wives are more likely to take offense at their treatment by farmers' wives. The monthly meetings of the Women's Rural Institute ("the Rural") and the Church Guild ("the Guild") are contexts where wives of farmers and shepherds congregate. I did not attend these meetings, but events purported to occur in them were referred to as exemplifying women's heightened sensitivity to class. In describing these meetings, women emphasized the same theme of social distancing through not mixing. It was said that at the meetings of the Women's Rural Institute, farmers' wives and shepherds' wives sit separately for the supper. Another woman who classified herself as a shepherd's wife related the following story:

> The house my mother lived in for over twenty-four years was near a farmer's house. My mother and the farmer's wife would speak to each other and get along fine. Both were members of the Rural and the farmer's wife would usually give my mother a ride to the meetings. But at the meetings, the farmer's wife would mix only with other farmers' wives and she wouldn't speak to my mother at the meetings.

Men, conversely, are said to be "less classy." The common explanation for farmers and shepherds being less overtly sensitive to class differences and the social practices that constitute them goes thus: men have a genuine common interest in sheep; they have to work together on the farm, and cooperation between farmer and shepherd is important for the success of sheep farming. As a result, in farm work contexts farmers and shepherds have to establish a "working relationship" and a mutual respect. They cannot afford to take offense every time class differences are implied by a farmer giving an instruction, deciding not to spend money on equipment or tups for a shepherd's hirsel, or not being available for sheep work because of other commitments (such as bookwork, overseas holidays, or leisure activities).

Class Mobility

A third feature of class relations that I found remarkable is the way in which farmers and shepherds (mis)construe each others' financial circumstances and responsibilities and their implications for the possibility of shepherds' class mobility. For both farmers and shepherds, the main obstacle to shepherds becoming farmers is the lack of capital that would enable them to buy a farm, to be considered by the Buccleuch Estate for a tenancy, or to purchase livestock. The pattern I am referring to can be illustrated by a short interchange between a shepherd and a farmer that I witnessed one September afternoon. I was at a farm where the shepherd Hamish was primarily responsible for the sale tups for the upcoming Lockerbie sales. We were at the folds near the shed where the tups were housed when a farmer, Walter, drove up.[6] Hamish turned to me and said that Walter was probably coming to have a look at the tups. As the farmer approached, the following interchange (and my interpretation) occurred:

> *Hamish* [in a joking manner]: Must be nice to be a farmer. (Interpretation: It must be nice to be a farmer who has so little work and lots of spare time to go around in his car in the afternoon to look at other people's tups.)

> *Walter* [in the same joking manner]: You couldn't cope with the worry. (Interpretation: There's more to farming than working. You could not cope with a farmer's responsibility of paper work, financial planning, getting European Community subsidies and grants, and making the farm financially viable as a business.)

Embedded in this brief exchange between Hamish and Walter are stereotypes of farmers and shepherds that farmers and shepherds use to explain why each is in his respective class position and more specifically why shepherds usually can not obtain the capital necessary to become a farmer. In the following, I closely paraphrase these stereotypes and group them according to which class expressed them and which class they supposedly characterized.

FARMERS ON SHEPHERDS. Shepherds waste their money drinking at the pub, so they cannot save enough to build up the capital to buy livestock or to be eligible for a bank loan for the livestock.

Shepherds lack discipline. They want immediate pleasure and put indulging themselves (i.e., drinking at the pub) before discipline and long-term planning.

Shepherding is a cushy job: they get steady wages, lots of perks (cottage, some utilities, potatoes, and coal), and limited responsibility.

FARMERS ON FARMERS. The personal drawings we (farmers) take from the farm are no different from the wages and costs of a shepherd. So we are not better off financially than shepherds.

We can't afford to drink at the pub; it's better to put the money back into the farm. Farmers have discipline; we put the farm as a whole before indulging ourselves (i.e., going to the pub a couple of times a week).

Farmers have a long-term commitment to the farm and the community (implying that shepherds do not have such a commitment because they do not have relations of tenure to a farm and do not own livestock).

In these stereotypes, farmers emphasize general personality traits of farmers and shepherds. The most important trait for a farmer in explaining class differences is discipline—manifest in a high level of financial restraint. Unlike shepherds, farmers do not spend money for immediate pleasure, but take a long-term perspective by using farm income to improve the farm business and finding pleasure in a successful farm. Further, most farmers thought that shepherds' wages are quite high, some even saying that "my shepherds make more than I do," that is, they pay shepherds more than they take from the farm for their own personal spending. Even if farmers have the potential to draw from the farm's earnings a personal income that is greater than that paid to shepherds, they have the discipline not to do so and to redirect the money into productive rather then pleasurable ends. There was an element here of class-serving misconstruction of the comparative financial situations of farmers and shepherds. It may be that if only the direct personal drawings by a farmer are considered, then in some cases the assertion that a shepherd earns more than a farmer is accurate in a narrow sense. Not only do farmers have a large capital base in livestock, machinery, and property, but, as one farmer recognized: "… it's an unfair comparison because a lot of things my shepherd has to pay for out of his wages are paid for directly out of the farm account and not out of my personal drawings … electrical power, petrol, vehicles, etc., aren't paid for out of my personal drawings."

What is not at issue in farmers' stereotypes is that shepherds have sufficient knowledge of livestock and the stockmanship skill to be a farmer. The reason why they are unable to "get a farm" is that they lack a long-term perspective and discipline necessary to save the money and to prove to bank managers they have the financial responsibility to run a successful farm. One farmer specifically addressed this issue in response to my remarking that it would be difficult

for a shepherd to become a farmer because of the lack of
start-up capital:

> I disagree. If shepherds really wanted to become farmers, they
> could obtain the capital though it would not be easy. I did it.
> Even though I came from a farming family, I raised enough
> capital on my own to become a tenant on this farm. I started
> from scratch ... worked for several years as a shepherd ... saved
> my salary and came into this farm with £5000 and borrowed
> heavily at the start.

He then explained how a shepherd might raise the capital to
become a tenant farmer:

> A shepherd makes £200 a week cash.[7] He and his family, by
> skimping [exercizing restraint and discipline] a lot, could live
> on £70 a week. Thus of his £10,000 a year cash salary, it would
> cost the shepherd about £3500 to live. To supplement the food
> he buys, the shepherd would have to be quick at getting dead
> sheep and grow vegetables to save money. By saving £6500 a
> year, in six years he would have capital of £39,000 plus interest.
> Any bank manager would be impressed with such a shepherd's
> ability to save money with discipline. In these circumstances,
> the bank would probably support financially the shepherd's
> bid for a farm tenancy.

SHEPHERDS ON FARMERS. Farmers have lots of money; they
drive around in BMWs and Rovers, take overseas vacations
and can afford to go curling in winter.

Farmers look after themselves; they could pay us more so
we could be the same (class), but they don't so they can
remain feeling superior—even though they are no better
than shepherds.

SHEPHERDS ON SHEPHERDS. We have the skills and abilities to
be farmers. We could do the farm work and the bookwork.

What is holding us back is having the money to buy into
a farm; and farmers look after themselves in deciding on who
gets a tenancy so that we can't get a farm.

Like farmers' stereotypes, those of shepherds also portray themselves as possessing the knowledge of livestock and
stockmanship to successfully be a farmer. Nor is the issue one
of their personality traits. Instead it is a lack of capital that
results from farmers who "indulge" themselves with expen-

sive cars and holidays instead of paying more wages to shepherds. Again, there is a converse similarity between farmers and shepherds in their class-serving misconstruction of each other's financial situations. For shepherds, farmers have plenty of money to do almost anything they please, so if they wanted to pay shepherds more to help them accumulate the capital for a farm, they could. But farmers do not want to do this because they want to maintain their dominant class position. Yet, again under some questioning by me, they admitted that there are lots of expenses in running a farm and that farmers have high levels of debt and overdrafts that they need to pay off to stay in business.

I have given detailed accounts of these dimensions of class practice—including people's talk about it—because for me they represent how farmers and shepherds play out in Teviothead what Jackson in the earlier quotation called "the impersonal forces of history ...." (1996:22). The issue now is to illustrate how the hill sheep farm refracts these impersonal forces of history "according to its own internal structure" (Wacquant 1992:17) to produce what I found to be some remarkable dimensions of class in Teviothead. In previous chapters on the division of farm space and labor for shepherding and breeding I have laid the groundwork for doing so.

The Spatial Organization of Class on Hill Sheep Farms

In Eskdalemuir, another valley of hill sheep farmers not too distant in time and space from Teviotdale, Littlejohn found that "Each person knows his or her place in the [local class] system" (1963:112). He is of course referring to "place" in a social sense of people being able to accurately ascribe their own and others' membership in a class category.[8] However, on hill sheep farms the sense of class-place is more than social; it is also spatial. Further, the spatial sense—and sensation—of class-place is constitutive of the particular social-sense of class-place and the asymmetry between classes. The spatiality of class is embedded in the distinctive territorial organization of sheep and division of farm labor such that farmers and shepherds each have a distinct place of responsibility on the farm and as a result are in a particular hierarchical relation to each other.

Recall that a hired shepherd's principal responsibility was to care for a hirsel of ewes and that the concept of hirsel refers simultaneously to those ewes and the place on the hill where they graze. The cottages where shepherds live are located as close as possible to their hirsels and often quite distant from the farmhouse. The spatial distance of hirsel and cottage from farmhouse and farmer is replicated in supervisory distance. Shepherds are largely independent from daily scrutiny by the farmer of their herding and sheep. They organize and experience their everyday lives in terms of what is appropriate for the proper care of their hirsel. Shepherds accept personal responsibility for the quality of the ewes of their hirsel and the lambs they produce. The lambs embody their stockmanship and personal value, and this is one of the reasons why the bids their lambs receive and the farmer is willing to accept at store auctions are taken seriously by shepherds. Thus, through their herding a hirsel, shepherds make their place on the farm in a spatial as well as a social sense. A shepherd's place, the hirsel, represents only a part of any hill sheep farm. Not only are there other hirsels on over half the farms, but all farms, even those with only one hill hirsel of sheep, have other income-producing operations, such as breeding park sheep and suckler cattle. In sum, then, a shepherd's sense of place on a farm revolves around his hirsel that links him to a specific area of the farm's land and with only part of the farm's flock of hill ewes.

A farmer's sense of place is the farm as a whole. The labor of the farmer and his family is spread over the entire range of farm operations including hill herding, caring and feeding park sheep and cattle, arable cultivation, and maintenance. Unlike shepherds, there is no "typical" hill sheep farmer in terms of the type of work activities performed; each farmer is different because of the personal preferences and stockmanship of the farmer and family members and the skills of other workers on the farm. Despite this, all farmers take responsibility for two of the farm's most important activities no matter what their stockmanship skills or personal preferences.

The first is overseeing the breeding program of the whole flock. We have seen how tups embody the stockmanship of farmers because they make or approve the choice of tup lambs, the rotation of tups around the farm's cuts, and the buying in of tups. Tups are rotated to different cuts every two years, and this had two consequences: tups are not linked spatially or expressively to any one hirsel or shepherd, and tups give the farm's flock its distinctiveness as a whole. Since farmers take a dominant role in selecting home bred tup lambs, in deciding how much to pay for which tups at auctions, and in organizing the rotation of tups around the farm's cuts, tups and the whole flock embody their stockmanship as well as the natural characteristics of the farm's land.

The other activity for which farmers or members of their families are responsible is a range of administrative, financial and business activities that are glossed by the term "bookwork." It includes consulting catalogs and ordering supplies, buying machinery, recording income from sales, keeping the VAT book (i.e., recording purchases that were exempt from Value Added Tax), long-term financial planning, keeping up with advances in veterinary procedures, filling in forms for the Department of Agriculture of the European Community, and reading and understanding all the United Kingdom and European Community agricultural regulations, subsidy programs, and development grant schemes. These tasks are essential to the success of a farm over time. Development grants were used to improve hill land; without subsidies farms would have been financially unviable; financial planning was needed to take advantage of inheritance tax legislation; and new medicines and vaccines improved the condition of ewes and lambs. I often asked shepherds if they thought they could be a farmer. All said they could in terms of the stockmanship and breeding, but many said that it was the bookwork that they would have trouble handling. Bookwork is thus seen as a particular responsibility of farmers that derives from their control of the means of production and demands special skills. In doing this bookwork, farmers have to adapt the farm as a whole—its sheep breeding, cattle rearing, and arable cultivation—to the policies and programs of the United Kingdom and European Community as well as to the familial relations between those involved in the business.

Breeding and bookwork relate to farms as a whole in yet another way. Hill sheep farms, like the family farms studied

by Abrahams (1991), Bouquet (1982), de Haan (1994), Salamon (1992), and Salazar (1996) are "an uneasy compromise
between its two constitutive principles" (Salazar 1996:93) or
domains: a moral domain of a domestic group constituted by
common residence, kinship relations, and cultural values
associated with "family"—affect, generalized reciprocity
(Sahlins 1974), disinterested cooperation, and long-term
generational continuity through marriage, birth, inheritance, and succession; and a commercial domain of a business enterprise combining ownership and managerial
control (see Gasson and Errington 1993) whose aim is to
realize profit and permeated by cultural values associated
with economics—rational calculation, interested cooperation, balanced reciprocity, and profit maximization (see Gray
1996a). Tup work addresses both domains of the family farm.
One of a farmer's aims is to manipulate genetically through
the selection and rotation of tups the body confirmation of
the flock so that its lambs are salable commodities and effective instruments of profit because they have characteristics
that conform to European Community standards and consumer demands. That rational calculation for profit maximization entered into breeding hill lambs is evident in a
conversation I had with a farmer while walking around the
hill. He said:

> Tastes and preferences in lamb have changed since we joined
> the EEC. Both the French and Italian consumer like smaller
> non fatty lambs around 44 lbs. killing weight. I remember when
> lambs had to have a lot of fat on them for them to bring a good
> price. But because of European Economic Community stan-
> dards and medical evidence, the trend is away from fatty meat.
> Farmers have to re-educate themselves and change the tups
> they select for breeding and the ewe lambs they retain for
> replacement stock so that they can produce lean lambs. Last
> year, there was a carcass competition held at an abattoir in
> Lockerbie. The judge of the competition was a Frenchman.
> I was astonished at the winning carcass—to me it was the
> thinnest and scrawniest of the lot, but it made me rethink my
> breeding program.

Simultaneously, tups and the flock serve as metaphors for
the family and its singular relation to the farm. As I will
describe in the next chapter, farmers usually formed legal

partnerships with other members of their families. In this respect, hill sheep farming families are corporate individuals that farmers personify. Through the breeding program, a farmer (and the family he signifies) and the characteristics of the land upon which sheep graze commingle in the tups and the flock. Further, the intergenerational association between a specific flock of sheep and a specific territory is an image of the wished-for continuity of a farm. Almost every farmer in Teviothead told me that the main objective is to keep the farm in and of the family. In bookwork, farmers have to combine rational calculation for cost minimization and profit maximization with the familial aim of passing the farm and the business onto the next generation. With respect to the former, farmers plot the best way to take advantage of European Community price subsidies and agricultural development grants. For most this means using the latter to improve and fence hill land so that more and more park lambs can be produced in order to maximize the former. Family partnerships are not formed for the usual commercial reason of raising capital to increase the scale and profitability of the enterprise. Rather, the motivation for partnerships is kinship. The switch from sole proprietorship to partnership is done because of the implications of the United Kingdom government's Capital Transfer Tax for inheriting the farm.[9]

Farmers are associated with the whole farm and with the most valued sheep, tups. Shepherds are associated with a part of the farm, the hirsel, and with the relatively less valued sheep, ewes. These spatial and value relations between farmer and shepherds on a hill sheep farm shape how hill sheep people experience the asymmetrical relations between the class of farmer and the class of shepherd. There is implicit in Marxist (see Frankenberg 1966) and Weberian (see Littlejohn 1963) accounts of class in rural localities of the United Kingdom a tendency to treat classes as distinct but sociologically equivalent social groups or categories making up the whole of society. The general line of analysis is that through their specific relations to the means of production, these class groups or categories are brought into existence, juxtaposed, ranked, and differentiated in terms of power and/or status (see Figure 9.1A). Based upon the spatiality of hill sheep farming practices, I am suggesting that the relations between farmer and shepherd classes are in a whole-part or encompassing-encompassed structure that Dumont (1980) argues was another form that asymmetry could assume (see Figure 9.1B).[10] Dumont (1980) identifies two core principles of such an encompassing-encompassed structure. The first is

Figure 9.1   Two Configurations of Class Relations

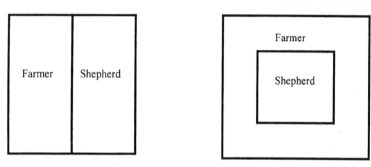

A. Equivalence Configuration   B. Whole-Part Configuration

that the whole is valued over the part, and the second is that the whole can contain its contrary. Based upon the whole-part spatial and value relations between farmer and shepherd that are embedded in hill sheep farming practices, this configuration provides a more accurate portrayal of their everyday sense of class-place and a mapping of most features of their class relations and stereotypes as follows:

Encompassing	:	Encompassed
Whole	:	Part
Valued	:	Less Valued/Devalued
Farm	:	Hirsel
Farmer	:	Shepherd
Domesticated	:	Wild
Tups	:	Ewes
Discipline	:	Indulgence
Dominance	:	Subordination
Control	:	Resistance

From this mapping we can discern the polysemous nature of hill sheep people's sense of place on a farm. It is an emplacement that is at once spatial, social, and moral and that imparts a particular inflection on how class relations are experienced on hill sheep farms. In this configuration of asymmetry, shepherds are associated with the outbye hirsels of wild and untamed land and sheep. It is not difficult to see the resonance between shepherds living and working on a farm's less disciplined hirsels and farmers' moral stereotype of shepherds as indulgent or lacking discipline, which in turn explains why they are unable to save the money necessary to get a farm and be a farmer. Further, we can see how the class(ic) themes of domination and resistance are played out on and refracted by hill sheep farms. The acknowledged resistance of hill sheep to the level of domestication of park sheep recalls shepherds' resistance to accepting what they see as the superiority practiced by farmers. One shepherd expressed his defiance as follows: "Farmers go around think- ing they are better than us workers ... I"ll not bow down to farmers. They are no better but I don't mix with them." In addition, shepherds are in no doubt about the existence and importance of class in their daily lives. Their stereotypes of farmers are used to explain their difficulty in becoming a farmer and to describe how farmers maintain their subor- dination and insinuate their inequality. Farmers share this view of shepherds as being more class conscious. One farmer typified farmers' perception when he commented upon this apparent greater sensitivity of shepherds to class: "There is class separation, a them-and-us attitude, but it's more from the shepherd's point of view." Conversely, farmers play down class membership—and their role in subordinating shep- herds—as a significant dimension of social relations and class position. Instead they stress those aspects of farm work and income in which they are similar to shepherds as a discourse of fundamental human equality underlying local circum- stances of class difference. In addition, farmers are associ- ated with the whole farm and, through bookwork and financial planning, with the Common Agricultural Policy. In this respect there is a resonance with the moral virtue of dis- cipline that they attribute to themselves and that explains their becoming and remaining farmers.

A final note that foreshadows an important theme of the next chapter: For both farmers and shepherds, sheep still suffuse their understanding of this whole-part configuration of class relation in two ways. First, sheep represent the whole of the hill sheep farming community in Teviothead and beyond—recall the earlier quotation in which a farmer said that involvement with sheep binds farmers and shepherds into a farming community that transcends, but does not negate, class differences. Second, farmers and shepherds explain the acquisition and transmission of class membership, belief, and action through a genetic metaphor of sheep breeding. One farmer told me:

> Class is bred into you, I'm sure it is. There are folks who have made a lot of money in business and step up a class, but it's obvious that they have stepped up a class—they don't fit in so well with the people who used to be above them. Class is not just having money, it's bred into you. You can get folk who are down and out but are still in the top class.

This is not much different from how a shepherd talked about class: "There are classes. I'm a peasant and I know that ... a farmer is a little higher up the social ladder. Our kind doesn't mix with their kind. If I wasn't brought up a peasant, I might accept being with them [farmers] and farmers are brought up thinking that they are better than workers." In these quotations are the same two processes, acquired behavioral adaptation and genetic transmission, that I described in Chapter 5 for the process of hefting on: the process of acquired behavioral adaptation is expressed as how someone was "brought up" to think and act like members of a class; and genetic transmission is expressed as class thinking and acting being "bred into" a person. Given the permeability between these two processes, this genetic metaphor allows the possibility of a shepherd becoming a farmer, not just in the sense of getting a farm and owning livestock, but also in the sense of being able to mix with farmers.

Notes

1. See also Frankenberg 1966 for a similar academic usage in other communities in Britain.
2. I am in no way suggesting that the Nepali *pariwar* and the Borders family hill sheep farm are similar in character, even though both are domestic domains. The nature and meaning of "domestic" is an issue for ethnographic analysis that cannot be taken for granted.
3. Since Littlejohn completed his research, most of the farms have been sold for forestry plantations. Thus there is little left of the community he described. It has been replaced by a Tibetan monastery as the center of a community of monks and followers. Having done major fieldwork in Nepal, I had the same sense of postmodern dislocation that Arjun Appadurai, Carol Breckenridge, and their son experienced when they travelled halfway around the world to India only to find that the Hindu priest, who was the chief informant for Carol Breckenridge's research, had departed to serve parishioners in Houston, Texas (Appadurai 1991:200-201).
4. There were another sixty nonfarming people living in cottages dotted around the valley.
5. I was partly responsible for the level of class consciousness in Teviothead through what Bourdieu calls the "theory effect" (1990a:129, 1992:249-250). By asking questions about the existence of classes and their effects on social life, I was assuming to be real and simultaneously imposing a scholarly derived vision of a division of society into classes. I have tried to neutralize this theory effect in the following analysis by focusing upon the way people in Teviothead struggled to make sense of what was an obvious division between those people they called farmers and those they called shepherds or workers.
6. Walter was one of the few farmers who occasionally went to the pub and mixed with shepherds. He was accordingly not criticized by shepherds for acting snobby, and Hamish got along well with him.
7. The amounts given by the farmer in this example have been revised to reflect wages and costs of living for the early 1990s.
8. Littlejohn's metaphoric usage of "place" is like Bourdieu's (1990a) notion of the "sense of one's place in social space" that I alluded to in opening this chapter.
9. I will give more details of family partnerships and their strategic importance for succession and advantages for inheritance taxes in the next chapter.
10. The differences between these two forms of social relatedness are aptly pictured in the Postface to the revised edition of *Homo Hierarchicus* (Dumont 1980:242) upon which Figures 9.1A and 9.1B are based.

Chapter 10

THE FARMHOUSE
Keeping the Farm in the Family

At the 1991 annual general meeting of the Teviothead Show Committee, the first item of business was the election of a new chairman. After announcing the retirement of the previous chairman, Willi Ballantyne of Linhope Farm, the secretary called for volunteers or nominations. When none were forthcoming immediately, he said, while looking at the previous year's show program where the Committee officers were listed by first initial and surname: "Why don't we just change the 'W' to an 'R'." By this he was suggesting that Willi's son Rob, who had previously been secretary and an active member of the Show Committee for many years, take over from his father as chairman. Rob's immediate response was: "Aren't there any other *families* in the valley? *Linhope* is always doing the kirk, the show and the school." By phrasing his protest in this way, Rob Ballantyne drew upon a taken-for-granted understanding of the relation between a family and a farm as different refractions of one phenomenon. In the first sentence, families were represented as the primary social units with responsibilities for the community ("the valley"). In the second sentence, Rob then used the name of the farm—where his family had lived and worked as tenants for three generations—to stand for his family as well as to give it a distinct social identity and status within the community. To him, his farm and family *are* inextricably linked. The same discursive merging of family and farm occurs in other con-

Notes for this section begin on page 239.

texts. For example, in talking about the people who are most active in organizing and participating in local church affairs, a woman remarked: "It's the same families who are active in the Kirk: Linhope, Hislop, Bowan Hill, and Caerlanrig [names of farms in Teviothead]."[1] Rob's usage echoed the spatialization of sixteenth-century reiving, in which discrete kin groups or families were constituted through the association of particular people with a specific place, and seventeenth-century Buccleuch Estate reforms, in which tenant families became associated with particular farms over time.

This everyday referential practice, reflecting and generating a link between a family and a farm, between a group of beings and a place, introduces the theme of this chapter: the nature of family farms in Teviothead derives from a particular sense of place rather than from the types of people and activities that comprise them, and this has important implications for our understanding of the family farm in the United Kingdom more generally. I have a sense of déja vu here, for the problems that sociologists and anthropologists are confronting in attempting to construct an analytic definition of the family farm in Europe are similar to those I encountered in my research in Nepal on the household (Gray 1995). In both ethnographic contexts, researchers adopt a "theoretical posture" (Bourdieu 1990a:60, 96) toward household and family farms, treating them as objects of knowledge. From this external stance, they use "instruments of objectification" (Bourdieu 1990a:60, 98) in the form of ideal typical constructs to define these phenomena in such a way as the definition contributes more to the aims of the academic discipline than to an understanding of the lived reality of a family farm.

Gasson and Errington's work is exemplary in this respect. They distance themselves from people's everyday understanding of family farming by purposely creating an ideal typical concept of the "farm family business," not the family farm, and they identify its six diacritical elements that "can be observed in real life" (1993:12). They state that the concept serves as a means "to raise [analysts'] awareness of relationships and to highlight their consequences" (18). In order to achieve these scholarly aims, they maintain that the elements of an ideal typical definition should unambiguously distinguish a family farm from other types of farms and social groups. One symptom of a well-defined analytic concept is that it has clear boundaries: "Deciding what is not a family farm business may help to clarify what it is" (20). On this basis, researchers can then engage in the taxonomic practice of classifying the social phenomena observed. Arguments about such definitions, therefore, concern which criteria are best in identifying those people, relationships or activities that demarcate the boundaries of the concept of the family farm.[2] For Gasson and Errington it is a combination of a form of relatedness (family) and a specific set of activities (ownership and managerial control) that provides clear boundaries between the farm family business and other types of farms; the other four elements of the family farm business do not by themselves demarcate the boundaries of the concept. For Djurfeldt (1995), it is the absence of hired labor, and, as we saw in the previous chapter, for others (Abrahams 1991; de Haan 1994; Salamon 1992; and Salazar 1996), it is the integration of two different domains of social relatedness and values—kinship and farming business.

The problem with all these definitions stems from the theoretical posture taken in constructing them. To paraphrase Bourdieu (1990a:60), there is an enormous difference between, on the one hand, trying to understand a family farm so as to reveal the strategies and practical intuitions of those living in them that go into building up farm production and a viable farm business in order to pass it on to children, and, on the other hand, trying to understand the family farm so as to construct a clearly bounded theoretical model of it. In Teviothead, hill sheep farmers' concept of "family farm" is not created consciously and self-reflexively with the aim of defining it as an object of knowledge. Their concept is a by-product of the daily activities, such as hill herding, tup breeding, lamb and tup auctions, through which they gain practical knowledge of family farming. Their aim is to reproduce their family farms not to define them for analytic purposes of theorizing, categorizing and typologizing. The concept of family farm that emerges in these practices tends not to be concerned with defining precisely the boundaries of the concept but with knowing the everyday operations of successful family farms. Intrinsic to these everyday operations is the singular and embodied attachment between a family and a farm and its reproduction over generations.[3] I now introduce the term "consubstantial" to characterize this particular sense of place through time, and I argue that it is fundamental to hill sheep farming people's experience and their actions that are constitutive of their family farms.

In some respects it might appear that there is little difference between my use of the concept of a consubstantial relation between a farm and family and the approach of de Haan (1994), Abrahams (1991), Salamon (1992) and Salazar (1996), who see the family farm as a synthesis of family relations and the business exigencies of farming. We all appear to make a similar analytic distinction between these two dimensions of family farms, and we all appear to see a family farm as integrating them. The difference, however, is that I do not posit as the source of family farmers' practices an explicit need to integrate these two domains. This is an imputed motivation developed by analysts to objectify and explain the family farm; it does not necessarily reflect the way family farmers experience the intimate association between their families and their farms, their often unspoken aims of being a family farmer, and the actions they undertake to achieve them. Instead, the strategies I will be describing in this chapter adopted by hill sheep farming people apparently to integrate family and business relations as a means of keeping the farm in the family are themselves the product of a more fundamental predilection toward consubstantiality. My use of the term "consubstantial" is meant to suggest that a family farm is more a way of being-in-the-world than a specific set of people, relations, activities, and/or domains of social life.

Again turning to Heidegger, but this time using his notion of ontology (1962, 1977), the essence of any human phenomenon is not its observable attributes but rather the particular structure of consciousness through which its attributes are revealed. Accordingly, the essence of a family farm in Teviothead is not a particular synthesis of two apparently contradictory domains—family and market (de Haan 1994), economic and noneconomic (Salazar 1996), family and farm business (Salamon 1992)—or a lack of hired labor (Djurfeldt 1995), or a particular combination of business and managerial control, kinship relations among principals, family labor, and intergenerational transfer, and residence (Gasson and Errington 1993), but a mode of apprehending that renders these things as "family-farm-like." This ontological approach reverses the relation between everyday things and concepts. From a theoretical posture, everyday things observed by investigators are used to define an analytic concept of family farm by delimiting its boundaries. From the perspective of everyday practice, these same things are revealed to people as family-farm-like by a structure of consciousness. The notion of consubstantial sense of place is meant to capture the essence of the structure of consciousness of family hill sheep farming in the Border hills.[4]

The task for this chapter, then, is to elaborate on the nature of this farm-family consubstantiality and to describe the processes through which it is passed on. In using the framework of genetic discourse to organize the narrative, I am suggesting that it also is an important dimension of the consubstantial structure of consciousness. Within this narrative framework, most of the previous chapters were about the practices through which farming families created or acquired their consubstantial relation to a farm.

Acquiring Consubstantiality

The essence of a consubstantial relation is that two phenomena, seemingly distinct in time, space, and/or nature, partake of the same substance and are therefore fundamentally different refractions of one phenomenon. On Teviothead hill sheep farms there are several instances of this type of consubstantial relation between being(s) and a place. Perhaps the clearest example is a heft, the everyday sheep farming concept referring to the relation between a distinct group of ewes and the territory where they dwell—a relation that is maintained and sensually understood by shepherds in going around the hill. Recall that in the process of hefting on, ewes acquire a special bond or attachment to a particular territory on the hill. In doing so they create both their own place and themselves as a distinct group of sheep. The use of the word "heft" (or "cut") reflects the unification of the group of sheep and the area of land to which they become attached. The interchangeability of family name and farm name in Rob Ballantyne's protest at the Show Committee annual general meeting and in everyday conversation among people in Teviothead represents the same relation, this time between a group of humans and a farm.

An essential part of this special attachment is that the ewes remain in the same heft throughout their lives and learn about and adapt to its specific topographical features, vegetation, soils, and parasites. Further, replacement stock is selected from the ewe lambs born of the heft so that it consists of a six-generation descent line of ewes. As a result, a cut of ewes is understood to genetically incorporate and transmit through selective breeding their acquired adaptations to the specific characteristics of the territory, thus giving each cut its distinctiveness. In this respect, ewes embody the land upon which they lived and are distinguished by it. My use of the term "embodiment" here is shorthand for the effects of the processes of hefting on and selective breeding that unifies a group of sheep related by descent and a place they create by living on it such that beings and place partake of a common substance and become different refractions of that common substance. But this is not the only way in which sheep are consubstantial. I also described in earlier chapters two other instances. The first concerns how through hill herding the stockmanship and personhood of a shepherd are embodied in the hirsel of ewes for which he is responsible; the second is how through the farm's breeding program (selection and rotation of tups) the stockmanship and personhood of a farmer is embodied in the tups and ultimately in the farm's flock. In both cases, a descent line of sheep, the personhood of a human being, and the characteristics of the land upon which they live become consubstantial—shepherd and hirsel, farmer and farm are united in sheep. And this relation between being(s) and place is repetitively reproduced every year in all the activities of rearing lambs for sale on the agricultural market.

The point of reviewing this ethnographic material here is to provide a basis for showing how the consubstantial relation between humans, sheep and the territory is both a lived metaphor (Jackson 1996:9) and mechanism for the relation between a family and a farm. As metaphor, a descent line of sheep—whether heft or flock—bonded to and embodying a particular territory over generations is an image of the consubstantial relation between family and farm that characterizes the family farming structure of consciousness and orients why farming families attempt to pass on the farm to the next generation. The metaphor goes further in suggesting how this relation is acquired by a family: a descent line of sheep simultaneously creates a place and its special attachment to it in the act of living and reproducing on it. Moreover, a descent line of sheep is not only an image of the relation between family and farm, but it also mediates the creation of the relation. In everyday herding and breeding activities on hill sheep farming, families become consubstantial with their farms in and through their sheep because both the farm places where the families live and the families themselves are consubstantial in the flock.[5]

These same practices are also mechanisms through which families and farms, being(s) and place, become consubstantial. In previous chapters I described the farming practices through which a consubstantial relation between a family and a farm is acquired: Chapter 4 showed how a family originally establishes a singular relation with a farm and constitutes itself as a discrete family through tenure; Chapter 5 analyzed how shepherding and breeding practices create a line of sheep that build and embody a place as one of the ways in which hill sheep farming people come to sense that they have a special relation to a territory; and the major themes of Chapter 6 were how in going around the hill shepherds forge a sentimental attachment to the hills where they feel at home and how by overseeing a farm's breeding program, a farmer produces a distinctive flock of sheep through which he (and the family he personifies) has a special attachment to the farm as a place. For both shepherd and farmer, their consubstantial sense of place is an internalization of the everyday relation between themselves, the sheep and the farm; it is also a technique of the body (Bourdieu 1984:466)—including the knowledge of sheep and the skills for herding them that constitute stockmanship—for building that relation in their farming activities.

In the remainder of this chapter I describe the strategies for keeping the farm in the family, that is, how hill sheep farming families in Teviothead organize relations among their members for transferring farm assets and operational authority to sons so that the acquired consubstantiality between the family and the farm is passed on to the next generation and is thus "bred into" the families. In this process, the concept of "family," that was constituted in the act of establishing a singular relation to a farm through tenure, takes on a further attribute. By successfully reproducing farm-family consubstantiality in the next generation, the concept of family acquires a temporal dimension as an agnatic descent line of discrete nuclear families.

Transmitting Consubstantiality

Gasson and Errington argue that intergenerational transfer of assets (inheritance) and managerial control (succession) is "not absolutely essential" (1993:20-21) to defining the boundaries of the ideal typical family farm business. The reason they cite for downgrading its importance is because it is not actually achieved on every family farm. The logic of this argument is that definitional importance is only produced by quantitative preponderance of actions. Still they ask: "Why then this search for continuity" (184)? And they provide a range of possible answers from the calculated to the sentimental—from offering "a livelihood to one or more children ... with few alternative opportunities" to preserving "the sense of identity ... associated not so much with the family business but with the land it occupies" and maintaining "the deeply-rooted and the resulting emotional bonds" to the land (184-185). While the latter answers resonate with my notion of the consubstantiality of family and farm, Gasson and Errington opt for an analysis that does not so much answer the question as to describe the patterns of observable conditions and rational actions for keeping the farm business in the family. In adopting this perspective, they put the observable things of the family farm before the family-farm mode of observing things; in other words, they do not identify the propensities that hill sheep farming families' consubstantial sense of place brings to the apprehension of their farms and to the improvisation of strategies for keeping them in their families. As we will see in the following analysis, farming people do much the same in being able to talk about the observable things and explicit actions they take to keep their farms in their families rather than about the family-farm mode of observing things that is immanent in their farming activities, their sheep, and their personhood.

If, through ownership or tenancy of a farm and through shepherding and breeding sheep, a family acquire a consubstantial relation with a farm, inheritance and succession give that relation a temporal extension over generations, so that, like sheep's relation to their place, a family's relation to a farm is bred into them. My own research in Teviothead suggests that keeping the farm *in* the family is taken literally. It includes not just the explicit legal transmission of the farm's assets and operational control to a successor but also the implicit reproduction the family's self-defining and consubstantial sense of place on the farm.

All farmers in Teviothead told me that they wanted their sons and their families to become farmers on their farms. Jock Turnbull of Craggierig Farm expressed the existence and strength of this goal when he said: "My philosophy is my family and farm come first. I'd like my sons to farm so I want to develop this farm, expand it, for my sons." When Jock told me this, his oldest son was just five and the actual event of his son and family getting Craggierig Farm was at least fifteen years in the future. His statement is indicative that the transmission process is *always* happening in the sense that passing the farm on to his son is invariably an essential factor in the way he thought about his farm and his family. Thus, whether or not his son will actually take over the farm from him does not negate that for him, as well as others in Teviothead, the continuity of association between a family and a farm over several generations, such that they are refractions and constitutive of each other, is what made hill sheep farms family farms.

A majority of farming families in Teviothead had been successful in passing on their farms and the consubstantiality that the farms embodied. During the 1980s, there were four farms that had been passed down from father to son for at least three generations; four others were in their second generation; and since 1980, seven families, both tenants and

owner-occupiers, had transmitted the farm to the next generation.[6] In all but one case, the farm had been passed to a
son. The exception was a farm that was transferred to a
daughter and her husband, but even in this case the parents
and their son had originally organized the legal and business
relations of the farm so that the son and his wife would take
over the farm. However, several years later and before his parents were to retire, the son decided that he did not want to be
a farmer and withdrew his share from the farm. Upon retirement, the parents transferred the farm to their daughter who
had married a farmer's son.[7]

In "successfully" passing on the farm to the next generation, the main concern is not the financial state of the farm
business per se but the relations among family members that
affect it.[8] The context for the process is British inheritance
laws under which all children have inheritance rights. If the
parents' estate is in cash or other liquid assets, then inheritance rights of children are equal. However, if the estate is in
landed property, such as a farm, then parents can apportion
inheritance rights unequally among children. This is an important legal distinction for farmers because, as I described in
Chapter 4, the social size of a hill sheep farm precludes two
families jointly owning or tenanting and managing it for
extended periods. In this respect, hill sheep farms were practically impartible; and therefore, the problem becomes how
to pass on the asset to all children without risking the farm's
financial viability, and thus its association with the family,
through liquidation or high levels of indebtedness. The problem is complicated by demography and the implications of
the acquired farm-family consubstantiality. For a significant
period of the transmission process, marriages of children
mean that two or more families, that is, nuclear family units
centered upon a married couple, are associated with a single
farm, each as a focus of interest in it. As a result, the issues for
transmission are to re-establish the singular relation between
one of these families and the farm and to sever the relation
between the other families and the farm while at the same
time fulfilling their legal rights to a share of the asset value of
the farm. Because of the inextricability of family relations
and farm relations created by consubstantiality, to change the
way individual family members are legally and financially

linked to the farm is simultaneously to change relations between family members; conversely, changes in relations among family members motivate changes in their relations to the farm. This is why the process of passing the farm on to the next generation is so delicate and can easily lead to tensions, "falling out," or "bust-ups" between family members. People in Teviothead are well aware of these problems and they described to me disputes that had occurred in Teviothead and typically arose between family members during the process of passing on the farm. All of these disputes had to do with the fragmenting effects of individuals representing the emerging separate families making moral and legal claims to the farm. These claims often led to "bust-ups" because they had the potential to divide up the farm asset to the point where it was not viable as a business able to support a succeeding family. Precisely because farm and family are consubstantial, practices that fragment one also fragment the other as well as severing the relation between them. Such problems are concentrated at the times when there are major changes in family relations that punctuate what might be called a farm-family cycle: birth of children and selection of a successor, marriage of the successor, and retirement of parents from the farm. Farm families in Teviothead adopt a number of strategies to deal with the fragmenting effects of family relations on the farm's financial viability and consequently on the transmission of farm-family consubstantiality to the next generation.

Birth of Children and Selection of a Successor

The first strategy is organizing relations between family members and the farm through the formation of partnerships. This is a relatively new tactic developed in response to the introduction of the Capital Transfer Tax (CTT) in the late 1970s. In the seven farming families that went through the process of intergenerational transfer since the early 1980s, the parents had come into or succeeded to the farm between 1937 and 1965 prior to the introduction of the CTT when death duties were still in force. As the name suggests, death duties were taxes levied on the entire value of the farm assets when a farmer died. Frequently, heirs to farms did not have the cash to pay death duties, necessitating the sale of farm assets and the consequent severing of the relation, often of several generations, between family and farm in order to acquit the liability. This happened to two farm families in Teviothead, one of which had been "in the family" for eighty-five years spanning three generations. Death duties, then, were a major impediment to reproducing the consubstantial relation between farm and family over several generations. When farming families were liable for death duties, forming family partnerships was not strategic because it was the heir who became liable upon taking possession of the asset regardless of the legal relations between the parents and between the parents and the heir.

The provisions of the CTT exempt or diminish the tax liability of transfers of agricultural land from farmers to their children. Parents may individually make limited tax-exempt "gifts" of farm assets to children as a legitimate mechanism for intergenerational transfers during their lifetimes thereby minimizing more quickly the value of the asset transferred to and the consequent tax liability incurred by the heir at their deaths. In order to take advantage of the provisions of the CTT for reproducing farm-family consubstantiality over generations, business partnerships between husbands and wives are formed. In these partnerships, each had a share in the value of the stock, equipment, and land (if the farm is under owner-occupancy). While in most cases, husbands and wives have equal shares, there were a few cases in which one partner, usually the husband, retained the largest share.[9] These partnerships add a legal framework to the practical definition of a family established through tenure. Reflecting an assumed commonality of interest, these legal partnerships formally make the married partners, who originally constituted the family, into a corporate individual which the farmer personifies and whose well-being motivates his work activities. Thus when a farmer's personhood is embodied in the farm's flock through his breeding skills, so is the identity and common interests of the family that he personifies through these partnerships.

Once such a partnership is formed, parents begin a long-term process of intergenerational transmission with the selection and incorporation of the successor into the partnership. Unless the family owns or tenants more than one farm, it is the oldest son who is considered the most likely to succeed to the farm. In six of the seven farming families that went through intergenerational transfers, the successor identified was the only son.[10] The other family, the Grahams of Hillend Farm, had four sons and two daughters. They thus had the problem of selecting a successor to the family's farm and getting a farm for the other sons who wanted to go into farming. It was a situation that all farmers in Teviothead empathized with because they knew that it often leads to severe tensions and family bust-ups, as inevitably happened in this case. It became evident early on that one of the Graham sons was not interested in farming; he found work and lived off the farm. The other three sons wanted to be farmers and went into a partnership with their parents. When the eldest married and started his family, his father was not ready to retire. Earlier in Chapter 4, we encountered a similar situation facing the Olivers of Burnthill Farm and their attempt to get a separate farm for their son because of the necessity for each family to establish a singular relation with a farm. In the current case, the Grahams were able to find a farm for this son. Another son was content to work under and with his father until the latter's retirement. But the other son, Warren, was not willing to wait. He demanded that his share of the farm be paid in cash immediately to him. In doing so, he threatened the viability of the family farm because to pay him out, the remaining partners had to dangerously increase their level of indebtedness. No one questioned Warren's legal and moral right to his share; thus in itself his exercising of this right was not the cause of the family bust-up. Instead, relations between Warren and the rest of the family became extremely acrimonious and were irretrievably severed because the way he demanded his share—immediately and in full—seriously jeopardized the continuing relation between the Graham family and the Hillend Farm. One person commented: "I didn't know a son could do a thing like that to his family."

The families of the other six farms in Teviothead were only in the early stages of the transmission process. They consisted of husband, wife and young children. Each had at least one son who was seen as the potential successor and heir. In these farms, the pattern of incorporating the son into the partnership was similar to the one followed by the seven farms that had recently completed succession. On these latter farms, the sons who wanted to become farmers began working on the farm as adolescents. Two were responsible primarily for a hill hirsel, one combined herding part of a hill hirsel with responsibilities for the farm's cattle, and the remaining four worked mostly with the farm's cattle with some responsibilities for herding during lambing. During this period of work, sons had to demonstrate their commitment to farming as a career and their abilities to be successful hill sheep farmers. Most did so by leaving school and working full-time on the farm for relatively little pay. There were two ways of paying them. One simulated employment by formally setting a weekly wage. The other was a less formal arrangement that involved parents providing "pocket money," clothes, and other personal needs, and usually a car. I could not discern a pattern between the form of tenancy a family had to the farm and the option of wage or pocket money. It seemed to be a choice that suited the particular personalities of family members; it was also a choice that could drift over time. For example, one farmer told me that when he first started working for his parents, they decided to give him a weekly wage. However, after several months, it slid toward a less formal arrangement that he said suited all of them. His parents provided a car, his personal needs, and when he needed cash for going out, he was freely given it. Whether a formal weekly wage or informal pocket money, the remuneration is small relative to hired workers, and this is taken into account years later when apportioning the estate among the children.

As the son approachs age twenty, the decision is made by the parents to take him into the partnership. One farmer explained: "Once a son has shown he wants to be a farmer by working on the farm, you take him on as a partner."[11] Sons are usually made partners before their marriages and are given a small share in the business. But almost immediately, each parent begins to use the gifting provisions of the CTT to transfer shares of the capital to the partner-successor at the maximum rate. This type of transfer takes place "on paper." As the son's share in the farm increases over time, the parents' share and concomitant CTT liability decreases. In addition, the son's work on the farm, like that of the other partners, has to be formally recognized in the farm's accounts for taxation purposes.

At the same time as shares are being transferred to the chosen successor and heir, provisions for other children who are not going into farming to receive their portions of the estate are made in such as way as to avoid paying out the shares in lump sums. Reflecting on what happened to the Grahams of Hillend Farm, one farmer became more concerned about the possibility of his other children doing the same. Even though he did not think they would do what Warren Graham did, he changed the legal arrangements of the farm so that they could not demand their entire shares to be paid out in one lump sum because, he said, "you never know what could happen." One way of paying out the other children's shares is to use the annual gifting provisions of the CTT so that the parents and/or successor do not need to sell off part of the farms or borrow against it in order to pay out the other shares in lump sums. Another is to include in the farm asset passed on to the successor son the obligation to pay the other children's share. In both cases, the transfer took place "in cash." Part of the farm's income is used to make periodic cash payments to the other children until the share/s are fully paid out. In the cases for which I have information, children who did not succeed to the farm and did not take up farming received a smaller share of the assets. The typical reason given for this unequal distribution is, as one farmer put it: "George [the successor] has spent all his life working on the farm for very little, so his sister's share is less than his … and his sister understands that." This is an accurate assessment not only of George's sister's attitude but also of siblings in other farm families who are not going into farming. There were no instances in Teviothead of such non-succeeding siblings disputing the apportionment of the inheritance, and farmers did not have stories of such disputes in other families.

Marriage of Successor: One Farm, One Partnership, Two Families

When the successor marries and starts his own family, the farm's family relations change to an extended form consisting of two generations of agnatically linked nuclear families. This situation is anomalous because it contradicts the singular and constitutive relation between a family and a farm in three ways. First, while both families are dependent upon one farm until the parents withdraw from the partnership through retirement or death, each, as we saw in Chapter 4, is understood to form a separate focus of interest in it. Second, while some members of both families (parents and son) form one unified partnership, the transfer of shares that occurs during this period continually produces a consciousness of two separate families. Third, while the successor is just one of the partners, he is a member of the two families and subject to their respective and potentially conflicting interests. Farmers told me that this anomalous situation has the capacity to cause conflict in the family and that such conflict is usually played out among the wives of the male partners. As a result, the strategies adopted for reproducing the relation between a family and a farm in the next generation focuses on these women.

The overt change in family relations during this period of the farm-family cycle is the incorporation of the successor's wife into the family farm, and this is double-edged. On the one hand, the son's marriage is the basis of forming the next generation of family that will succeed to the farm and is thus necessary for realizing the goal of keeping the farm in the family. On the other hand, a daughter-in-law from outside the family and the partnership becomes a claimant upon the farm's assets, and should the marriage fail, she could bring about the loss of the farm in the settlement. Farm families in Teviothead use the timing of when a daughter-in-law is taken into the family partnership and how much of a share is retained by the parents to minimize her legal interest in the farm business during the early years of the marriage. Some families made the son's wife a partner right after the marriage but retained majority share; others delayed making her a partner for several years to see if the marriage was successful or until just before the parents' retirement from the farm and their withdrawal from the partnership; and in some families, it was not until the parents died that the son's wife became a partner. I was told about the Burns family of Braehead Farm who had set up a complex, multileveled business organization to minimize their daughter-in-law's share in the farm. The parents, Charles and Jane, had not been "pleased with the marriage" of their son, William. As a result, from the outset they did not get along well with their daughter-in-law, Sarah. People in Teviothead said that Charles and Jane had expected there to be a divorce and in anticipation they set up the farm business so that Sarah's share was limited to one-quarter of the farm's livestock, a figure that represented less than a tenth of the farm's total asset value. This was achieved by the parents jointly owning the landed property, the two couples forming a separate four-member business partnership that owned the livestock and machinery and leased the land from the parents. There was no divorce but, due to the message about family relations the parents inscribed in their design of partnerships, there continued to be strained relations between William's parents and his wife that eventually caused a family bust-up after the parents retired.

Given my ethnographic experience of household dynamics in Nepal, for me a remarkable feature of the way people in Teviothead represent the danger to family relations and to the continuity of family-farm consubstantiality during this period is that wives, not the sisters, of the male partners are construed as the primary cause of tensions.[12] The following is typical of the accounts I was given of family bust-ups blaming wives as the source of conflict between either a set of brothers or a father and son:

> It's common for wives [of brothers] to stir up trouble. Wives get jealous of each other. The eldest son [of a farmer] might get the big house [after the father retires] and the younger son gets a cottage so the wife of the younger brother gets jealous and the wives end up not speaking. Wives are the biggest problem of married brothers working together on a farm.[13]

Earlier in Chapter 4, I described how people treated farms as socially too small for two families. This is an explicit recognition that tensions and jealousies between men in the family can occur on farms during the period when more than one family is in the partnership. In farm families with more than one son interested in becoming a farmer, it is a time when relations between brothers are being affected by their changing relations to the farm. As partners in the farm, they have a socially equivalent relation to it. But this changes when the elder brother or son, who is designated to succeed to the farm, starts to exert his authority and to "build his own empire." This happened in a neighboring valley to a tenant farm family in which two brothers were partners. In order to accommodate the younger brother, the partnership purchased another very small farm primarily to provide a place where the younger brother could have a separate residence on a separate "farm." This partially enabled each family to be associated with a separate farm; but the second farm was not big enough for the second brother to build a separate empire financially or socially. So, there was the inevitable "falling out" between the brothers over the control of farm policy on the main farm and the splitting of the partnership. In a comment about this situation that reaffirmed the singular and constitutive relation between a family and a farm, a farmer said: "You're always better on your own." Even in cases where the brothers fall out, it is still their wives who are seen to exacerbate such tensions to the point of causing the bust-up. One farmer, George, told me about the situation among some of his distant relatives. A man and three sons formed a partnership on a tenanted farm. "Duncan and his brothers got on fine when they were working together on the same farm when they were teenagers. But there's some squabbling going on there now. One brother thinks one day that he's getting more of the work to do." At this point in the narration, George's wife interjected: "There's also pressure from the wives that increases the squabbling, that's why it's necessary for brothers to get separate farms."

Most farmers knew of farms where there had been short-lived partnerships between brothers. That tensions would arise between the brothers is so taken for granted that some families organize their business relations to minimize them. One farmer told me how, after his father died, he and his brothers had formed a two-tiered business structure. Together, the brothers formed a partnership whose purpose was to provide a strong financial basis for each brother to get his own farm. Once each brother and his family had become the sole tenant on a separate farm, their accountant advised them to dissolve their joint partnership before their family relations inevitably deteriorated. Other farmers approved of the accountant's advice, but again implicated the brothers' wives as the most likely cause of any deterioration in relations between them: "That's sound advice. On a farm with two or three brothers [in partnership], they can work hard together and get along fine. But after they get married, friction starts between their wives. The women start getting niggled over one getting more than the other—one gets a fridge and the other doesn't. Once a niggle starts, its gets bigger and bigger until the brothers can't get along any more."

Retirement of Parents from Farm

Since 1981 when I began fieldwork in Teviothead, demography seemed to favor the farming families going through the process of transmission because most of them had only one son. As a result, the problems they faced in passing on the farm tended to emerge in the lineal axis (i.e., between father and son and/or between mother-in-law and daughter-in-law) during the retirement phase of the process. Even though almost all people designate age 65 as the time of "retirement," the practical moment of retirement is difficult to define because farmers use it to refer to a number of situations. There seemed to be four events that can be indicative of retirement. Retirement can be marked by: (1) the son taking on full responsibility for management and farm policy symbolized in his control of the business checkbook; (2) all the parents' shares in the business partnership being transferred to the son; (3) the father-farmer ceasing full-time work on the farm; and/or (4) the son and his family moving into the farmhouse and the parents finding another residence, often off the farm. All cases of retirement from Teviothead farms involved one or a combination of these events, but no one instance was exactly the same. There was one case in which the parents retired in the senses of the father-farmer ceasing to work full-time and passing on management and financial control to the son and his family but the parents stayed in the farmhouse. There was another case in which, to everyone concerned, the parents had not retired in the senses that the father-farmer continued to work full-time and the parents had retained majority shares in the business but they moved out of the farmhouse. On one farm, the farmer died before fully retiring in the senses of transferring all the shares to his successor and giving up full-time work, but his wife remained residing in the farmhouse. And there was one case that was closest to being "classic" in the sense that all four events indicative of retirement occurred relatively simultaneously. If retirement entails one or more of these events, then it is a phase that can take a number of years to complete rather than all at once. During retirement, each event is a potential source of tension between parents and the successor: the timing and extent of the transfer of management, decision-making on farm policy, and financial control; the timing and amount of the transfer of the parents' shares in the farm business; the timing of the father-farmer ceasing full-time work and the corollary issue of what work, if any, the retiring farmer would do; and the timing of the successor moving into the farmhouse. All farmers could relate stories of their own or other families in which tensions arose over one or more of these events of retirement. It is perhaps a testament to the strong disposition of Teviothead hill sheep farmers to re-produce the acquired consubstantiality between family and farm that they manage the process of retirement without all families falling out.

Depending upon the financial arrangement parents have made, there are various strategies farmers use to complete the process of asset transfer to the heir and to secure their income during retirement in a way that does not fragment the asset. One strategy is to remain in the partnership and to receive a retirement income from the farm business that is in proportion to their remaining share. In this case, the complete transfer of assets occurs at the death of the parents, but the CTT liability has been minimized by previous transfers. Another strategy—available principally to owner-occupied farms where the value of the assets is greater than on tenanted farms—is for the heir to borrow against the value of the farm to pay out the parents' share in a lump sum upon their retirement, thereby leaving no CTT liability. A third strategy, available to farmers who have other sources for retirement income, such as insurance policies and annuities, is to transfer "on paper" all remaining shares to the heir upon retirement. There are provisions of the CTT that make this last strategy particularly advantageous for keeping the farm in the family. Not only does the heir not have to borrow to pay out his parents' share, but also, if they live more than seven years after the transfer, there is no tax liability for the heir. In this case, parents often purchase a term life insurance policy to cover the decreasing liability over the seven-year period.

During the retirement processes I was able to follow in Teviothead over several periods of fieldwork from 1981 to 1995, there were few instances or accounts of tensions arising between a retiring farmer and his son over transfer of management and changes in farm policy. From my perspective, there is the potential for a son to niggle his father by making changes in farm policy or for a father to niggle a son by resisting any changes. Though people in Teviothead were unsure of the exact nature of the dispute, they thought that argument over control of farm policy was the most likely cause of the falling out among the Grahams and of Warren Graham demanding an immediate payout of his share in the family farm. Otherwise, no one mentioned tensions arising between father and son over farm policy as typical of the retirement phase. When I asked about this, the reason given was similar to one used to explain why men were less sensitive to class differences. During years between the son becoming a partner and the father's retirement, the men work together on the farm and jointly develop a common understanding of the farm policy. I often heard farmers and sons discussing future changes in farm operations, particularly in light of how they understood the possible effects of changes in the Common Agricultural Policy. Thus, when the Sheep Meat Regime was introduced, farmers and sons discussed the merits of increasing the number of inbye sheep to take advantage of the variable premium; and when the Beef Special Premium was introduced in the early 1990s, several farms, where the farmer and his son were jointly working, shifted policy by increasing the number of suckler cattle on the farm. In both these circumstances, there were no bust-ups between the fathers and sons involved. On one farm, the son was more interested in cattle than sheep. When he returned to his family farm after several years of working on a dairy farm in another part of Britain, his parents who were the sole partners, decided to buy in a number of cattle in an effort to make a "place" for the son on what was largely a hill sheep farm. The general point is that because father and son have worked together over several years in jointly developing farm policy, the actual event of transferring control does not have a great effect on the character of the farming operations and thus on the relations between father and son. The transfer of farm management and control does seem to have a greater effect on their wives.

Just as in the previous phase in which wives of brothers in a farming partnership are often blamed for the breakup of families and the severing of the relation with a farm, after the retirement of the parents it is troubled relations between mothers-in-law and daughters-in-law that threaten the continued consubstantiality of family and farm. The focus of the problems is the farmhouse. The changing of residences usually accompanies the transfer of control over the farm to the son and his family. The women's position in relation to the farmhouse is analogous to the position of their spouses in relation to farm policy in the sense that for the women the farmhouse is their domain within the farm; thus, moving into the farmhouse signals the transfer of control from the parental to the successor's family. Several women told me that it was not a good idea for mother-in-law and daughter-in-law to live next to each other. Typical was a farmer's wife, Liz, who had recently moved out of the farmhouse to make way for her son, his wife, and their children: "Mothers-in-law and daughters-in-law can become a problem by living too near each other ... mothers-in-law may interfere too much. Bossy mothers-in-law try to keep their daughters-in-law right." Then, referring to the Burn family of Braehead Farm that was currently going through a bust-up, she added: "After moving into the farmhouse, Sarah started to niggle Jane by making big alterations to the house, which was already beautiful.[14] It's not a good thing to be too close ... I couldn't live close to my son and his wife. You get to see too much of each other ... that's when you fall out."

The problem identified by Liz concerns the difficulty a mother-in-law has in giving up her authority over the farmhouse and domestic operations (buying and cooking food, caring for children) symbolized by the interior decoration. A similar sentiment was expressed by a woman who had married a farmer's son. Even though there was a cottage on the family farm, the couple moved into a house in another valley while her husband's parents remained in the farmhouse until the father's retirement. She said: "When I first married, I did not want to live in a cottage on the farm ... I would have felt too near Alex's [her husband's] mother" who others told me was "a bit domineering." Apparently, the feeling of being too close physically and socially were mutual because when the parents retired and the young couple moved into the farmhouse, the parents took up residence in a nearby town rather than on the farm.

Figure 10.1 Falnash Farmhouse

As Liz indicated, if resentment arises between the women, it is often because the daughter-in-law makes changes to the decorations of the farmhouse as her means of signaling the transfer of control to her family and of exerting her control over the domestic operations of the farm. Like their husbands who are building their empires in farm operations, women are building theirs in the farmhouse. One farmer said: "When a young couple moves into the farmhouse, they have to make some changes to make it their own, but the old folks often don't see it that way ... it upsets them because for them it was fine." In another case where the two families did live close together, building an empire included struggles for dominance and independence that were carried out over whether or not to share a washing machine: the daughter-in-law wanted both women to share her machine and the mother-in-law wanted to have her own machine. The level of recognition of tensions arising over the farmhouse was evident to me when one woman told me how she and her daughter-in-law had explicitly discussed the potential for resentment between them and had "agreed not to get offended with the way each of us felt about the taste of the other" over changes that the daughter-in-law might make in decorating the farmhouse. By letting go of her taste controlling the interior decoration, the mother-in-law was signaling that she was also letting go of her authority over the domestic domain of the farm.

In most cases (five of seven), such tensions are minimized by the distancing of separate residences off the farm. But they do have the potential to cause the family to lose the farm. This was the danger in the bust-up of the Burns family at Braehead Farm. As this tale goes, after the young couple moved into the house, the extent to which relations between Jane [mother-in-law] and Sarah [daughter-in-law] had deteriorated was expressed through Sarah's actions in relation to the farmhouse. I was told how she "ripped out" much of Jane's decorating, which was interpreted by people in Teviothead as reprisal for the way Sarah felt she had been treated by her parents-in-law. In addition, Sarah's feeling of absolute control over the farmhouse, and by implication the control of her husband over farm policy, was declared in her never inviting Jane back into the farmhouse she had lived in for over twenty years. Her declaration was successful in that these tensions affected relations between Charles and William to the point that Charles ceded complete control of farm policy to William by moving far away from Teviothead for several years. In addition, Charles and Jane wanted to completely withdraw their share from the farm. They explored several avenues of achieving this, but all of them jeopardized keeping their farm in their family because of the high level of indebtedness William would have to incur to pay out his parents' share in the business partnership and well as to purchase the landed property from them. The only way seemed to be for the parents to remain owners of the land, for William and Sarah to buy out the parents share in the business partnership, and for the latter to continue leasing the land from the parents. This organization of relations between family members and the farm aimed at keeping the farm in the family seemed to have beneficially affected the strained relations between the family members themselves. Several years later, William and Sarah were still farming Braehead, they were making plans to pass the farm onto their son, and relations with the parents had improved sufficiently for Charles and Jane to return to the Borders. This result indicates how they improvised their business and family relations to ensure consubstantiality between Braehead Farm and the Burns family.

The Genetic Metaphor

Throughout the transmission process, which begins with the birth of a child and ends with the death of the parents, the goal of the strategies adopted by farming families is to ensure there is a financially viable farm that can be *legally* passed on to the next generation of the family. Yet I have also argued that what makes a family-farm business (to use Gasson and Errington's term) a family farm to people in Teviothead is a consubstantial rather than a legal relation between family and farm so that these strategies by themselves are not sufficient to reproduce that relation over time. Herein lies the significance of the genetic discourse that was described in previous chapters. It is used metaphorically in Teviothead to explain how people acquire a range of attributes including their individual personality, the behavior patterns and attitudes characteristic of a social class and/or region, and the skills, aptitude, and temperament for farming. These attributes are said to be "bred into" a person, that is, acquired and transmitted through genetic processes such that they inhere in the person's body. The metaphorical quality of this understanding is that farmers' knowledge of the genetic mechanism of sheep breeding gained in their everyday farming activities is used to conceive of the process through which people acquire and transmit attributes. One farmer explicitly recognized the metaphorical character of using breeding in this way: "People around here have been breeding sheep for a long time and they get ideas from this … so they explain the likeness in family members from watching bloody sheep!" It was evident to this farmer that the metaphor builds upon how consubstantiality is produced and reproduced in sheep through shepherding and breeding practices. As we have seen above, hill sheep farmers "know" that sheep acquire, embody, and transmit genetically a range of attributes—not just body confirmation, meat-to-fat ratio, ability to produce milk for lambs, and quality of wool, but also their temperaments, adaptations to the particular vegetation, pests and soils of the hills where they graze, the skills of the shepherd who herds them, and farmer who selects the tups for breeding. It is this practical knowledge of sheep breeding that "gives them ideas" for explaining the attributes of people.

When used in relation to farming, the metaphorical extension of this practical knowledge is epitomized by two phrases that Teviothead farmers used often in talking about each other: "farming is bred into you" and "good farmers come from farming families." In these phrases they are propounding a theory of a genetic mechanism for the acquisition and intergenerational transfer of those attributes that are necessary to be a farming person. In such a theory, the aptitude for farming is corporeal such that personhood and farming commingled in a common substance that appears to be transmitted genetically in the same way that sheep embody the hills and farming people. One farmer described hill sheep farmers in the Borders as follows: "They are a special kind of farmer in Britain. They will put up with bad times and stick with their farms until good times come again. Such 'stick-to-it-ness' is bred in them." The metaphor is also behind the way farmers talk about themselves. Almost the first thing farmers told me about themselves or about other people was to place themselves or others in a genealogy of farming families. The implication was that people acquired and inherited their farming prowess from their families. The following are two examples of this:

> James is a good farmer. His family has been on Bowan Hill farm for over 100 years. In the 1870s, James's great-grandfather came to Bowan Hill from a farm in Ettrick. At the time, James's grandfather was twelve years old. His mother's father was a shepherd at Falnash Farm for twenty-nine years, then he became the shepherd at Bowan Hill working for James's father. Before his work at Falnash, James' mother's father was a shepherd at Craik. James's wife's family are farmers at Bonchester; his wife's sister is still in farming. She and her husband own a farm in South Eden.
>
> I'm from a farming family who have [been in] Catslackburn Farm in Yarrow for generations. My two brothers are still on that farm.

This genetic metaphor is also applied to the relation between particular families and particular farms through the mediation of sheep. As I described earlier, the farm's land and the family inhere in the flock's genetic constitution through breeding practices, and these same practices transmit the adaptations and the consubstantiality of sheep, farm land, and farm family to succeeding generations of sheep to form a genealogical line that is characteristic of the farm as a whole. As a result, sheep are both the embodiment and the icon of the consubstantiality that is a family farm. Further, farmer's knowledge of these processes provide a practical understanding of the nature of consubstantiality: it is a corporeal association of a descent-based group with a specific territory over generations. Through both the genealogical bias in tenancy laws and the strategies adopted by family farmers to ensure the legal and financial transfer of a farm to their children, family farms have come to resemble their flocks' relation to the hills where they graze: both are descent groups associated with a particular territory over several generations. But sheep as a metaphor transpose the legal and financial mechanisms of transfer into genetic mechanisms so that it is also farm-family consubstantiality that is passed on to the son and his family. It explains why I never heard of any son buying in a new flock when he took over a farm from his father no matter how strained the family relations. And it was on this basis that the Ballantyne family and Linhope Farm were used interchangeably by Rob Ballantyne in the 1991 annual general meeting of the Teviothead Agricultural Show Committee; they were two ways of referring to the same thing. At that time, Rob had recently married and assumed managerial and financial control of Linhope Farm. Through living, working, marrying, rearing children, *and* continuing the breeding of the flock that his father and grandfather had bred on the farm, he demonstrated that he had inherited genetically his parents' aptitude for hill sheep farming; in doing so, he genealogically extended and replicated his parents' nuclear family's consubstantial relation to the farm and its place in the community.

Notes

1. This usage was extended to people living in cottages so that the name of the cottage stood for the family living in it.
2. See Netting, Wilk and Arnould (1984) and Yanagisako (1979) for similar debates in relation to defining a household.
3. The difference between an analytical and practical concept of the family farm I am describing here is similar to Burling's distinction between trying to define color concepts in terms of drawing borders or selecting the focus, the 'truest' example, of each color (1970:46-49). Burling points out that this latter practice is more typical of the way people use color concepts in everyday life. Daniel found a similar difference between how the Indian government defines a village in terms of cartographic boundaries and how Tamil villagers conceptualize it in terms of the important places that demarcate its spatial center (1984:74). For my purposes, Burling and Daniel suggest that our aim is to identify the focal dimensions of family farming as the basis of the concept. This shifts attention away from criteria that demarcate differences between farms as a means of creating exclusive categories to the focal activities and ideals of family farms as a means of understanding the similarities between them.
4. While I have not explicitly used the term here, it would be appropriate to say that I am treating the consubstantial relation between family and farm as a dimension of what Bourdieu would call "habitus," an acquired and embodied disposition operating "below the level of consciousness and language," both reflecting and constituting family farms (1984:466-467).
5. In saying that the farming family was consubstantial with the flock is to foreshadow material discussed later in the chapter where through forming family partnerships the farmer becomes a personification of his family. Thus when through breeding practices the flock embodies the farmer, they also embody the family that he personifies through the partnership.
6. While I have not done so in the text, there would be some legitimacy in including the managed farm in the group because, as described in Chapter 4, the position of manager also passed from father to son.
7. Since 1981 when I began fieldwork in Teviothead, five farms were not passed on to the next generations. The reasons were as follows: the tenant decided to leave farming (one case), the tenants were unmarried and had no children to whom to pass the farm (one case), the tenants had to come out of the farm because of financial difficulties (three cases, see chapter 4). In these cases, the lack of passing on the farm to the next generation was not due to disputes and tension among family members.
8. I have put "successfully" in quotation marks to indicate that passing the farm on to a successor can be completed but it may also cause tensions among family members. If the latter is the case, there is an ambiguity about how "successful" the process has been from the family's perspective.
9. These partnerships took on even more significance with the introduction of quotas on the number of ewes eligible for subsidies under changes to the European Union Ewe Premium Scheme in the early 1990s. The quota was set at 1000 ewes per partner. As a result, many farms in the United Kingdom with more than 1000 ewes set up what were called "instant partnerships" to increase the number of ewes eligible for the ewe premium. Eventually, only partnerships formed before the changes were recognized as giving each partner the 1000 ewe quota.
10. I am including here the one farm cited earlier where the only son was originally designated as the heir but severed his relation with the farm.

11. One farmer told me that many farmers waited a long time before taking the successor son into the partnership and this caused problems especially if one of the parents died unexpectedly. This left the successor with tax liabilities more like death duties.

12. In Nepal, villagers blamed women for the breakup of their households. However, it is important to treat this overt similarity with caution. It is a similarity between one specific dimension in two complexes of social relations in different cultural worlds. We should not make the mistake of assuming that it betokens a similarity between the whole family and household systems.

13. There are resonances here with the way wives were portrayed as more sensitive to expressions of class differences. One person made this explicit: "Farmers' wives are the most into status and jealousy … they've almost come to blows over it … if one [wife] gets something, the other has to get something better."

14. It was clear to me in the way Liz expressed this niggle that she empathized with Jane. There may even have been a measure of projection of her own feelings about her situation in that there were rumors of some tensions between Liz and her daughter-in-law also arising from the changes that the latter had made to the farmhouse.

AFTERWORD

Hill sheep farming in the Scottish Borderlands is imbued with a distinctive sense of place. Through herding ewes on the hill, breeding tups, selling lambs and tups at auctions, and passing their farms onto the next generation, hill sheep farming people incarnate a consubstantial relation between a family and a farm such that human being and place are experienced as partaking of the same substance and thus as refractions of a single phenomenon. The way sheep dwell and reproduce on the hill is both a metaphor and a mechanism for this sense of place. In bringing the book to an end, I wish to build upon this ethnographically specific understanding of a particular sense of place in Teviothead to suggest a way of rethinking rural. I hope that these closing remarks speak equally to those living in rural and those studying rural. In this phrasing of the issue, I purposely use the adjectival form of the word "rural" ungrammatically without a noun that it modifies to disturb us into to recognizing that is it the referent of the word that I am treating as problematic.

In the Introduction, I situated my account of hill sheep farmers' sense of place within a predicament of emplacement and a concomitant upsurge in the awareness of people and anthropologists of the importance of placedness in social life. At the same time, there is also a mounting interest in and critical stance being taken toward the notion of the rural. This is largely motivated by a parallel predicament of rurality that is evident in the Common Agricultural Policy's conflicting aims of promoting economic efficiency and preserving inefficient family farms and the rural society they sustain that I analyzed in Chapter 3. If the hill sheep farmers of Teviot-

head are any indication, it is a predicament felt by people of
the countryside. It emerges from their recognition of the
destruction of rural landscapes and marginalization of family
farming and rural localities despite a continuing societywide
commitment to a romantic image of the rural as the haven
for social harmony, community, and moral values in the context of the industrialization of agriculture, urbanization of
society and counter-urban movement of urban people seeking to live the "rural idyll" (Creed and Ching 1997; Halfacree
1996; Williams 1975).

Much like the deterritorialization of the concept of culture discussed in the Introduction, there has been an analogous de-spatialization of the concept of the rural: "almost any
inhabited space can be experienced as either rural or urban"
(Creed and Ching 1997:13); "the social representation of the
rural was becoming increasingly divorced from the rural
space which it nominally represented" (Halfacree 1993:33);
and "there is a continually spatial loosening of the elements
once considered indicative of differences between rural and
urban areas" (Lobao 1966:89). And again like the ironic
heightening of the importance of placedness to deterritorialized people, there is a similar re-emphasis by despatialized
rural and urban people of the differences they see between
life in rural and urban places despite the inability of geographers and rural sociologist to analytically define the distinctiveness of the rural (see Creed and Ching 1997:2ff;
Halfacree 1996). In fact, this may be another form of Bourdieu's "theory effect" (1992:249-250). As scholars, largely
from urban locations, analytically marginalize the concept of
rural space (Pahl 1966; Newby and Buttel 1980; Hoggart
1990) because its demographic, economic, and social characteristics can not be unambiguously distinguished from
urban space, they contribute to the marginalization people,
who consider themselves to be living in rural areas, are experiencing. In response people living in rural areas have a
heightened sense of their distinctiveness from and vulnera-
bility to urban areas. Certainly this was paramount in some
Teviothead hill sheep farmers' worry about the escalating
prices of rams that I mentioned in Chapter 8: they were concerned that excessively high-priced rams reported in newspapers would give people in urban areas the wrong impression

of the precarious financial position of farmers in rural locations and jeopardize the government subsidies that sustained them. It is also expressed in the lines of a ballad, "The Forest and the Farm," composed in the early 1980s by Tim Douglas, a contemporary Borders hill sheep farmer:

> The cities, like some greedy beast,
> have gobbled up the land.
> Their rate of feast has now increased.
> Their appetite expands.

If the rural is not a distinctive type of geo-social space, an alternative scholarly strategy is to consider "'the rural' and its synonyms" (Halfacree 1993) to be a form of everyday language practice about a type of space—discourse (Pratt 1996), social representation (Halfacree 1993), or grounded metaphor (Creed and Ching 1997). The claimed advantages of this way of defining the rural are that it reveals how ordinary people in different social locations express and understand rurality and how different political interests are promoted through the use of rural discourse. Unlike the search for one distinct type of rural space, there are now as many ruralities—from valued place-images of country life, to devalued place-images of rural backwardness, stasis, and decay, to the invisibility of the rural within a dominant urban-based worldview—as there are social positions from which it was constituted in discourse.

In these definitions of the rural, the proponents focus their arguments on the nature of the rural as an object of scientific knowledge: the rural is a type of locality, a form of discourse, representation, or metaphor. Throughout this ethnography I have used an approach inspired by phenomenology to describe hill sheep farmers' everyday experience of their farms—how their sense of place becomes embodied in and through their ordinary farming activities. It is an approach that distinguishes between the immediate lived experience of people, their life-world, and the distanced reflexive knowledge of those studying and explaining the life-world of people (Jackson 1996). By not giving unquestioning priority to the latter, phenomenology shifts the definitional issue from the rural as an object of scientific knowledge suffused with the presuppositions of what the investigator takes for granted to the subjects living the rural—to "things as they are" (Jackson 1996) in consciousness of people, that is, to the rural as it is in everyday, practical experience. In this perspective, the rural is a mode of being-in-place, a sense of place, a form of embodied experience uniting self and space (Casey 1996), a particular way of experiencing a mutually defining *relation between human being and place* that is an aspect of social life. It is this relational quality of the rural as a sense of place that is missing from its characterization as a locality or discourse, as space or place-image.[1] Heidegger's notion of dwelling is evocative in its assertion that a fundamental dimension of being-in-the-world is being-in-place: "the way in which you are and I am, the manner in which we humans *are* on the earth is … dwelling" (Heidegger 1975:147, italics original). "Heidegger's term 'dwelling' succinctly describes the way that people are on earth, it is a verb which conveys a sense of a continuous being which unites the human subjects with their 'environment'" (Thomas 1993:28).

It is a long way to go from suggesting that the rural is a form of being-in-place to describing experience(s) characteristic of a rural sense of place. As one who has lived most of my life in urban locales, my long-term fieldwork in Nepal and the Scottish Borders has led me to reflect comparatively upon my sense of place as a urban dweller and the senses of place I encountered while dwelling with Nepali villagers and Borders hill sheep farming people, both of whom were in no doubt that they lived in rural places that were different than urban places. Villagers in Nepal continually distinguished life and conditions in their village *(gaun)* from the crowds and dirtiness of the city *(sahar)*, and as I described in the Introduction, farming people in Teviothead often told me that they did not like towns and cities and could not live in them. From this in-depth experience in two self-defined agrarian-based rural locales, my somewhat intuitive, somewhat reflective, and certainly speculative description of a rural sense of place highlights the intimate and mutually constitutive embodied relation between human being(s) and a particular tract of land that I found in both Nepal and the Scottish Borders.

The origin tale and genealogy *(Bangshwali)* of the group with whom I did fieldwork in Nepal describes how their patrilineage was formed (Gray 1995:160ff). After traveling from northern India to the city of Patan in the Kathmandu Valley, a Brahman befriended the king and married a pure virgin of another caste. This was the beginning of a new clan. From the third generation, agnatic descendants left Patan and established settlements in various sparsely or uninhabited areas of the Kathmandu Valley where they could engage in subsistence agriculture. Each of these settlements was the origin place of a distinct lineage within the clan, and each of these lineages was distinguished linguistically by the name given to the village that was founded and where their descendants continue to live and produce their subsistence. Further, through consuming the crops grown on the specific land with which they are identified, the lineage embodies the place they created and that created them (Gray 1995:173). Thus, founding a separate lineage entails dwelling in a separate place such that lineage and place become inextricable. I think we can recognize in this very Nepali sense of place something of what I have suggested is a rural sense of place in which human beings and place are embodied refractions of each other.

I hope that my account of Borders hill sheep farming people's consubstantial sense of place was effective enough in expressing the culturally distinctive way in which a particular family and a particular hill sheep farm are inextricable so that I do not need to reiterate it here. However, it may be that this intimate and embodied fusion of self and land of a rural sense/sensing of place is partly what British urban dwellers seek to experience when they flee the city on holiday to live in farm cottages and walk the country landscape. The European Community's paper on the *Future of Rural Society* perhaps implicitly perceived this rural emplacement experience in its recognition of the countryside "assuming an increasingly important role as the most popular location for relaxation and leisure" (CEC 1988:5). I end by illustrating my point with two poems composed by Tim Douglas. They manifest and extend this rural sense of place in using the nature of Borders rural landscape as a metaphor to express the nature of Borders people and their place in the Scottish nation.

The Border

Have you ever seen the heather
on the blue hills of the border,
the birch's silver lining,
or the rowan berry's fire?
With the hill sheep roaming, grazing,
all scattered in disorder,
and the brown burns gently chiming
through the hawthorn and the briar?

Have you seen the salmon leaping
on a silver singing river,
or the brown trout, sharply biting
at a feather-fashioned fly?
Have you seen the hillsides weeping?
Has the frost mist made you shiver?
Have you watched the wildfowl flighting
on a shaded evening sky?

Have you seen the adder curling
on the scree beside the gate?
Have you watched the water swirling
when the burn is full of spate?
Have you heard the barn owl hooting?
Seen the stealing fox slip past,
or the sparrow-hawk, swift, swooping
on a field-mouse in the grass?

Have you felt a ghost go stealing
in a shadow on the breeze?
Have you felt a peaceful feeling
in a clearing in the trees?
And would you sing a song to this,
and would your words ring true?
Do you feel that you belong to this?
Does this belong to you?

For these are the hills the reivers rode
in the days of sword and lance.
This was the minstrel's last abode,
and the birthplace of romance.
From the Merse of Tweed to the Solway Firth
where the hills are a gasp for breath,
this was the stage of Scotland's birth
when the play was life or death.

These were the sights our grandsires knew,
that their sons and daughters know.
These are the lands where Scotland grew,
where they fought that we might grow.
These are the hills that gave us birth
and our heritage of bliss.
They fought for this, the best of earth,
and our heritage is this.

The days are wide awake, at last,
and life more soft and pleasant.
But, let us not forsake the past,
nor stagnate in the present.
And let us not give up the fight
to alter what is wrong.
To fill the darkness bright with light,
and, stubborn, fight for what is right,
determined, firm and strong.

Jedwater

When the sky of the Autumn glows sunny
on landscapes of orange and red,
there is nowhere on Earth half as bonny
as down by the banks of the Jed.
There are few in Jedwater would barter
an island of tropical stars
for the heathery slopes of the Carter,
or Hundalee's red sandstone scaurs.

Jedheads, and its wild moorland reaches;
then Sou'den's old kirk, tumbledown,
through the hills to the ashes and beeches
of Edgerston. On to Camptown:
Past the banks that its waters have weathered,
and down below Dolphinston Braes,
past the ghosts of the past at Auld Jethart,
where the sheep of the present now graze.

Mossburnford stands above Jacob's Ladder.
With a rush and a twist and a turn,
the swirl of the waters grows madder
as it sweeps the Willowford Burn,
Glendouglas, and Swinnie Burn's entry
where many a reiver was nursed,
for, up on the hill like a sentry,
stands sternly the bold Ferniehurst.

Lintalee, and the banks are a glory
of beeches and hazels and saughs.
The Capon Tree weeps its sad story
by Hundalee's hawthorns and haughs.
The waters have never a master.
The abbey looks down from its ridge,
where the flow of the stream appears faster,
and turns to the Cannongate Bridge.

Past Bongate, and on to Bonjethart,
the spate tugs at many a root,
and the spoil of its passage has weathered
fertility down to Jedfoot.
The mist that once kissed parts of Cheviot,
feeding numerous steadings and mills,
now loses itself in the Teviot
and sings its farewell to the hills.

The colours of Autumn are shedding
and stark are the shapes of the trees,
the rhones are all choked in the steading,
as the leaves are swept up by the breeze.
The rain is too much for the gutter
and the mist slaps a cap on the hills.
There is life in the swirl of brown water,
as it froths over caulds as it fills.

In the spate, when the big fish are running,
there are shadowy shapes by the rocks.
They melt to the trees with a cunning
much greater than that of a fox.
Meek tameness is not man's attendant
where the blood of the reivers runs red,
and the folk are a bit independent
that bide by the banks of the Jed.

The storms of the Autumn keep tally,
and lapsed is the soft Summer's lease.
Yet still in the Jedwater valley
lie landscapes of beauty and peace.
The cattle chew cud in the meadows.
The plough turns the stubble and lea.
The fox steals away to the shadows,
and the Jed wends its way to the sea.

And man, that indigenous creature,
with his love for the land of his birth,
is at one with the landscape and nature;

his feet planted firm on the earth.
No matter how far he may wander;
wherever his footsteps shall roam;
his mind, like the Jed, will meander
and set his heart yearning for home.

For home, where the landscapes are bonny,
'though the wind of the Winter blows cold
whether misty, or snowy, or sunny,
to a love that is richer than gold.
For home, where our hearts keep returning
wherever our footsteps are led:
We are filled with a desperate yearning
to be back by the banks of the Jed.

Note

1. What I am identifying as the experience of being-in-place is different than the experience of the rural-urban distinction in terms of contrasting images of landscape and forms of social life (Jedrej and Nuttall 1996:23; Creed and Ching 1997:2). Falk and Pinhey's phenomenologically based notion of "sense of rural" (1978:553) captures the spirit of my conception without the emphasis on the rural as an experience of being-in-place.

REFERENCES

Abrahams, R. 1991. *A Place of their Own: Family Farming in Eastern Finland*. Cambridge: Cambridge University Press.

Adejuyigbe, O. 1989. Identification and Characteristics of Borderlands in Africa. In A. I. Asiwaju and P. O. Adeniyi, eds. *Borderlands in Africa: A Multidisciplinary and Comparative Focus on Nigeria and West Africa*. Nigeria: University of Lagos Press.

Agnew, J., and J. Duncan, eds. 1989. *The Power of Place: Bringing Together Geographical and Sociological Imaginations*. Boston: Unwin Hyman.

Alverez, R. R. 1995. The Mexican-US Border: The Making of an Anthropology of Borderlands. *Annual Review of Anthropology* 24:447–470.

Anderson, J. L. 1986. *Profitability of Farming in South East Scotland 1984/85*. Edinburgh: The East of Scotland College of Agriculture, Agricultural Resource Management Department.

Appadurai, A. 1988. Introduction: Place and Voice in Anthropological Theory. *Cultural Anthropology* 3(1): 16–20.

_____. 1991. Global Ethnoscapes: Notes and Queries for a Transnational Anthropology. In R. G. Fox, ed. *Recapturing Anthropology: Working in the Present*. Santa Fe, New Mexico: School of American Research Press.

_____. 1986. Introduction: Commodities and the Politics of Value. In A. Appadurai, ed., *The Social Life of Things: Commodities in Cultural Perspective*. Cambridge: Cambridge University Press.

Auge, M. 1995. *Non-places: Introduction to an Anthropology of Supermodernity*. London: Verso.

Basso, K. H. 1996. *Wisdom Sits in Places: Landscape and Language Among the Western Apache*. Albuquerque: University of New Mexico Press.

Bell, C., and H. Newby. 1971. *Community Studies*. London: George Allen and Unwin.

Bender, B., ed. 1993. *Landscape: Politics and Perspectives.* Oxford: Berg Publishers.

Berdoulay, V. 1989. Place, Meaning, and Discourse in French Language Geography. In J. Agnew and J. Duncan, eds. *The Power of Place: Bringing Together Geographical and Sociological Imaginations.* Boston: Unwin Hyman.

Bernstein, L., and S. Sondheim. 1957. Somewhere. From *West Side Story.*

Bhabha, H. K. 1994. *The Location of Culture.* London: Routledge.

Bouquet, M. 1982. Production and Reproduction of Family Farms in South West England. *Sociologia Ruralis* 22:227–244.

Bourdieu, P. 1984. *Distinction: A Social Critique of the Judgement of Taste.* Cambridge: Harvard University Press.

_____. 1987. The Force of Law: Toward a Sociology of the Juridical Field. *Hastings Journal of Law* 38: 209–248.

_____. 1990a. *In Other Words: Essays Towards a Reflexive Sociology.* Stanford: Stanford University Press.

_____. 1992. The Practice of Reflexive Sociology (The Paris Workshop). In P. Bourdieu and L. J. D. Wacquant, *An Invitation to Reflexive Sociology.* Chicago: University of Chicago Press.

Bowler, I. 1985. *Agriculture Under the Common Agricultural Policy: A Geography.* Manchester: Manchester University Press.

Burling, R. 1970. *Man's Many Voices: Language in Its Cultural Context.* New York: Holt, Rinehart and Winston.

Camden, William. 1695 [1971]. *Britannia.* A Facsimile of the 1695 Edition published by Edmund Gibson. London: David & Charles Reprints.

Casey, E. S. 1997. *The Fate of Place: A Philosophical History.* Berkeley: University of California Press.

_____. 1996. How to Get From Space to Place in a Fairly Short Stretch of Time. In S. Feld and K. Basso, eds. *Senses of Place.* Santa Fe, New Mexico: School of American Research Press.

Clifford, J. 1997. Spatial Practices. In *Routes: Travel and Translation in the Late Twentieth Century.* Cambridge, Mass: Harvard University Press.

Cohen, A. P. 1982. Belonging: The Experience of Culture. In A. P. Cohen, ed. *Belonging: Identity and Social Organisation in British Rural Cultures.* Manchester: Manchester University Press.

_____. 1985. *The Symbolic Construction of Community.* London: Tavistock.

Combe, I. 1983. *Shepherds, Sheep and Sheepdogs.* Lancaster: Dalesman Books.

Cosgrove, D. 1984. *Social Formation and Symbolic Landscape.* London: Croom Helm.

Creed, G. W., and B. Ching. 1997. Recognizing Rusticity: Identity and the Power of Place. In G. Ching, and G. W. Creed, eds. *Knowing Your Place: Rural Identity and Cultural Hierarchy.* London: Routledge.

Daniel, E. V. 1984. *Fluid Signs: Being a Person the Tamil Way.* Berkeley: University of California Press.

Debord, G. 1994. *The Society of the Spectacle.* New York: Zone Books.

de Certeau, M. 1984. *The Practice of Everyday Life.* Berkeley: University of California Press.

de Haan, H. 1994. *In the Shadow of the Tree: Kinship, Property and Inheritance among Farm Families.* The Hague: Het Spinhuis.

Department of Agriculture and Fisheries for Scotland, Leaflet AIS(EC) 1. 1986. Agricultural Improvement Scheme, Improvement Plans: Explanatory Leaflet.

Djurfeldt, G. 1995. Defining and Operationalising Family Farm—the View of a Sociologist. Paper presented in Working Group 6 (Family Farming—Conceptual and Operational Issues), 16th Congress of the European Society for Rural Sociology, Prague.

Dominy, M. 1995. Toponymy: Positionality and Containment of New Zealand High Country Stations. *Landscape Review* 2:16–41.

Donnan, H. and T. M. Wilson. 1994. An Anthropology of Frontiers. In H. Donnan and T. M. Wilson, eds. *Border Approaches: Anthropological Perspectives on Frontiers.* Lanham: University Press of America.

Douglas, M. 1966. *Purity and Danger: an Analysis of Concepts of Pollution and Taboo.* Harmondsworth: Penguin Books Ltd.

Dumont, L. 1977. *From Mandeville to Marx: The Genesis and Triumph of Economic Ideology.* Chicago: Chicago University Press.

_____. 1980. *Homo Hierarchicus: The Caste System and Its Implications* (revised edition). Chicago: University of Chicago Press.

Duncan, J. S. 1990. *The City as Text: The Politics of Landscape Interpretation in the Kandyan Kingdom.* Cambridge: Cambridge University Press.

Entrikin, J. N. 1991. *The Betweenness of Place: Towards a Geography of Modernity.* London: Macmillan.

European Community – Commission (CEC). 1987. *The Regions of the Enlarged Community: Third Periodic Report on the Social and Economic Situation and Development of the Regions of the Community.* Luxembourg: Office for the Official Publications of the European Communities.

_____. 1988. *The Future of Rural Society.* Bulletin of the European Communities, Supplement 4/88. Luxembourg: Office for the Official Publications of the European Communities.

Falk, W., and T. Pinhey. 1978. Making Sense of the Concept Rural and Doing Rural Sociology: An Interpretative Perspective. *Rural Sociology* 43:547–558.

Feld, S., and K. H. Basso. 1996. Introduction. In S. Feld and K. H. Basso, eds. *Senses of Place*. Santa Fe, New Mexico: School of American Research Press.

Fernandez, J. W. 1974. The Mission of the Metaphor in Expressive Culture. *Current Anthropology* 15(2):119–45.

_____. 1986. Edification by Puzzlement. In *Persuasions and Performances: The Play of Tropes in Culture*. pp 172–188. Bloomington: Indiana University Press.

Flynn, D. K. 1997. "We Are the Border": Identity, Exchange, and the State Along the Bénin-Nigeria Border. *American Ethnologist* 24(2):311–330.

Folmer, C., et al. 1995. *The Common Agricultural Policy Beyond the MacSharry Reform*. New York: Elsevier Science.

Foucault, M. 1970. *The Order of Things: An Archaeology of the Human Sciences*. London: Tavistock.

_____. 1972. *The Archaeology of Knowledge*. London: Tavistock.

_____. 1977. *Discipline and Punish: The Birth of the Prison*. London: Penguin Books.

_____. 1991. Nietzsche, Genealogy, History. In P. Rabinow, ed. *The Foucault Reader*. London: Penguin Books.

Frankenberg, R. 1966. *Communities in Britain: Social Life in Town and Country*. Harmondsworth: Penguin.

Fraser, G. M. 1971. *The Steel Bonnets: The Story of the Anglo-Scottish Border Reivers*. London: Pan Books Ltd.

Friedmann, H. 1978. World Market, State and Family Farm: Social Basis of Household Production in the Era of Wage Labour. *Comparative Studies in Society and History* 20:545–586.

_____. 1986. Patriarchy and Property: A Reply to Goodman and Redclift. *Sociologia Ruralis* XXVI(2):186–193.

Gasson, R., and A. Errington. 1993. *The Farm Family Business*. Wallingford, UK: CAB International.

Geertz, C. 1975. Deep Play: Notes on the Balinese Cockfight. In C. Geertz. *The Interpretation of Cultures*. London: Hutchinson.

Gray, J. N. 2000. The Common Agricultural Policy and the Re-Invention of the Rural in the European Community. *Sociologia Ruralis* 40(1).

_____. 1996a. Cultivating Farm Life on the Borders: Scottish Hill Sheep Farms and the European Community. *Sociologia Ruralis* 36(1):27–50.

_____. 1996b. Irony and Paradox in the Scottish Borderlands: Hill Sheep Farms and their Relations with the European Union and United Kingdom. *The Australian Journal of Anthropology* 7(3):191–217.

_____. 1988. Work, Technology and the Experience of Class Relations on Scottish Hill Sheep Farms. *Ethnos* 53(1–2):78–103.

_____. 1984. Lamb Auctions on the Borders. *European Journal of Sociology* 24: 54–82.

_____. 1995. *The Householder's World: Purity, Power and Dominance in a Nepalese Village.* New Delhi: Oxford University Press.

Gray, J. N., and D. J. Mearns. 1989. *Society from the Inside Out: Anthropological Perspectives on the South Asian Household.* New Delhi: Sage Publications.

Greenblatt, S. 1991. Resonance and Wonder. In I. Karp and S. D. Levine, eds. *Exhibiting Culture: The Poetics and Politics of Museum Display.* Washington, D.C.: Smithsonian Institution Press.

Grigg, D. 1989. *English Agriculture: An Historical Perspective.* Oxford: Blackwell.

Gupta, A., and J. Ferguson. 1992. Beyond "Culture": Space, Identity and the Politics of Difference. *Cultural Anthrpology* 7(1):6–23.

Gupta, A. and J. Ferguson. 1996. Discipline and Practice: "The Field" as Site, Method and Location in Anthropology. In A. Gupta and J. Ferguson, eds. *Anthropological Locations: Boundaries and Grounds of a Field Science.* Berkeley: University of California Press.

Gupta, A., and J. Ferguson. 1997a. Culture, Power, Place: Ethnography At the End of an Era. In A. Gupta. and J. Ferguson, eds. *Culture, Power, Place: Explorations in Critical Anthropology.* Durham, N.C.: Duke University Press.

_____. 1997b. Beyond "Culture": Space, Identity, and the Politics of Difference. In A. Gupta and J. Ferguson, eds. *Culture, Power, Place: Explorations in Critical Anthropology.* Durham, N.C.: Duke University Press.

Halfacree, K. H. 1993. Locality and Social Representation: Space, Discourse and Alternative Definitions of the Rural. *Journal of Rural Studies* 9(1):23–37.

_____. 1996. Out of Place in the Country: Travellers and the 'Rural Idyll'. *Antipode* 28(1):42–72

Hansen, N. 1981. *The Border Economy: Regional Development in the Southwest.* Austin: University of Texas Press.

Hastrup, K. 1995. *A Passage to Anthropology: Between Experience and Theory.* London: Routledge.

Hastrup, K. and K. F. Olwig. 1997. Introduction. In K. F. Olwig and K. Hastrup, eds. *Siting Culture: The Shifting Anthropological Object.* London: Routledge.

Heidegger, M. 1962. *Being and Time*. New York: Harper and Row.
_____. 1975. Building, Dwelling, Thinking. In *Poetry, Language, Thought*. New York: Harper and Row, Publishers.
_____. 1977. *The Question Concerning Technology and Other Essays*. New York: Harper Torchbooks.
Herzfeld, M. 1991. *A Place in History: Social and Monumental Time in Cretan Town*. Princeton: Princeton University Press.
Hill Farm Research Organisation. 1979. *Science and Hill Farming: Twenty-Five Years of Work at the Hill Farming Research Organisation, 1954–1979*. House o' Muir, Scotland: Hill Farming Research Organisation.
Hill, B. 1993. The 'Myth' of the Family Farm: Defining the Family Farm and Assessing Its Importance in the European Community. *Journal of Rural Studies* 9(4): 359–370.
Hirsch, E. 1995. Landscape: Between Place and Space. In E. Hirsch and M. O'Hanlan, eds. *The Anthropology of Landscape: Perspectives on Place and Space*. Oxford: Clarendon Press.
Hirsch, E., and M. O'Hanlan, eds. 1995. *The Anthropology of Landscape: Perspectives on Place and Space*. Oxford: Clarendon Press.
Hogg, J. 1872. *The Works of the Ettrick Shepherd* (2 volumes). Centenary Edition. London: Blackie & Son.
Hoggart, K. 1990. Let's Do Away with Rural. *Journal of Rural Studies* 6:245–257.
H-SAE. 1998. Site Identification Thread. *Society for the Anthropology of Europe (SAE) Web Site at H-Net*. Http://h-net2.mus.edu/~sae/threads/id.htm.
Jackson, M. 1995. *At Home in the World*. Sydney: HarperCollins Publishers.
_____. 1996. Introduction: Phenomenology, Radical Empiricism, and Anthropological Critique. In M. Jackson, ed. *Things As They Are: New Directions in Phenomenological Anthropology*. Bloomington: Indiana University Press.
Jedrej, C., and M. Nuttall. 1996. *White Settlers: The Impact of Rural Repopulation in Scotland*. Luxembourg: Harwood Academic Publishers.
Kearney, B. 1991. In J. Marsh. *The Changing Role of the Common Agricultural Policy: The Future of Farming in Europe*. London: Belhaven Press.
Kopytoff, I. 1986. The Cultural Biography of Things: Commoditization as Process. In A. Appadurai, ed., *The Social Life of Things: Commodities in Cultural Perspective*. Cambridge: Cambridge University Press.

Lightfoot, K. G., and A. Martinez. 1995. Frontiers and Boundaries in Archaeological Perspective. *Annual Review of Anthropology* 24:471–492.

Littlejohn, J. 1963. *Westrigg: The Sociology of a Cheviot Parish.* London: Routledge and Kegan Paul.

Lobao, L. 1996. A Sociology of the Periphery versus a Peripheral Sociology: Rural Sociology and the Dimension of Space. *Rural Sociology* 61(1):77–102

MacAloon, J. J. 1984. Olympic Games and the Theory of Spectacle in Modern Society. In J. J. MacAloon, ed., *Rite, Drama, Festival, Spectacle: Rehearsals Toward a Theory of Cultural Performance.* Philadelphia: Institute for the Study of Human Issues.

Macaan, C. 1993. *Four Phenomenological Philosophers.* London: Routledge.

Macdonald, J .S. M. 1991. *The Place-Names of Roxburghshire.* Hawick: The Hawick Archaeological Society.

Macdonald, S. 1993. Identity Complexes in Western Europe: Social Anthropological Perspectives. In S. Macdonald, ed. *Inside European Identities: Ethnography in Western Europe.* Oxford: Berg.

Mahar, C., R. Harker, and C. Wilkes. 1990. The Basic Theoretical Position. In R. Harker, C. Mahar, and C. Wilkes, eds. *An Introduction to the Work of Pierre Bourdieu: The Practice of Theory.* London: The Macmillan Press Ltd.

Marriott, M. 1959. Interactional and Attributional Theories of Caste Ranking. *Man in India* 39:92–107

———. 1968. Caste Ranking and Food Transactions: A Matrix Analysis. In M. Singer and B. S. Cohn, eds. *Structure and Change in Indian Society.* Chicago: Aldine.

———. 1976. Hindu Transactions: Diversity without Dualism. In B. Kapferer, ed. *Transaction and Meaning: Directions in the Anthropology of Exchange and Symbolic Behavior.* Philadelphia: Institute for the Study of Human Issues.

Marsh, J. 1991. Initial Assumptions. *The Changing Role of the Common Agricultural Policy: The Future of Farming in Europe.* London: Belhaven Press.

Martinez, O. 1994. Border People: Life and Society in the U.S.-Mexican Borderlands. Tucson: The University of Arizona Press.

Momoh, C. S. 1989. A Critique of Borderland Theories. In A. I. Asiwaju and P. O. Adeniyi, eds. *Borderlands in Africa: A Multidisciplinary and Comparative Focus on Nigeria and West Africa.* Nigeria: University of Lagos Press.

Munn, N. 1983. *Gawan Kula: Spatiotemporal Control and the Symbolism of Influence.* In J. Leach and E. Leach, eds. *The Kula:*

New Perspectives on Massim Exchange. Cambridge: Cambridge University Press.

Murdoch, J., and A. C. Pratt. 1993. Rural Studies: Modernism, Postmodernism and the 'Post-Rural'. *Journal of Rural Studies* 9(4):411–427.

Nadel-Klein, J. 1991. Reweaving the Fringe: Localism, Tradition, and Representation in British Ethnography. *American Ethnologist* 18(3):500–517.

Netting, R. McC., R. R. Wilk, and E. J. Arnould, eds. 1984. *Households: Comparative and Historical Studies of the Domestic Group.* Berkeley: University of California Press.

Neville, G. K. 1979. Community Form and Ceremonial Life in Three Regions of Scotland. *American Ethnologist* 6(1):93–109.

_____. 1989. The Sacred and the Civic: Representations of Death in the Town Ceremony of Border Scotland. *Anthropological Quarterly* 62(4):163–174.

_____. 1994. *The Mother Town: Civic Ritual, Symbol and Experience in the Borders of Scotland.* Oxford: Oxford University Press.

Newby, H. 1979. *Green and Pleasant Land? Social Change in Rural England.* Harmondsworth: Penguin Books.

_____. Rural Sociology and Its Relevance to the Agricultural Economist: A Review. *Journal of Agricultural Economics* 33:125–165.

Newby, H., and F. Buttel. 1980. Towards a Critical Rural Sociology. In F. Buttel and H. Newby, eds. *The Rural Sociology of Advanced Societies.* London: Croom Helm.

Newby, H., H. Bell, C. Rose, and P. Saunders. 1978. *Property, Paternalism and Power.* London: Hutchinson.

Nicolaisen, W. F. H. 1976. *Scottish Place-Names: Their Study and Significance.* London: B.T. Batsford, Ltd.

Oliver, J. R. 1887. *Upper Teviotdale and the Scotts of Buccleuch: A Local and Family History.* Hawick: W. and J. Kennedy.

Olwig, K. F., and K. Hastrup, eds. 1997. *Siting Culture: The Shifting Anthropological Object.* London: Routledge.

Ortner, S. 1989. *High Religion: A Cultural and Political History of Sherpa Buddhism.* Princeton: Princeton University Press.

Pahl, R. R. 1966. The Rural-Urban Continuum. *Sociologia Ruralis* 6:299–327.

Parish, S. M. 1996. *Hierarchy and Its Discontents: Culture and the Politics of Consciousness in Caste Society.* Philadelphia: University of Pennsylvania Press.

Pearce, J. 1981. *The Common Agricultural Policy: Prospects for Change.* London: Routledge and Kegan Paul.

Pickles, J. 1985. *Phenomenology, Science, and Geography: Spatiality and the Human Sciences.* Cambridge: Cambridge University Press

Porteous, J. D. 1990. *Landscapes of the Mind: Worlds of Sense and Metaphor.* Toronto: University of Toronto Press.

Pratt, A. C. 1996. Discourses of Rurality: Loose Talk or Social Struggle? *Journal of Rural Studies* 12:69–78.

Rabinow, P. 1977. *Reflections on Fieldwork in Morocco.* Berkeley: University of California Press.

Rapport, N. 1993. *Diverse World-Views in an English Village.* Edinburgh: Edinburgh University Press.

Relph, E. C. 1976. *Place and Placelessness.* London: Pion.

_____. 1981. *Rational Landscapes and Humanistic Geography.* London: Croom Helm.

_____. 1985. Geographical Experiences and Being-in-the-World: The Phenomenological Origins of Geography. In D. Seamon and R. Mugerauer, eds. *Dwelling, Place and Environment: Towards a Phenomenology of Person and World.* Dordrecht: Marinus Nijhoff Publishers.

Riddell, Henry Scott. 1871. *Poetical Works of Henry Scott Riddell.* Edited with a Memoir by James Brydon. Glasgow: Maurice Ogle and Co.

Ridpath, G. 1776. *The Border History of England and Scotland.* Berwick.

Robinson, M., ed. 1985. *The Concise Scots Dictionary.* Aberdeen: Aberdeen University Press.

Robson, M. J. H. 1977. *History and Traditions of Sheep-Farming in the Scottish Borders: A Study of Customary Life and Practices Among the Sheepfarming Community of the Central Hill Areas Before 1900.* Ph.D. Thesis, University of Edinburgh.

Rodman, M. C. 1992. Empowering Place: Multilocality and Multivocality. *American Anthropologist* 94(3):640–656.

Rogers, S. C. 1991. *Shaping Modern Times in Rural France: The Transformation and Reproduction of an Aveyronnais Community.* Princeton: Princeton University Press.

Sahlins, M. 1974. *Stoneage Economics.* London: Tavistock

_____. 1977. Colors and Cultures. In J. L. Dolgin, D. S. Kemnitzer, and D. M. Schneider, eds. *Symbolic Anthropology: A Reader in the Study of Symbols and Meanings.* New York: Columbia University Press.

_____. 1981. *Historical Metaphors and Mythical Realities: Structure in the Early History of the Sandwich Islands Kingdom.* Association for the Study of Anthropology in Oceania, Special Publication No. 1. Ann Arbor: University of Michigan Press.

_____. 1985. *Islands of History.* London: Tavistock.

Sahlins, P. 1989. *Boundaries: the Making of France and Spain in the Pyrenees.* Berkeley: University of California Press.

Salamon, S. 1992. *Prairie Patrimony: Family, Farming, and Community in the Midwest.* Chapel Hill, N.C.: The University of North Carolina Press.

Salazar, C. 1996. *A Sentimental Economy: Commodity and Community in Rural Ireland.* Oxford: Berghahn Books.

Scott, Sir Walter. 1814. *The Border Antiquities of England and Scotland Comprising Specimens of Architecture and Sculpture, and Other Vestiges of Former Ages, Accompanied by Descriptions.* London: Longman, Hurst, Rees, Orme, and Brown.

_____. 1932. *Minstrelsy of the Scottish Border,* volume I. Revised and edited by T. F. Henderson. Edinburgh: Oliver and Boyd.

Scottish Agricultural College. 1993a. *Profitability of Farming in Scotland 1991/92.* SAC Economic Report No. 42. Edinburgh.

_____. 1993b. Prices for Budgeting. *Monthly Economic Survey* 19(10):1–4.

_____. 1997. Prices for Budgeting. *Monthly Economic Survey* 23(5):1–4.

Seamon, D. 1984. Heidegger's Notion of Dwelling and One Concrete Interpretation as Indicated by Hassan Fathy's *Architecture for the Poor.* In M. Richardson, ed. *Place: Experience and Symbol. Geoscience and Man,* vol. 24. Baton Rouge: Department of Geography and Anthropology, Louisiana State University.

Shields, R. 1991. *Places on the Margin: Alternative Geographies of Modernity.* London: Routledge.

Sinclair, P. R. 1980. Agricultural Policy and the Decline of Commercial Family Farming: A Comparative Analysis of the U.S., Sweden and the Netherlands. In F. Buttel and H. Newby, eds. *The Rural Sociology of Advanced Societies: Critical Perspectives.* London: Croom Helm.

Smith, S. J. 1993. Bounding the Borders: Claiming Space and Making Place in Rural Scotland. *Transactions, Institute of British Geographers* (ns) 18:291–308.

_____. 1995. Where to Draw the Line: A Geography of Popular Festivity. In A. Rogers and S. Vertovec, eds. *The Urban Context.* Oxford: Berg Publishers.

_____. 1996. Bordering on Identity. *Scotlands* 3(1):18–31.

Smout, T. C. 1985. *A History of the Scottish People, 1560–1830.* London: Fontana Press.

Soja, E. W. 1989. *Postmodern Geographies: The Reassertion of Space in Critical Social Theory.* New York: Verso.

Taylor, C. 1979. Interpretation and the Sciences of Man. In P. Rabinow and W. M. Sullivan, eds. *Interpretative Social Science: A Reader.* Berkeley: University of California Press.

The Scotsman, 28 March 1993:23

Thomas, J. 1993. The Politics of Vision and the Archaeologies of Landscape. In B. Bender, ed. *Landscape: Politics and Perspectives.* Oxford: Berg Publishers.

Tilley, C. 1994. *A Phenomenology of Landscape: Places, Paths and Monuments.* Oxford: Berg Publishers.

Torgovnick, M. 1990. *Gone Primitive: Savage Intellects, Modern Lives.* Chicago: University of Chicago Press.

Tsing, A. L. 1993. *In the Realm of the Diamond Queen: Marginality in an Out-of-the-Way Place.* Princeton: Princeton University Press.

Tuan, Y-F. 1977. *Space and Place: The Perspective of Experience.* Minneapolis: University of Minnesota Press.

Turner, V. 1967. *The Forest of Symbols: Aspects of Ndembu Ritual.* Ithaca: Cornell University Press.

Wacquant, L. J. D. 1992. Toward a Social Praxeology: The Structure and Logic of Bourdieu's Sociology. In P. Bourdieu and L .J. D. Wacquant, *An Invitation to Reflexive Sociology.* Chicago: University of Chicago Press.

Watson, G. 1985 [1974]. *The Border Reivers.* Warkworth, Northumberland: Sandhill Press.

Weber, M. 1978. *Economy and Society,* Vol. 1. Berkeley: University of California Press.

Weiner, J. W. 1991. *The Empty Place: Poetry, Space and Being Among the Foi of Papua New Guinea.* Bloomington: Indiana University Press.

Weingartner, R. H. 1959. Form and Content in Simmel's Philosophy of Life. In K. H. Wolff, ed. *Essays on Sociology, Philosophy and Aesthetics by Georg Simmel et al.* New York: Harper Torchbooks.

Whyte, I. D. 1995. *Scotland Before the Industrial Revolution: An Economic and Social History c1050–c1750.* London: Longman.

_____. 1997. *Scotland's Society and Economy in Transition, c. 1500–c.1760.* London: Macmillan Press Ltd.

Williams, R. 1975. *The Country and the City.* Frogmore, St Albans, Herts: Paladin.

Wilson, T. M., and H. Donnan. 1998. Nation, State and Identity at International Borders. In T. M. Wilson and H. Donnan, eds. *Border Identities: Nation and State at International Frontiers.* Cambridge: Cambridge University Press.

Yanagisako, S. J. 1979. Family and Household: the Analysis of Domestic Groups. *Annual Review of Anthropology* 8:161–205.

INDEX

262 | Index

Common Agricultural Policy
(C.A.P.), 64–82
see also European
Community
and family farm, 69
and image of rural space, 69
and rural fundamentalism,
70
formulation of, 64
review of C.A.P., 72
Stresa conference,69
Treaty of Rome, 69
Common Ridings, 3–5
consubstantiality, 122, 212–38
cuts, 111–13, 115–6, 123, 126, 142
see also hefts

D

deCerteau, M, 8, 9, 126–7, 136,
189
death duties, 222
discourse, 29–30, 64, 113, 126,
174, 216, 236–38
genetic discourse, 113, 126,
216, 236–38
discourse of primitivism,
29–30
discourse of aesthetics, 174
discourse of rurality, 64
division of labour, 122, 125,
203–210
see also class, capital, hill
sheep farms.
Dumont, L., 189, 208

E

embodiment, 116, 120–21, 126,
142–43, 148, 155, 157, 161,
172, 175, 217
enclosures, 53–58
encompassing-encompassed
structure, 208
Eskdalmuir, 50, 188–91, 203
three tiered class structure
191

European Community, 6, 64–82
agricultural policy, 64
Sheep Meat Regime, 6,
73–74
Commission's report, 65
integration, 66–67
paper on the future of
rural society, 69
ewe premium, 74, 89, 118–21
exchange, (Kula), 171

F

family farms, 51–63, 69, 96–103,
122–46, 212–38
family farming 122, 125,
212–38,
family production units, 69
ideal-typical concept of,
213–14
inheritance rights, 59–63,
219–238
inter-generational transfer
of assets, 219–38
farmers, 173,188–210, 216–19
gentleman farmers, 191–2
stereotypes, 192, 200–203
farmer-shepherd
distinction, 125, 173
fat lambs, 74, 108, 161–67
E.C. Fat Lamb certification,
74, 108, 141, 147, 150,
161
fat lamb auctions, 161–67
Fernandez, J., 139–140
Foucault, M., 9, 14, 26, 46–63
disciplinary space (spatial
discipline), 48, 51–52,
57–63
discipline and punishment,
47
functional sites, 47, 52,
57–63
frontier (concept of), 22–43

CPSIA information can be obtained
at www.ICGtesting.com
Printed in the USA
LVHW051536090321
680996LV00011B/1359

9 780857 451798